EVIDENCE, RESPECT AND TRUTH

Can we rely solely on statistics when we judge what is true and just? This book takes a holistic approach to addressing this question. It considers the legal trial as its paradigmatic case study before analysing a wide range of different cases, including profiling, the use of algorithms to predict students' grades, and the authorisation of automated cars.

The book suggests that when we make judgements about the truth or about justice, approximations are not good enough. Truth and justice are uncompromising. They must be so, because the value that underlies them both is respect; and respect takes no compromise. Thus, in the search for truth as in the search for justice, a body of evidence that imposes a statistical compromise will not do. Only evidence that in principle allows reaching the truth and doing justice is good evidence. Once such evidence has been traced, the burden is on us to make good use of the evidence and reach truth and justice. We might or might not succeed, but once we have done our best on evidence that allows success, our judgements are justified; and as such, they can resolve conflicts over the truth and over justice.

Evidence, Respect and Truth

Knowledge and Justice in Legal Trials

Liat Levanon

•HART•
OXFORD • LONDON • NEW YORK • NEW DELHI • SYDNEY

HART PUBLISHING

Bloomsbury Publishing Plc

Kemp House, Chawley Park, Cumnor Hill, Oxford, OX2 9PH, UK

1385 Broadway, New York, NY 10018, USA

29 Earlsfort Terrace, Dublin 2, Ireland

HART PUBLISHING, the Hart/Stag logo, BLOOMSBURY and the Diana logo are trademarks of Bloomsbury Publishing Plc

First published in Great Britain 2022

A catalogue record for this book is available from the British Library.

A catalogue record for this book is available from the Library of Congress.

Library of Congress Control Number: 2022940549

ISBN: HB: 978-1-50994-265-7
ePDF: 978-1-50994-267-1
ePub: 978-1-50994-266-4

Typeset by Compuscript Ltd, Shannon

For Neta, Yotam and Tali

PREFACE

This book has evolved out of my interest in 'naked statistical evidence'. Like many others, I found the reluctance of courts to decide liability based on statistics alone both obvious and intriguing. I shared the courts' intuition that liability should not be decided on statistics, but reason seemed to have pointed in a different direction. After all, why not? I observed with interest the growing curiosity of non-lawyers about legal evidence, and the emergence of parallel evidential puzzles outside the legal context. Heated public debates over the use of statistics to determine students' grades following the Covid-19 lockdowns made it clear that there was much to be explored. So did disputes over the use of artificial intelligence in a range of other contexts.

I started my journey as any lawyer would, with a search for practical aspects of legal judgments that had not been considered before, and that could explain the reluctance to decide on statistics alone. This led to an article on the tragic nature of false convictions based on 'bad character evidence', published in *Legal Studies*. I then moved on to examine the possibility that legal judgments might have epistemic aspects in addition to practical ones, or that legal institutions were in fact interested in the formation of rational belief and knowledge. Statistics are one type of evidence that cannot generate rational belief and knowledge. I used the concepts of responsibility and legitimacy as links connecting epistemic norms with legal institutions. To my pleasant and complete surprise, the *Modern Law Review* article outlining my conclusions won the journal's Wedderburn Prize. By that point I came to think that this was the tip of an iceberg: there was much to explore and unpack about the practical and epistemic aspects of the law, and about the ways they play out in the context of legal institutions. I became more sensitive to a proximity between the search for the truth and the search for justice, especially where they form part of an institutionalised resolutive exercise. I explored some of these issues in another *Legal Studies* article before turning to this book.

The book takes the examination to a higher level of abstraction. At this level, the link that connects epistemic norms with practical norms in the legal context is respect for persons. It is respect for persons that legal institutions are responsible for maintaining, and on which their legitimacy depends; and it is respect for persons that underlies their dual epistemological and ethical project, whose goal is to resolve conflicts over truth and justice. And because respect for persons is, by definition, uncompromising, so are the searches for the truth and for justice. Probabilistic compromises will not do.

Liat Levanon
London
May 2022

ACKNOWLEDGEMENTS

I am grateful to *Legal Studies* and to the *Modern Law Review* for the heart-warming support I received in the process of bringing my articles to publication, and for allowing me to use parts of them in this book. For invaluable thoughts, comments and suggestions along the way, my special thanks to Mark Dsouza, David Enoch, Conor Gearty, Henry Mares, David Nelken, Federico Picinali, Jonathan Rogers, Paul Roberts, Re'em Segev, Andrew Simester, Martin Smith, John Stanton-Ife, Alex Stein, Bruce Wardhaugh, Lorenzo Zucca, the participants in the LSE Criminal Law and Criminal Justice Forum (2018), the participants in the Assize Seminar on Cutting Edge Criminal Law (2019) and the participants in KCL's KCrim seminar (2020). I am immensely indebted to the wonderful team at Hart Publishing, and especially to my editor, Kate Whetter, and to Tom Adams, Linda Goss and Catherine Minahan, for their immeasurable support during the writing of this book, and for bringing it to publication.

CONTENTS

PART II
THE PRACTICALITY OF LEGAL FACT FINDING

PART IV
BEYOND LEGAL FACT FINDING

Introduction

When we make judgements about the truth or about justice, approximations are not good enough; we are after uncompromising answers, or at least as uncompromising answers as the human condition allows for. This has evidential implications for the resolution of conflicts over the truth and over justice; and these implications are apparent in the practice of legal proof.

This book seeks to understand legal practice as legal practice understands itself. Since legal practice understands itself with reference to truth, justice and the resolution of conflicts over them, understanding legal practice involves taking a close look at each, drawing on the distinct bodies of research that explore each, and consolidating them into a unity that underlies legal practice. Accordingly, this is a work in theorising legal practice and in examining the implications of this theory, rather than an attempt to philosophise legal practice by way of subsuming it under conceptions of knowledge or of justice.

The emerging theory should be conceived as a first moment of reflection, whereby what defines legal practice is the resolution of conflicts over truth and justice. It is a necessary first step on the way to further reflection. In such subsequent reflection, the coexistence of truth and untruth, and of justice and injustice, within legal practice will be acknowledged, understood and accepted; it will be conceived as an additional constituent of legal practice against which truth and justice always pull and thereby establish themselves. But for such further reflection to be at all possible, the practice of legal proof should first be understood on its own terms. This is the task of this book.

If there is one thing that legal proof teaches us, it is that the search for the truth and the search for justice are one: if a body of evidence allows knowing the truth, it allows doing justice. Truth and justice are uncompromising, so in the search for truth as in the search for justice, a body of evidence that imposes a compromise will not do. There is no settling for evidence that can only lead to the 'somewhat true' or to the 'relatively just'. If this is all that the evidence can lead to, the evidence is faulty or not fit for purpose. Thus, only evidence that in principle allows reaching the truth doing justice is good evidence. Once such evidence has been traced, the burden is on us to translate principle to practice, to make good use of the evidence, to exhaust its potential, to eliminate the risk of error and thereby reach truth and justice. We might or might not succeed, but once we have done our best on evidence that allows success, our judgements about truth and justice are rational; and as such, they can resolve conflicts over the truth and over justice. The book will unfold these claims and examine their implications inside and outside the legal context.

In its attempt to provide appropriate resolutions for conflicts over the truth and over justice, the law attaches value to knowing the truth and to doing justice. Accordingly, the question that the legal decision maker asks herself is whether she can rationally judge that she knows the truth and that she acts justly. The book will follow the law by considering the rationality on the evidence of judgements about the truth and about justice. The examination will show that where the evidence does not allow reaching the truth and doing justice even in principle, but rather forces the legal decision maker to accept as ineliminable the risk of error, it is irrational for the decision maker to judge on it that she knows the truth or acts justly. It is irrational, because such evidence essentially leads the decision maker to hold inconsistent beliefs that cannot all be truthful, and to act inconsistently with justice. Accordingly, legal fact finding prohibits exclusive reliance on such evidence. The condition of legal fact finding is thus *error eliminability*: legal evidence must not only increase the likelihood that a fact is true and an action is just, but also logically allow total elimination of the risk of error.

As the examination progresses, the sources of this evidential convergence of the search for truth and the search for justice will come to light, and so will its value for the law. First, error eliminability is logically demanded by all things uncompromising, like truth and justice. When we say that truth and justice are uncompromising, we say that they pose a demand to reach them in full. We thus presume that we can, in principle, deliberately access truth and justice. When it comes to the truth, such deliberate access is knowledge. When it comes to justice, it is the doing of justice. Yet in practice, given human limitations, the imperative to access the uncompromising can entail just this: that we only conclude our search where there is no better or similarly good alternative to that which we entertain. In such circumstances, our judgements are as uncompromising as the human condition allows. And this imperative is nothing but error eliminability: as long as the risk of error is ineliminable on the evidence, there is at least one other alterative that is as good as that which we entertain, and the imperative is not met. The condition of rational judgements about all things uncompromising is thus one and the same, namely, error eliminability.

Second and relatedly, error eliminability is logically demanded by one of the values that underly both human knowledge and justice. This value is respect for persons. The law cares about knowing the truth and about doing justice because it cares about respecting persons, as it must. Reasons of respect might play out differently in different contexts, but what they require is always the same, and it is always uncompromising. Respect for persons requires treating persons in thought and in action in ways that are consistent with their value. Thus, it requires rejecting any probabilistic compromise in the treatment of persons in thought and in action; it requires rejecting any compromise in the form of 'probably respecting', as such a compromise projects value that is lower than the value of persons. Respect for persons must therefore presuppose and require the possibility of uncompromising relations between persons, like knowing the truth about each other's valuable human properties, and subsequently treating each other in ways that in fact project the value of these properties and hence also do justice. In evidential terms, this means that respect for persons requires, first and foremost, that error eliminability be met; it requires that reasons be available on the evidence to think that the risk of error has in fact been eliminated entirely. Accordingly, when the law seeks truth and justice by setting error eliminability as its evidential condition, it guarantees a value that underlies them, namely, respect for persons.

This commitment to respect for persons allows effective and legitimate resolution of conflicts over the truth and over justice. Clearly, that error eliminability is met, and reasons are available on the evidence to think that the risk of error has been eliminated, does not yet mean that these reasons are always correctly identified. Often they are not correctly identified, and error occurs. For this reason, disagreements in the search for uncompromising truth or justice are inevitable. This can pose a problem where truth and justice are sought as a way of resolving a conflict. But where an authority is entrusted with resolving such a conflict, meeting error eliminability as required by reasons of respect allows a way forward. It opens the door for all parties to have a go at exposing the relevant reasons that are at play and that should provide a basis for the authority's judgement. In this way, it guarantees that all parties can intentionally contribute to the generation of the judgement, thus preventing fresh conflict over an affected party's agency, and further dismantling any reasonable grounds for rejecting the authority's judgement as unacceptable. The parties and the general public might rationally and reasonably wish to appeal its content, but they would not (reasonably) 'leave the game' by considering the judgement non-binding on them.

As one might expect, it is not only legal fact finding that is guided by a condition of error eliminability. First, all practical contexts in which reasons of respect are relevant, and hence justice is relevant, demand meeting error eliminability. Thus, distributive and retributive social policies that would logically prohibit elimination of the risk of error do not get off the ground; and subsequent evidential principles that do not allow elimination of the risk of error in application of the remaining policies should also be rejected. The book will consider several examples. Second, all theoretical contexts in which a truth is sought demand error eliminability. The discussion in this book of these contexts, which include the scientific context and arguably also the aesthetic context, is brief. Since the focus of the book is practical-legal, a fuller exploration of these contexts must be pursued elsewhere.

Chapters 1 and 2 consider the legal search for the truth. They discuss its uncompromising nature and its evidential implications. The search for the truth is a search for deliberate and full access to the truth, or for knowledge. When we know, we have gained access to the truth, and we have done so based on good reasons provided by the evidence we have. Accordingly, the evidence must give us good reasons to think that we have gained access to the truth, or indeed to rationally believe that we have. Furthermore, if we are to know the truth (rather than merely hold a rational belief that we have reached the truth), we must identify those reasons accurately and believe based on them. There are, of course, other approaches to knowledge, and these chapters consider them too; but the focus is on the above-mentioned approach, which fits well with legal reasoning and practice.

Chapter 1 examines the rationality of believing that a proposition is true. It does so based on legal practice, which is interpreted here as a practice of knowledge generation. Legal practice demonstrates that it is rational to believe that a proposition is true if the evidence not only increases the likelihood that it is true, but also logically allows elimination of the risk of error entirely. While it might be practically impossible to eliminate the risk of error because of human fallibility, the evidence must be such that it logically allows us to do so; it must provide reasons to think that the risk of error has been eliminated, even if it is never guaranteed that we accurately identify the reasons that the evidence provides. This condition for rational, and hence justifiable, belief is termed 'error eliminability.' After introducing error eliminability, the chapter considers its relation to some other conditions of rational belief or of knowledge that have been proposed in the literature; and it further discusses its affinity with Jonathan Cohen's insight that the law, like experimental sciences, draws many of its inferences by way of eliminative induction, thus opening a gulf between provability and probability.

Chapter 2 shows that error eliminability allows handling concerns about error that go beyond any specific legal judgment. These concerns go to the general ability to make legal judgments about facts and indeed any epistemological judgements. To show this, the chapter first introduces sceptical challenges, one of which is the challenge about error. According to the challenge about error, we can never know anything because we can never know that we are not erring in the case at hand. The implications of this and other sceptical challenges are then considered. If sceptical challenges are valid, it is impossible to make any legal judgments or other knowledge judgements. Next, the chapter shows that error eliminability can help in withstanding the sceptical challenge about error. Other familiar sceptical challenges are also considered, and it is shown that provided that some plausible a priori assumptions are made, error eliminability can help in withstanding those too.

Chapter 3 is a transition chapter: it introduces the difficulties in uniting a discussion of the search for truth with a discussion of the search for justice. The reasons that rationally support a belief that a proposition is true might not be the reasons that rationally support any action, including just action. At least a priori, there is no reason to think that epistemological justification might overlap with any practical or moral justification. The rationales underlying the epistemological search are different from those underlying the practical. Accordingly, a rich discussion has developed in the literature about the possible relation between knowledge and action. Some of this discussion seeks to identify the practical value of knowledge, and some of it seeks to identify the epistemological value of reasons for action. The chapter introduces these discussions and shows that they culminate without definite conclusions. The following chapters then proceed to unpack the relation between knowledge and just action.

Chapters 4 and 5 move on to considering justice. They show that error eliminability is a condition of justice for wronged persons and for those accused of wrongdoing.

They further suggest that this is because justice is grounded in respect for persons, and respect for persons is uncompromising. This claim is unfolded with reference to Joseph Raz's account of respect. According to this account, to treat persons with respect is to treat them in thought and in action in ways that are consistent with their value. Yet any thought or action that is based on probabilistic value estimates projects lower value than the true value of persons. Accordingly, it is disrespectful. Respect thus requires first and foremost refraining from probabilism and meeting error eliminability: the risk of error in the form of disrespect must be entirely eliminable through reasoning, rather than merely probabilistically eliminable. Clearly, respect has independent moral significance. In addition, respect can guarantee what we commonly refer to as 'justice'. Reasons of respect make it irrational in all circumstances to bring about errors (disrespect) by imposing disastrous consequences on individuals for the sake of other social goals. After unpacking the relation between respect and justice, these chapters will further reflect on chapters 1 and 2 and suggest that respect for persons is also one of the values that underly the search for knowledge. We seek knowledge because, without it, our essentially probabilistic beliefs cannot comply with reasons of respect for persons.

Chapter 4 introduces respect and considers its implications for the treatment of wrongdoers and of wronged persons. It argues that respecting wrongdoers and wronged persons requires the state to investigate evidence of wrongdoing and to subsequently assert that wrongdoing has been committed. To develop this argument, the chapter first introduces the above-mentioned account of respect for persons, demonstrating that error eliminability is the first condition of respectful thoughts and actions. The chapter then considers respect for wronged persons. It notes that wrongdoing mounts a challenge against reasons to respect wronged persons. This challenge is moral and epistemic. As a moral challenge, wrongdoing demonstrates that there are no effective reasons to respect the wronged person. As an epistemic challenge, wrongdoing indicates that it is irrational to believe that there are reasons to respect the wronged person, because there might not be such reasons at all. The value that the wronged person in fact possesses then provides reasons to counter this twofold challenge. This requires making an assertion, which reflects a belief warranted by error eliminability, that wrongdoing has been committed against the wronged person. Next, the chapter moves on to examining respect for wrongdoers; the focus here is exclusively on legal judgments. It is shown that when the state decides to legally engage with wrongdoers, it must do so respectfully. Accordingly, any legal action that targets wrongdoers should be based on error eliminability; legal judgments about liability and its consequences should thus be founded on epistemically warranted assertions.

Chapter 5 considers the concept of justice. It does so with the prospect of identifying principles of evidence that reflect justice to those accused of wrongdoing. The chapter begins with examination of distributive justice. It offers a reconstruction of Rawls' Justice as Fairness. This reconstruction is evidential in nature. It is shown that Rawls' procedures of fairness help identify reasons of respect, which in turn provide the foundation for justice. To pursue this argument, it is shown that in the public sphere, reasons of respect cannot be decisively identified; there remains an ineliminable possibility that they are not in operation. And in such conditions, it is not always irrational to impose on some members of the public disastrous consequences for the sake of other social goals. The Rawlsian veil of ignorance then works to alter these conditions, so that reasons of respect can be decisively identified based on error eliminability. This has both epistemic and practical implications: subsequently, it is rational to believe that impacted persons are valuable in themselves; it is irrational to adopt any substantive distributive or indeed retributive principles that allow the bringing about of disastrous (and disrespectful) consequences for individuals for the sake of other goals; and, it will be further shown, it is irrational to adopt evidential rules that forbid successful application of the substantive principles, or compliance with reasons of respect in each specific case. Thus, it is irrational to adopt evidential rules that do not incorporate error eliminability.

Chapters 6 and 7 consider the pragmatic resolution of conflicts over truth and justice. They show that a search for truth and justice that is based on error eliminability and meets reasons of respect is well-suited to the resolution of such conflicts: it shields against escalation of the conflict and brings the legitimate results that the parties seek in a conflict over truth and justice in fact. Furthermore, such a search is also well-suited to a pragmatic system of resolution that seeks to prevent unnecessarily high social costs of error.

Chapter 6 demonstrates that error eliminability guarantees that the resolution offered by the legal system indeed resolves the conflict and allows the parties to move on from it. Drawing on the theory and practice of conflict resolution, the chapter shows that in conflicts over uncompromising truths, the appropriate resolution that the parties seek includes assertion of the truth by a third party. And to resolve the conflict successfully, such assertion should shield the parties from the danger of a fresh conflict. Such fresh conflict might arise if the assertion were erroneous, and thereby the losing party's ability to direct her life would be undermined. Error eliminability and the procedures associated with it shield the parties from such escalation. They do so by guaranteeing that the parties take agential part in generating the resolution: the parties are called upon to offer new hypotheses that are consistent with the evidence and to engage in elimination of the risk of error. In such conditions, all parties intentionally contribute to the generation of the resolution. Thus, fresh conflict does not emerge even where the judgment is erroneous. The resolution offered by the legal system then really resolves the conflict; it is acceptable and likely to be accepted by the parties and the public; and subsequently, the legal system maintains its legitimacy and can carry on resolving conflicts.

Chapter 7 shows that in the criminal context, cost analysis supports the adoption of error eliminability as much as do reasons of respect. The chapter demonstrates that false convictions based on evidence that fails to meet error eliminability are profoundly tragic in the Aristotelian sense. The tragedy is twofold: it is the tragedy of the falsely convicted defendant, and it is also the tragedy of the falsely convicting state. This aesthetic characteristic has moral implications that go beyond disrespect: tragedy manifests erosion of the value of human choice; the choice of the tragic hero ends up undermining rather than strengthening her ability to shield herself from arbitrary forces. Tragic errors thus have particularly high negative value; they are more costly than other errors. Accordingly, the case for error eliminability can also be made with reference to simple decision-theoretic principles: in the evidential conditions of the criminal justice system, maximin requires ruling out the most tragic error; and this can only be achieved by way of adopting error eliminability.

Chapter 8 examines the implications of the analysis for the responsibility of legal decision makers. The chapter first unfolds the epistemic responsibility of decision makers for assertions of the truth, and it clarifies why having decision makers who are epistemically responsible is socially valuable. The chapter further considers the practical and moral responsibility of decision makers. It notes that legal decision makers are responsible for the impact of errors on the parties, and it highlights the value of such responsibility for the legitimacy of legal institutions. Moreover, legal decision makers who decide based on error eliminability can carry Scanlonian substantive responsibility for the burden that they shoulder in cases of error. Such substantive responsibility is valuable, because it means that decision makers have no valid claims against the legal system in cases of error. Decision makers are thus not treated unfairly by the legal system and, moreover, there is no internal conflict within legal institutions that might independently further undermine their legitimacy.

Chapter 9 is the final chapter. It examines some of the implications of the proposed analysis of the search for truth and justice outside the domain of legal determinations of liability. There are various such implications in a range of contexts, and the chapter is only meant to highlight some of these. It begins with consideration of artificial intelligence, noting that its evidential substrate cannot meet error eliminability, and thus reliance on it might be problematic in all contexts that require judgement about truth and justice. Next, specific contexts in which artificial intelligence is used or might be used are examined, as well as specific contexts in which humans seek to rely on evidence that fails to meet error eliminability. The focus is on social and political contexts. These include the following: algorithmic sentencing; algorithmic prediction of students' grades; algorithmic allocation of resources in public and private domains; the authorisation and use of automated cars (and other dangerous machinery); profiling and risk prediction based on group affiliation in different contexts; the development of personal attitudes about individuals; and the generation of personal beliefs about groups.

There is no concluding chapter for this book; the conclusions can be summed up in several sentences: if we are to resolve conflicts over truth and justice, we must treat all those involved in them respectfully, as they are due to be treated. Such treatment should begin with the right thoughts, indeed the right beliefs; and it should proceed with the right acts that are based on these right beliefs. Yet as we are fallible, all we can and must do is ensure that the evidential conditions allow success.

PART I

The Epistemology of Legal Fact Finding

1

The Rationality of Belief and Error Eliminability*

The law is interested in the truth. Legal practice demonstrates that the law is interested not only in reaching the truth, but also in holding rational beliefs about the truth. There is a difference between the two: if all we are interested in is the truth, our methods of proof would be such that bring us as close as possible to the truth; but such methods might not ground rational belief that we have in fact reached the truth. Legal practice requires that the evidence be capable of grounding rational belief that the truth has been reached; subsequently, courts assert in their judgments that the truth has been reached.

This characteristic of legal practice finds the clearest expression in the legal reluctance to decide on evidence that cannot ground rational belief. Such is 'naked statistical evidence', like evidence that 95 per cent of defendants who have the same characteristic as the defendant who stands trial are in fact liable for the wrong at issue. Legal practice would forbid making a finding of liability based on such evidence; and this practice coincides with epistemic accounts according to which it is irrational to believe that the defendant is liable based on such evidence, and knowledge cannot be generated based on it.

This chapter introduces the legal take on the conditions of rational belief and knowledge. Taking the legal perspective leads to the identification of error eliminability as a condition for rational belief and subsequently of knowledge. According to error eliminability, for it to be rational to believe that a proposition P is true based on evidence E, the evidence E should logically allow for the elimination of the risk that P is in fact false on E. The chapter then considers the relation between error eliminability and Robert Nozick's truth-tracking condition for knowledge, and between error eliminability and LJ Cohen's identification of eliminative induction as the method for legal proof and for the justification of belief.

* An initial presentation of some of the ideas in this chapter can be found in L Levanon, 'The Probable and the Nonarbitrary: Evidential Foundations for a Finding of Guilt' (2021) 41 *Legal Studies* 294.

I. Epistemology and Proof Paradoxes: A Very Brief Introduction

To examine legal practice and its relation to rational belief and knowledge, we can begin by setting some epistemological background. Most epistemological accounts define knowledge as true justified belief; and the justification of belief is based on a standard of rationality. Some epistemological accounts define knowledge as true justified belief that meets an additional condition. Yet other accounts take knowledge to be a primary concept. Whichever option is used, all epistemological accounts would deny that we can know based on naked statistical evidence.

The inability of naked statistical evidence to generate knowledge is demonstrated with reference to proof paradoxes, namely, cases in which, if we rely on the evidence to generate epistemic claims, we will end up with a contradiction. Some familiar proof paradoxes are Rodeo Stadium and Blue Bus. In Rodeo Stadium, 950 out of 1,000 spectators gatecrashed.[1] For each spectator, the probability that she gatecrashed is 0.95, and therefore it is rational to believe that she gatecrashed. If it is rational to believe for each spectator that she gatecrashed, it is also rational to believe that all of them gatecrashed. But given the evidence that only 950 of the 1,000 gatecrashed, it is irrational to believe that all the spectators gatecrashed. In Blue Bus, 60 out of 100 buses in town are operated by the Blue Bus company, and the rest are operated by the Red Bus company; a bus whose colour is unknown has caused an accident.[2] Based on the evidence about the distribution of buses, it is rational to believe for each bus that it is blue and hence a blue bus caused the accident. Yet it is also irrational to believe as we are then obliged to believe that all buses are blue.

To respond to such proof paradoxes, different epistemological accounts identify different epistemic conditions that need to be met for a belief to be rational or for knowledge to be generated. For example, an account based on normalcy suggests that it is irrational to believe that a proposition is true if it is normal for the proposition to turn out to be false.[3] Thus, it is irrational to believe that a specific spectator gatecrashed in evidential conditions where there would be nothing abnormal or requiring special explanation if it turns out that this specific spectator did not gatecrash; and it is irrational to believe that a blue bus caused an accident in evidential conditions where there would be nothing abnormal or requiring special explanation if it turns out that a red bus in fact caused the accident. Or, to take another example that will be considered further in section IV, an

[1] This is a numerical variation on Cohen's Rodeo Stadium example in LJ Cohen, *The Probable and the Provable* (Oxford, Clarendon Press, 1977) 74–75.

[2] This is a variation on the American case of *Smith v Rapid Transit, Inc* 58 NE 2d 754 (Mass 1945). See discussion in GL Wells, 'Naked Statistical Evidence of Liability: Is Subjective Probability Enough?' (1992) 62 *Journal of Personality and Social Psychology* 739.

[3] M Smith, *Between Probability and Certainty: What Justifies Belief* (Oxford, Oxford University Press, 2016).

account of knowledge that is based on sensitivity suggests that where our belief that a proposition is true would hold even if the proposition were false, this belief cannot qualify as knowledge.[4] The belief that a specific spectator gatecrashed is not sensitive to the truth, and thus it cannot generate knowledge. The same is true for the belief that a blue bus caused the accident.

II. Legal Practice: Logically Ineliminable Errors

We can now turn to legal practice and take the first step in identifying a condition of rational belief and knowledge that emerges out of it. Legal practice has specific interest in the risk of error. Accordingly, the kind of naked statistical evidence that the legal system has been reluctant to decide on is a special one: it is evidence that does not logically allow eliminating the risk of error; often, it even logically entails errors.

Let us begin with evidence that logically entails error. The evidence logically entails errors in the sense that if it is decided on systematically for all the members of the relevant reference class, errors would be a certainty. This is because the evidence that supports a proposition P presumes that there are as a matter of certainty cases of no-P in the reference class it captures. Such is the evidence that gives rise to proof paradoxes, and that the legal system has been reluctant to decide on. Consider Rodeo Stadium, where 950 out of 1,000 members of the audience gatecrashed. If we convict all 1,000 members, we are certain to have 50 errors. The same goes for Blue Bus, where the Blue Bus Company operates, say, 60 out of 100 of the buses in town, and a bus whose colour is unknown has caused an accident. Assume that all 100 buses were on the road at the time of the accident. If, based on this evidence, we make a judgment with respect to each of the buses that it was blue, we are certain to have 40 errors.

Let us now move on to evidence that does not logically entail error but also does not allow elimination of the risk of error. Consider 'cold-hit' DNA evidence, where a crime-scene DNA sample is compared with DNA profiles held by the authorities until a sufficiently high level of match is traced. In the case of cold-hit DNA evidence, it is possible that the set of people whose DNA profile matches the crime-scene sample at a level like that of the defendant and to whom the sample does not belong is empty; accordingly, errors are not logically certain. But crime-scene samples hardly ever provide a full DNA profile; it is not impossible that they would provide a full sample (more will be said about this later), but usually they only provide a partial or a contaminated DNA profile. In such conditions, the risk of error cannot be eliminated even if the full probative potential of the evidence is unfolded: it remains possible that the DNA profiles of the defendant and of another person differ only in the parts that were missing from the crime-scene sample. Errors are thus not logically certain, but their possibility cannot be eliminated.

[4] R Nozick, *Philosophical Explanations* (Cambridge, MA, Harvard University Press, 1981) ch 3.

The same is not true with respect to other statistical and non-statistical evidence on which the legal system routinely relies. Here, the evidence logically allows eliminating the risk of error. First, reliance on such evidence does not entail errors as logical certainty, because such evidence does not presume that, in the reference class that the evidence captures, there are as a matter of certainty cases for which the proposition in question would be false. Second, if the proposition in question is true and the full probative potential of the evidence is unfolded, the emerging narrower reference class that the evidence captures will include only cases for which the proposition is true; and if the proposition is false and the full probative potential of the evidence is unfolded, the emerging narrower reference class will include only cases for which the proposition is false. Hence, the risk of error is eliminable on the evidence.

To see this, consider, for example, 'case-specific' explanatory evidence, such as first-hand testimony. The proposition in question concerns the truthfulness of such testimony. Once the testimony is examined for signs of truth and the reference class of similar testimonies is accordingly narrowed down, it becomes possible for the emerging reference class of testimonies that show various signs of truth to include no untruthful witnesses (so no cases for which the proposition about the truthfulness of the testimony is false in the reference class). It is thus not logically certain that errors will occur when relying on such first-hand testimonies. Furthermore, if the proposition about the truthfulness of the specific testimony is true, the maximally perceptive and best hypotheses-generator factfinder would be able to narrow down the reference class of first-hand testimonies with such signs of truth to include only truthful testimonies. And if the proposition is false, this factfinder would be able to narrow down the reference class of testimonies with such signs of untruth to include only untruthful testimonies, and she would therefore not conclude that the testimony is truthful. It is accordingly logically possible to avoid errors entirely; the risk of error is logically eliminable.

The same is true for 'case-specific' evidence that supports predictions, like evidence that the defendant had a motive to commit the crime. After the evidence is examined, it is possible that the emerging narrow reference class of such defendants with such strong motives contains no members who will not have committed the crime (so no cases for which the proposition that the defendant committed the crime is false). Errors are thus not logically certain to occur. Furthermore, if the proposition that the defendant committed the crime out of this motive is true, the maximally perceptive and best hypotheses-generator factfinder will be able to identify this narrow reference class (it is possible that in such matters, the relevant narrow 'reference class' would include only the defendant at issue). And if the proposition is false, this factfinder would narrow down the reference class of defendants with characteristics X, Y, Z and so forth, and a motive with characteristics A, B, C and so forth, so that the emerging narrow reference class includes only defendants who do not act on such motives. She would therefore not conclude that the proposition is true. Thus, the risk of error is logically eliminable.

At other times the bare evidence already suggests that the existence in the reference class of cases for which the proposition in question is false is not a certainty, or even that the likelihood that there would be such cases in the reference class is negligible, and accordingly errors are not logically certain. And further, if the proposition is true and all the full probative potential of the evidence is uncovered, the risk of errors is eliminated. Examples would include evidence that an apple fell off its tree, leading, together with the laws of gravity, to the conclusion that the apple fell by the tree; or evidence that Ernie dropped a garbage bag down the chute, leading, together with the laws of gravity, to the conclusion that the bag is now in the basement.[5] In such examples, there may well be no cases for which the proposition is false in the reference class (no cases of a different course of development in the exact same conditions), and hence errors when relying on such evidence are by no means a logical certainty.[6] And if our theoretical hypotheses are true and the full probative potential of the evidence is uncovered, the risk of error will be eliminated: if we uncover all the information about the conditions in which the apple fell off the tree, or Ernie dropped the bag, we will be able to entirely avoid error in believing P based on E.

III. Rational Legal Belief

Now that we have identified a difference between the evidence that courts are willing to decide on and the evidence that courts are unwilling to decide on, let us consider whether this difference might make beliefs rational or irrational respectively.

A. Error Avoidability

It is irrational to believe based on evidence that does not allow eliminating the risk of error. To see this, we can first work with Rodeo Stadium as a running example; remember that in Rodeo Stadium some errors are a logical certainty. A court convicts a randomly selected member of the audience of 1,000, out of which 950 gatecrashed. Is it rational to believe that the conviction is a true one? If the court were to repeat the same exercise systematically with respect to each of the 1,000 members of the audience, the court would convict all of them and would

[5] E Sosa, 'How to Defeat Opposition to Moore' (1999) 13 *Philosophical Perspectives* 141. A similar example has been introduced by J Vogel, 'Tracking, Closure, and Inductive Knowledge' in LF Steven (ed), *The Possibility of Knowledge: Nozick and His Critics* (Totowa, NJ, Rowman & Littlefield, 1987) 197, 206. In this example I leave ice cubes in a glass outside on a hot day; after several hours I can be said to know that the ice cubes have melted. For some additional attempts to explain these examples, see D Pritchard's discussion in 'Anti Luck Virtue Epistemology' (2012) 109 *Journal of Philosophy* 247, esp at 251–52: and see also Pritchard's original statement of anti-luck epistemology in *Epistemic Luck* (Oxford, Oxford University Press, 2005); S Roush, *Tracking Truth: Knowledge, Evidence, and Science* (Oxford, Oxford University Press, 2005) esp in section 2(3).

[6] If at all, no-P will only happen in rare cases that include unexpected developments that alter the presumed factual conditions (ie exclude the case from the reference class).

err 50 times. The probability that one of these errors occurs when convicting the randomly selected member of the audience is equal to the probability that it would occur in each of the 999 remaining repetitions. In such circumstances, there is no reason for the court to believe the error does not occur when convicting the randomly selected member of the audience. For there to be such a reason, the probability of error when convicting the randomly selected member should be lower than the probability of error in any of the possible repetitions. As the probabilities are all equal, there is no reason to believe that the court is not erring in the case at issue. Since the court has no reason to believe that the error does not occur when convicting the randomly selected member, believing that error does not occur in that case is irrational. The irrationality of the belief that the court is not erring in convicting the randomly selected defendant is inconsistent with a belief that the conviction is a true conviction. Accordingly, the court's belief that it is right in the case at issue and that the randomly selected member of the audience is in fact guilty is irrational.

Let us now compare this with the justification for belief based on evidence that does not entail errors as logical certainty. A court convicts a defendant based on consistent first-hand testimony. Is the conviction justified? If the court were to repeat this exercise systematically with respect to all defendants against whom such consistent first-hand testimony is available, it is logically possible that the court would never get it wrong; errors are not a logical certainty. The reason for this is that if the testimony is truthful, the probability of error would decrease with every sign of truth that the court identifies in the testimony, and additional signs of truth can always be identified until only reliable testimonies are captured in the reference class. In the same way, if the testimony is untruthful, the probability of error in judging it truthful would increase slightly with every sign of untruth that the court identifies in the testimony, and additional signs of untruth can always be identified until only unreliable testimonies are captured in the reference class. In such conditions, it is logically possible that the risk of error in judging that the defendant is guilty based on the first-hand testimony in the current case is zero. It is thus not irrational to believe that the court is not erring in the case at issue.

Accordingly, if P and P* are competing but not mutually exclusive propositions, the following necessary condition for rational legal belief can be proposed:

> *Error Avoidability:*
>
> *E can support belief in P only if E does not logically entail erroneous beliefs when relied on for P and for every competing proposition P*.*

B. Error Eliminability

But this is hardly enough, and we should also examine the rationality of belief where errors are not a logical certainty but the risk of error is logically ineliminable even if P is true. Recall that such is the case in the context of most cold-hit DNA evidence. Cold-hit DNA evidence presumes that it is possible that the set of people with a level of match identical to that of the defendant is empty – there are no such people.[7] Error is thus not a logical certainty. Yet courts that choose to convict on such cold-hit DNA evidence could still face a challenge about the rationality of the belief that the crime-scene sample belongs to the defendant. We said earlier that for first-hand testimony, the probability of error decreases or increases slightly with each additional sign of truth or untruth that the court identifies in the evidence, and that hence it is logically possible that the court has managed to narrow down the reference class to the point where the risk of error for each member of the subsequent narrow reference class is zero or one. But the same is not true for all cold-hit DNA evidence; it is not true in the more common case where the crime-scene sample does not provide a full DNA profile. In such cases, there always remains a possibility that another person exists whose DNA profile differs from the defendant's only in those areas of the DNA that have been left out of the sample. It is then logically impossible to reason out entirely the risk of error in judging that the crime-scene sample belongs to the defendant based on match levels. Accordingly, while the probability of error is low, it is positive and equal for all cases in the reference class, or for all persons with a similar level of match (the defendant and any other person, if such a person exists).

In such circumstances, there can be no reasons available to support the proposition that if an error occurs, it does not occur in the case at issue. It is therefore irrational to believe that if an error occurs, it does not occur in the case at issue. Rather, it is only rational to believe that if an error occurs, it might occur in the case at issue. But such a belief is inconsistent with belief that an error does not occur, and hence is impossible, in the case at issue. Accordingly, the court's belief that it is right in the case at issue and that the crime-scene sample belongs to the defendant is irrational.

Thus, a condition for belief can be proposed that will reflect the concern of courts with the possibility of error on the evidence. For belief to be rational, the evidence on which it is based must logically allow the courts to reason out further and further the possibility of error in believing propositions based on the evidence, to the point where the risk of such error will have been eliminated. This does not mean that the court should in fact reach this point for its determinations to be rational; a standard of rationality does not entail such a requirement, which would also have been impractical. But the condition for belief in the legal context requires that the evidence does not bar the court from reaching this point, if the proposition in question is indeed true.

We can therefore term the condition for belief that can be generated out of courts' evidential practices *error eliminability*. Error eliminability requires that if the proposition is true, the evidence would allow the court to reason out entirely the possibility that the proposition is false; and if the proposition is false, the evidence

[7] The moment it is presumed that there is even one more person with the same level of match, the defendant can no longer be convicted on the evidence.

would allow the court to reason out entirely the possibility that it is likely to be true on the evidence. We can construct error eliminability formally as a necessary and sufficient condition for belief (rather than only a necessary condition). For this purpose, it will be assumed that it is irrational to believe a proposition if the probability that it is false is higher than the probability that it is true; and probabilities here are Bayesian.

> *Error Eliminability:*
>
> *E supports belief that P is true if and only if:*
>
> (1) *Without further examination, E increases the posterior probability that P is true given E so that it is higher than 0.5; and*
> (2) *if P is true, E logically allows reducing to zero the posterior probability that P is false given E; and*
> (3) *if P is false, E logically allows reducing to zero the posterior probability that P is true given E.*

Notably, the question whether evidence E meets error eliminability depends on the scope of information of which this evidence consists. The evidence is the information on which rational belief is based. This information might include only information relating to P that is already apparent on the evidence (and accordingly has been identified by the agent who formed belief). Alternatively, it might further include information that there exists more information relating to P that is not yet apparent (and accordingly has not been identified); this unidentified information logically allows determining with certainty if P is true given E. Error eliminability requires the second. It requires that the evidence on which belief is based would include (i) apparent (and thus identified) information relating to P, and (ii) 'information that there is more information', which logically allows eliminating the risk of error on the evidence.

As we shall see in the next chapter, epistemologists are divided between externalists and internalists. Externalists suggest that it is justified to believe a proposition P only when reality in fact gives reasons to believe P, or when P is true. Internalists suggest that it is rational and hence justified to believe a proposition P when reality gives the observer reasons to believe P, even if P is untrue (or even if reality gives the idealised observer reasons to believe P is untrue). Error eliminability reflects a predominantly internalist view, as it allows for rational belief in false propositions. But error eliminability also assigns significance to the reasons that in fact exist, as it requires information about their availability. If the evidence gives no reason to believe that a proposition is not false, error eliminability would forbid belief. Error eliminability thus provides a conception of rational belief as responsiveness to the content and the existence of reasons.

Before moving on, an objection to error eliminability needs to be considered. It is arguable that while it might be logically impossible to eliminate the risk of error, it is still realistically possible to avoid error. Under the assumption that we do not develop beliefs with respect to all members of relevant reference classes, it is surely practically possible that we avoid error in all the beliefs that we do develop. Thus, why should we concern ourselves with errors in beliefs that will never be generated?

There are several replies to this objection. First, the fact that it is practically possible to eliminate error does not yet make it rational to believe that error does not occur. Maybe we should not worry about the rationality of belief and subsequently about knowledge at all, but if we do need to worry about it then we should worry about the possibility of error rather than only about actual errors. Second, it is arguable that epistemology is about developing rational beliefs based on available reasons (which often take the form of available evidence). The starting point is then the evidence, not this or that belief that we have already somehow developed on the evidence and whose rationality we now consider in retrospect. Once we encounter the evidence, the task is to identify the propositions we can rationally believe on this evidence. And if the starting point is the available evidence, and the epistemological project concerns the beliefs that can be rationally held based on it, then the beliefs that we should care about are all the beliefs that we can rationally develop on the evidence, together with the likelihoods that we err when we develop each of them.

Yet perhaps the more important response to this objection is still to be developed in the rest of the book. It concerns the dual epistemic and practical significance of error eliminability. Error eliminability is the condition that allows respect for persons; and respect for persons is one of the values that underly both the epistemological project and the moral project. More to come in the following chapters.

IV. Error Eliminability and Truth Tracking

Error eliminability captures Nozick's insight about the place of truth tracking in knowledge. Partly in response to challenges about statistical evidence, Nozick suggested that knowledge is only generated where a true belief tracks the truth. Thus, knowledge is generated only where a proposition P is true; an agent S believes that it is true; if P were not true, S would not believe that P; and if P were true, S would believe it.[8] Where these conditions are met, the agent's belief is sensitive to, or tracks, the truth of P.[9]

[8] Nozick (n 4) esp 172–76.

[9] See also Roush (n 5) esp in section 2(3). For additional introductions and analyses of the sensitivity principle, and of alternative principles like safety, see K Becker and T Black (eds), *The Sensitivity Principle in Epistemology* (Cambridge, Cambridge University Press, 2012); K Becker, *Epistemology Modalized* (New York and London, Routledge, 2007); D Pritchard, 'Sensitivity, Safety, and Anti-luck Epistemology' in J Greco (ed), *The Oxford Handbook of Skepticism* (Oxford, Oxford University Press, 2008) 437.

Error eliminability resembles Nozick's sensitivity in that it too tracks the truth: what error eliminability seeks to ensure is that the truth is trackable on the evidence.[10] In error eliminability, if the truth is not trackable on the evidence, believing this truth is irrational and unjustified. In Nozick-type knowledge, if the truth is not trackable by a belief, this belief might still be rational and justified, but knowledge is not generated.

There are, however, differences between Nozick's sensitivity and error eliminability. What matters on error eliminability is whether the evidence is truth-tracking, and subsequently whether the agent treats it as such, rather than whether the agent's belief tracks the truth. And what is important is that the agent's search for the truth on this evidence is not futile to begin with (because of the nature of the evidence), rather than merely that there is a tracking connection between the agent's belief and the truth.

The difference between the account proposed here based on legal practice and Nozick's sensitivity account stems from Nozick's analysis of evidential support. Nozick assumes that information is evidence for P whenever it is likely to exist if P is true and unlikely to exist if P is false.[11] The choice to conceive evidential support this way might be reflecting a deeper view according to which evidence supports falsities almost by definition. Nozick notes 'we know mediately, not directly. This leaves room for a divergence between our beliefs and the truth. It is as though we possessed only two-dimensional plane projections of three-dimensional objects.'[12] Under this view, the existence of evidence has only limited value in identifying the truth, and accordingly it should only play a secondary role in the generation of knowledge.

I do not wish to wrestle with these assumptions here. It can be briefly noted that such assumptions about the existence of evidence-transcendent information can be questioned, and the law does not seem to reflect them. It can be plausibly suggested that the only relevant truth consists of our perceived 'two-dimensional' reality, or alternatively that the evidence provides us with three-dimensional plane projections. In the next chapter we shall see that there might be reasons to support an a priori assumption that such is the case.

Instead of confronting these assumptions head on, I will only comment as follows: it is possible that Nozick would nevertheless have only limited issue with

[10] Accordingly, some of the criticisms that have been directed at sensitivity can allegedly be directed at error eliminability. Some of these criticisms will be considered in chapter 3. Note, however, that error eliminability fares well against other criticisms. Take, for example, Kripke's variation on Fake Barn in S Kripke, *Philosophical Troubles: Collected Papers*, vol 1 (Oxford, Oxford University Press, 2011) ch 7. This variation demonstrates that in the face of red barns and façade not-red barns, sensitivity suggests that the agent knows that there is a *red* barn in front of her but not that there is a barn in front of her. On error eliminability, the agent rationally believes (and knows) that there is a red barn in front of her.

[11] Nozick (n 4) esp 261 ff.

[12] ibid 203.

the different conception of evidence proposed here. The reason for this is that Nozick's sensitivity condition would deny knowledge based on evidence that does not logically allow elimination of the risk of error; and error eliminability would, arguably, deny knowledge where a belief is (attractively) not sensitive. The two conditions thus do the same epistemic work.

To see this, consider the situations in which the evidence does not allow elimination of the risk of error. One such situation would arise in a sceptical scenario whereby the truth is beyond all evidence. Sceptical challenges are discussed in the next chapter, but it can already be noted that Nozick concedes that where it comes to such sceptical scenarios, our beliefs are not sensitive and knowledge cannot be generated. Alternatively, evidence does not allow elimination of the risk of error where error is discernible on some information but this information is to be found on other pieces of evidence that I do not possess. Consider, for example, partial cold-hit DNA evidence. In contrast with Enoch and Fisher's interpretation,[13] Nozick's theory does not seem to allow knowledge based solely on partial cold-hit DNA evidence. When it comes to cold-hit DNA evidence, the relevant question is whether a partial crime-scene sample belongs to the defendant.[14] Evidence in the form of a high level of match would, in Nozick's terms, weakly track the truth, as it *might* not have been identified had the sample not belonged to the defendant. Thus, for Nozick, it can support belief in the proposition that the sample belongs to the defendant. But as far as the analysis of knowledge is concerned, Nozick would say that belief based on such 'weakly truth-tracking' evidence does not track the truth as it should, because error is indiscernible on the evidence: even if the crime-scene sample did not belong to the defendant, any observer would still believe it did. Because a partial crime-scene sample does not allow narrowing down of the reference class so that it only captures the defendant, belief on the evidence does not meet Nozick's tracking condition for knowledge.

[13] In D Enoch, L Spectre and T Fisher, 'Statistical Evidence, Sensitivity, and the Legal Value of Knowledge' (2012) 40 *Philosophy and Public Affairs* 197, fn 38, and in D Enoch and T Fisher, 'Sense and "Sensitivity": Epistemic and Instrumental Approaches to Statistical Evidence' (2015) 67 *Stanford Law Review* 557, it is argued, I think mistakenly, that Nozick's condition would allow knowledge based on cold-hit DNA evidence.

[14] Enoch and Fisher deny this, relying on a 'possible worlds' interpretation, according to which the relevant question is whether the crime-scene sample would appear at all had the defendant been innocent (so, their relevant close possible world is one in which the defendant is innocent, and the sample would not have appeared in such a world). But DNA evidence is not evidence of guilt; it is evidence that the defendant's tissues found their way into the crime scene. Juries are accordingly asked to consider whether the sample belongs to the defendant and, only if so, whether this means that the defendant is guilty. When we focus on the first question, it is evident that there is no sense in thinking of the relevant close possible world in which the sample does not belong to the defendant, and concluding that in that case it would not have appeared. Rather, in the relevant close possible world in which the sample does not belong to the defendant, the sample would in fact still have appeared.

It remains to be seen whether error eliminability denies knowledge where a belief is not sensitive. To consider this question, we should introduce Gettier cases.[15] Gettier cases are examples seeking to show that justified true belief does not constitute knowledge; and one of the main attractions of Nozick's account is that it works effectively to deny knowledge in Gettier cases. Consider a true belief about the temperature in an oven based on a broken thermometer that happens to show the right temperature. On Nozick's account, such a true belief might well be justified given the evidence, but it is not sensitive, and thus knowledge is not generated.

What about error eliminability? At first glance it seems that the belief in the broken thermometer case is justified based on error eliminability: the thermometer includes the information that it is broken, and accordingly errors are discernible on it; in such conditions, it looks like error eliminability is met. Under the assumption that knowledge is justified true belief, knowledge is then unattractively generated. If this is correct, error eliminability does not do all the epistemic work that sensitivity does, and an additional condition of knowledge should be identified as part of a fuller account.

Yet it is arguable that, in fact, error eliminability is not met in such Gettier examples, and subsequently knowledge is not generated even on the 'true justified belief' view. Where a proposition is true, error eliminability requires this: that the evidence would allow reducing to zero the probability that the proposition is false. In the broken thermometer case, the belief about the temperature is true, yet the evidence (the thermometer) does not logically allow reducing to zero the probability that it is false. Rather, the additional information of which the evidence consists only allows increasing the probability that the belief is false. The thermometer includes information that it is broken, and given this additional information, the belief is most probably false. The risk of error is thus logically ineliminable on the evidence. In such circumstances, the belief that the temperature is as indicated by the thermometer is irrational and unjustified. Subsequently, knowledge is not generated in such Gettier cases, much like in Nozick's sensitivity account.

A possible objection to this application of error eliminability might run as follows: it is hard to deny that error eliminability would be met where the broken thermometer shows the wrong temperature and I develop a false belief based on it. The probability that my false belief is true can then be reduced at least very close to zero on the evidence. Potentially, it can be reduced to zero. Such is the case where, for example, the thermometer has an identifiable fault that makes it consistently inaccurate; or where it is apparent on the thermometer that it froze when the temperature could not have been the same as it is when I form my belief. Accordingly, my belief is rational and justified on error eliminability. However, the difference in outcomes when applying error eliminability to the two broken

[15] E Gettier, 'Is Justified True Belief Knowledge?' (1963) 23 *Analysis* 121.

thermometer cases (where the belief is accidentally true and where the belief is false) is, arguably, counter intuitive. After all, I rely on the exact same information where I happen to get the temperature wrong and where I happen to get it right; why should my belief be rational only when it happens to be wrong?

In response to this objection, it can first be noted that this difference in outcomes might not be counter intuitive after all. In fact, the suggestion that the two beliefs are not equivalent resonates well with the normal and intuitive responses to them. When I discover that I generated a false belief based on a broken thermometer, I will tend to say that there was nothing 'wrong' or irrational about my belief; it was based on good evidence that could have guided me well but unfortunately did not. But when I discover that I generated a true belief accidentally based on a broken thermometer, I will tend to say that my belief was skewed, and that it was based on bad evidence that could not have guided me well. Furthermore, this difference in responses is not arbitrary. It is rooted in the fact that where my belief is false, the possibility that it might be false is apparent on the evidence and accordingly appropriately addressed; but where my belief is accidentally true, the possibility that it might be accidentally true is not apparent on the evidence and accordingly not addressed at all. This possibility comes to this: that my belief is supported only by evidence that I do not possess, or only by reasons whose existence is not apparent to me. If rationality is responsiveness to the existence of reasons for belief, my belief is rational only in the case where it ends up being false like the thermometer indicated to me that it might be. This is what the difference in the two applications of error eliminability captures.

If this is correct, error eliminability does the full epistemic work that sensitivity does. Yet this might not be the end of the epistemic discussion, because sensitivity has been criticised over the way it handles scepticism. We can postpone the discussion of scepticism until the next chapter.

V. Error Eliminability and Eliminative Induction

We can now examine the relation between the legal condition of rational belief and logical forms of inference. Cohen's insight that legal proof takes the logical form of eliminative induction will be at the centre of attention in this section. The relation between eliminative induction (as a logical form) and error eliminability (as a condition of rational belief) will be considered. It will be shown that error eliminability is not only a condition of rational belief; it is also an essential logical component of eliminative induction, and hence logical inferences based on eliminative induction meet the legal condition of rational belief.

The move from a discussion of the condition of belief to a discussion of logical forms of inference might imply inferentialism (the idea that beliefs can only be justified based on inferences from other beliefs). If error eliminability is taken as a component of a logical inference that justifies belief, inferentialism is essentially presumed. This conclusion is resisted if the argument is more modest: that some logical forms of inference incorporate error eliminability, but error eliminability does not necessitate an inference. I prefer this more modest suggestion: inferentialism is controversial, and many reject it in favour of foundationalism (the idea that some basic or foundational beliefs can be justified directly on perception without any inference). There is thus no advantage in committing to inferentialism if it is possible to move on without doing so. I will nevertheless say a few words on inferentialism and the arguments that support it; foundationalists are invited to skip this part.

A. Inferentialism

The root of many controversies in epistemology lies in a disagreement over the way beliefs are formed and justified: how does one come to conclude that there is a window in front of one? What are the mental processes that lead to this conclusion? Foundationalists suggest that while some beliefs are justified based on inference from other prior beliefs, others are not: foundational beliefs are justified directly on perception and without any inferences of reason. Inferentialists suggest that the perceptual is meaningless absent inferential reason; thus, all beliefs can only be formed and justified based on inferences from other beliefs.

There is no space or need to consider these positions here. Instead, we can briefly mention several arguments in favour of inferentialism. First, any belief includes concepts (linguists would say that it includes words); concepts are the products of reason, and at least some accounts of concepts take the application of concepts in relation to the perceptually given to be itself inferential.[16] Relatedly, it is doubtful if the perceptually given can have any normative force (ability to justify contentful or meaningful belief) when it stands on its own and outside any inferential framework of content and meaning giving.[17] Furthermore, even foundationalists would agree that beliefs provide a basis for inferences of reason; but if this is true, any belief based on perception presumes at least a notion of inferential significance that is prior to this belief.[18] Last, if the notion of belief refers to human belief, foundationalism cannot properly confine this notion; it implies that animals with perceptual abilities also hold beliefs.[19]

[16] Without adopting Brandom's interpretation of Rotry in full, the following comment is instructive, '[T]o talk of facts is to talk of something that is conceptually structured, propositionally contentful, something, that is, with the right shape to stand in inferential and hence justificatory relations. And that is a shape something can only be given by a vocabulary. Conceptual norms are creatures of vocabularies: no vocabularies, no conceptual norms.' RB Brandom, *Perspectives on Pragmatism* (Cambridge, MA, Harvard University Press, 2011) 124.

[17] ibid 123–24.

[18] This is what Brandom (ibid 103–05) describes as the 'Sellars-Kant' point.

[19] Notably, while Brandom suggests that animals do not hold beliefs, there is philosophical disagreement over this question. For discussion of some of the positions in the literature, see F Dreckmann,

If these and other available arguments in favour of inferentialism are found to be convincing, the condition for the justification of legal belief can be stated with reference to logical forms of inference (that incorporate error eliminability); otherwise, error eliminability can stand on its own feet, as suggested thus far.

B. Logical Inferences: Syllogisms and their Propositional Structure

The logical analysis of inferences goes back to Aristotle.[20] In Aristotelian logics, the structure that includes a transition from an initial proposition to a new proposition is a syllogism. The initial proposition is the premise; the transition that is based on logical norms is often referred to as the inference; and the new proposition is the conclusion.

Let us consider in more detail each of the propositions of an inference, starting with the premises. The premises might introduce an object [O]. This object can, for example, be a thing (a medicine or a drug) or an action (prescribing or selling a medicine or a drug). We can take a running example whereby O [Mr Smith's actions]. In addition, the premises provide information about [O]. Where this information is empirical, it takes the form of evidence [E]. Such evidence would include specific information about [O] that can be denoted [E1]; and it might further include generalised information about [E1] that can be denoted [E2]. We can take as an example E1 [Ms Jones' testimony] and E2 [testimonies like Ms Jones' are truthful]. The combination [O] and [E] is a propositional structure that can be called [P1O]. In our example, P1O [(Ms Jones testifies that she saw Mr Smith selling illegal drugs) + (testimonies like Ms Jones' are truthful)]. P1O then allows a logical transition to additional propositions about [O] that function as the conclusion in the syllogism; these can be called [P2O]. In syllogisms like the one we are considering here, [P2O] consists of a single proposition about [O]. In our example, P2O [Mr Smith sold illegal drugs]. Notably, [O] is an element shared by [P1O] and [P2O]; [E] belongs only in [P1O] and allows the logical move to [P2O].

Let us now pause to further consider [P2O]. [P2O] contains the concluding proposition of the logical inference; we can call it 'the main proposition'. From this proposition, additional propositions are logically deducible; and their validity

'Animal Beliefs and Their Content' (1999) 51 *Erkenntnis* 93; and SB Lesson, B Tinklenberg and K Andrews, 'Belief and Representation in Nonhuman Animals' in S Robins, J Symons and P Calvo (eds), *The Routledge Companion to Philosophy of Psychology*, 2nd edn (London, Routledge, 2019) ch 23.

[20] Aristotle, *The Works of Aristotle: Organon or Logical Treatises of Aristotle*, vol 2, tr T Taylor (Dilton Marsh, Prometheus Trust, 2001).

works to affirm the validity of the main proposition. These affirming propositions deny competing realities that are inconsistent with the main proposition. The main proposition [Mr Smith sold illegal drugs] is thus affirmed by the truth of deducible propositions that deny inconsistent realities, such as the proposition [it was Mr Smith rather than anyone else who sold the illegal drugs]; or the proposition [it was illegal drugs rather than legal medicines that Mr Smith sold]. To take another example, consider a syllogism where the main proposition is [bees distinguish colours to navigate]. Here, the main proposition is affirmed by a set of propositions that work to deny realities that are inconsistent with it, including for example [bees distinguish colours rather than scents to navigate] or [bees distinguish colours rather than shapes to navigate].[21] And consider further a syllogism where the main proposition is [Bobby is a dog]. Here, the main proposition is affirmed by propositions like [Bobby is a dog rather than a duck]. There may be a very large set of such affirming propositions.

There is no need for us to consider in detail the logical status that the affirming propositions might or might not have within the syllogism.[22] The affirming propositions do not necessarily have any logical status as part of the syllogism; they are not necessarily part of the logical consequence that is derived from the premises. But while not essentially part of [P2O], the affirming propositions can be part of [P2O] in some forms of logical inference. To see when this might be the case, we need to move on to examining logical forms of inference.

C. Logical Forms of Inference in Legal Practice

The transition from the premises to the conclusions in a syllogism reflects one of several logical norms or forms of inference. These forms of inference are usually thought to include deduction, various forms of induction (including enumerative induction and several variations of non-enumerative induction) and abduction that has received various interpretations in the literature. Some further add inference to the best explanation as another form of inference.[23]

In crude terms, deduction is an inference in which the truth of the premises makes necessary the truth of the conclusions;[24] induction is inference from the truth of particulars to a universal truth;[25] and abduction is the adoption of

[21] This example builds on Cohen's discussion of Karl von Frisch's work on bees in Cohen (n 1) ch 13, para 42.

[22] Full consideration of this question requires an analysis of the notion of logical consequence. The field is rich.

[23] See GH Harman, 'The Inference to the Best Explanation' (1965) 74 *Philosophical Review* 88; DA Schum, *The Evidential Foundations of Probabilistic Reasoning* (Evanston, IL, Northwestern University Press, 1994) 468–69.

[24] ibid 23

[25] ibid 323–24.

a hypothesis that explains known facts.[26] Inference to the best explanation is a term that was originally coined in artificial intelligence literature.[27] It involves the generation of hypotheses and the selection of the most plausible one, and, as Schum notes, it mixes abductive and inductive tasks.[28]

Analyses of legal proof with reference to logical forms of inference have captured the fact that legal conclusions include affirming propositions. Ronal Allen and Michael Pardo, and then Ronald Allen and Alex Stein, have suggested that legal practice is based on inference to the best explanation.[29] According to Allen and Stein, legal practice should and does compare the parties' competing narratives of reality, or their competing explanations, and judges in favour of that which is more plausible on the evidence.[30] Plausibility is defined based on a standard of the layperson; and it brings into consideration consistency, coherence, simplicity, consilience, coverage of the evidence, completeness and causal articulation.[31] In such an account, some of the affirming propositions are logically derived from [P1O] and receive a logical status as part of [P2O].

Yet this account raises difficulties in terms of logics and in terms of law;[32] and more importantly for current purposes, it raises difficulties when it seeks to provide a normative basis for the use of inference to the best explanation in law. The authors mention that inference to the best explanation offers the most promising way to get to the truth in an individual case,[33] but this is surely not so: probabilistic inferences that take no count of similarly probable alternative explanations could well be more accurate. They further suggest that inference to the best explanation makes one narrative epistemically superior to another,[34] but it is not clear why this is the case; and as noted by Enoch,

[26] For different interpretations of abduction and for its distinction from induction see ibid 460–63.

[27] ibid 468. It is important to note that logically, it is impossible to infer from the fact that a hypothesis is the most plausible one out of several identified hypotheses that this hypothesis is correct or true. Only if all possible competing hypotheses have been identified and negated is it possible to infer that the one non-negated hypothesis is true. We shall see the significance of this later, when considering eliminative induction.

[28] ibid 468–71.

[29] MS Pardo and RJ Allen, 'Juridical Proof and the Best Explanation' (2008) 27 *Law and Philosophy* 223; RJ Allen and A Stein, 'Evidence, Probability, and Burden of Proof' (2013) 55 *Arizona Law Review* 557.

[30] Pardo and Allen (ibid); Allen and Stein (ibid) 567–69 and 577–79.

[31] Allen and Stein (n 29) 568.

[32] In terms of logical theory, the authors' version of inference to the best explanation at least partly overlaps with eliminative induction. It seems to rid itself of the need to systematically search for competing hypotheses, but this merely weakens its logical power compared with eliminative induction. Further, it is not clear that the authors accurately capture the way syllogisms feature in law. In the authors' account, the competing hypothesis is a full narrative of reality rather than a localised hypothesis about the origin of any single piece of evidence (see Allen and Stein (n 29) 567). As the authors acknowledge, the law does not require defendants to provide full independent narratives, and for good reasons: such a requirement will place a burden on defendants that is better resisted. Last, it is not entirely clear why the fact that a narrative makes sense to a layperson makes it plausible; to the extent that this is just the definition of plausibility, its logical power is contestable.

[33] ibid 597.

[34] ibid 597.

Spectre and Fisher, even if it is the case, it is not clear why this should matter for the law.[35] Lastly, the authors mention that inference to the best explanation provides for better-reasoned decisions.[36] Yet they do not properly explain why reasons to prefer one narrative over another are better than reasons to think one narrative true. Relatedly, the authors concede that there always remains statistical likelihood that the more plausible narrative is false; all they suggest is that we should not think about the inference in statistical terms. But again, it is not clear in what way such form of reasoning is better than its statistical counterpart, where all the available information is considered and mathematically evaluated. Still, the authors' somewhat brief and unsubstantiated glance at the logical forms of inference remains important.

A different familiar attempt had been made by LJ Cohen, and as we shall see in the next section, this attempt too captures the fact that in legal practice, the affirming propositions form part of the conclusions. Cohen proposed that legal proof is based on eliminative induction that gives rise to measurable levels of 'inductive probability.' His account was motivated by the thought that induction is essentially probabilistic in nature, but the theory of probability failed to represent some of the limitations of inductive reasoning. Induction is essentially probabilistic because the observed does not make any generalisations necessarily true but only probabilistically true. Theories of probability fail to represent the limitations of inductive reasoning because, if they can meaningfully generate the probability of a single event at all, they do not give numerical representation to the level of completeness of the information on which a probability is determined.

To see this more clearly, consider the two dominant theories of probability. Frequentist probability defines the probability of an event as the number of times the event occurs over the total number of trials, in the limit of an infinite series of equiprobable repetitions. Frequentist probability assumes that meaningful frequency ratios are given by observed data and that they are fixed (or at least close to that) within infinite series of these variables. Yet these assumptions are beyond proof.[37] This has led to the criticism that the definition of probability in terms of relative frequency is circular: 'it assumes that repeated trials have the same probability of outcomes – but it was the very notion of *probability* that we were trying to define in the first place!'[38] In principle, all that can be described by frequentist

[35] Enoch, Spectre and Fisher (n 13).

[36] Allen and Stein (n 29) 597.

[37] They reflect Occam's razor (or the parsimony principle), which is a presumption rather than a provable premise. For a brief introduction to Occam's razor, see HA Van Den Berg, 'Occam's Razor: From Ockham's via Moderna to Modern Data Science' (2018) 101 *Science Progress* 261.

[38] R Trotta, 'Bayes in the Sky: Bayesian Inference and Model Selection in Cosmology' (2008) 49 *Contemporary Physics* 71, section 2.11.

probability is the ratio of the variables, and the probability of any single event is indeterminate.[39]

The second theory of probability is the Bayesian theory. Bayesian probability is a measure of the degree of belief about a proposition. Bayes' theorem computes the appropriate change in degree of belief following the introduction of new data. Thus, given an initial degree of belief (the prior probability), Bayes' theorem allows calculation of the degree of belief following the introduction of new data (the posterior probability). The prior probability can be determined subjectively or objectively. If it is determined subjectively, its value would depend on the belief holder's subjective assumptions, which are accepted as they are. The eventual posterior probability would then not reflect the completeness of the data on which the belief holder formed her initial assumptions. If the prior probability is determined objectively based on observed data, Bayes' theorem too must rely on the unprovable assumption that observed data about variables allow predictive generalisations.[40]

These difficulties led Cohen to propose a new account of inductive practices and their relation to probabilities. In *The Probable and the Provable*,[41] Cohen focused on Bacon's original account of eliminative induction. In eliminative induction, which is commonly used in the experimental sciences, generalised hypotheses are established through systematic observation of specific instances whereby they might be negated. In Cohen's words, in eliminative induction we work to 'eliminate alternative, antecedently not unlikely, explanations of the phenomenon'.[42] Cohen then relied on this method of inference (eliminative induction) to develop a method of quantification that he termed 'inductive probability'.[43] Inductive probability seeks

[39] Charles Sanders Peirce already noted this characteristic of frequentist probability. See CS Peirce and P Weiss (eds), *Collected Papers of Charles Sanders Peirce*, vol V: *Pragmatism and Pragmaticism*, book I: *Lectures on Pragmatism* (Cambridge, MA, The Belknap Press of Harvard University Press, 1934) paras 21–24; in para 21, Peirce notes 'In this view of the matter, we note, to begin with, that a given species of event considered as belonging to a given genus of events does not necessarily have any definite probability. Because [it may be the case that] the probability is the ratio of one infinite multitude to another. Now infinity divided by infinity is altogether indeterminate, except in special cases.' This characteristic of frequentist probability is one reason why Bayesians reject it.

[40] Bayes' theorem was developed in Rev T Bayes, 'An Essay toward Solving a Problem in the Doctrine of Chances' (1763) 53 *Philosophical Transactions of the Royal Society of London* 370. Bayes' theorem itself cannot help here, because the data could be given an infinite number of explanations (there could be infinite functions that incorporate observed data), and Bayes' theorem is constrained where the series under consideration is infinite. For the relevance of Occam's razor for Bayesians, especially in the context of determining prior probabilities, see E Sober, *Ockham's Razors: A User's Manual* (Cambridge University Press, 2015) 84 ff.

[41] Cohen (n 1).

[42] ibid 130.

[43] A qualification regarding the differences between inductive reasoning and inductive probability is due. Cohen (ibid 41–42) stresses that '[i]nductive probability is not just a special form of inductive support … Roughly, the inductive probability of a first order, singular proposition S on the evidence of another, R, will turn out to vary directly with the inductive support that exists for the first order generalization of which the conditional making S consequent upon R is a substitution instance … Thus whereas inductive support belongs most intimately and directly to universally quantified conditionals, in relation to the results of testing them, inductive probability belongs rather to the consequents of substitution-instances of such conditionals relatively to their antecedents.'

to give numerical expression not only to observed data, but also to their completeness relative to a set of possible hypotheses. Part of Cohen's argument was that eliminative induction and inductive probability work to explain a wide range of evidential practices, including those of legal proof and those of the generation of knowledge.

Referring to the law, Cohen suggested that legal propositions of responsibility and guilt are often inferred in the same way as the general hypotheses of the experimental sciences, namely, through eliminative induction (negation of competing hypotheses). Accordingly, relevant probability estimations would be the ones of inductive probability. And in inductive probability, evidence such as 'naked statistical evidence' about which the law has been ambivalent lacks any weight. The reason it lacks weight is that it does not serve to negate competing hypotheses or to deny possible realities that are inconsistent with the main proposition. In other words, such evidence is not probative because it does not allow establishing the affirming propositions of [P2O].

As for belief, after demonstrating the irrationality of belief based on mathematical probability, Cohen identifies its root in the fact that mathematical probability does not measure the comprehensiveness of the information that produces it. He shows that this can be rectified if belief is based on inductive probabilities. His proposed condition of belief is accordingly as follows:

> For any singular proposition S about the individual or individuals a1, a2, … a(n), accept S if and only if for some R you know that R states all the relevant evidence about a1, a2, … and a(n) and that P1[S,R]≥K where K has to be greater than zero but its precise level is to be determined in accordance with the nature of the subject matter and the best available list of relevant variables for tests on generalisations about that subject matter.[44]

Thus, Cohen in fact suggests that the justification for belief depends on the extent to which we can reason out error, the exact values of which would depend on the range of possible errors in the specific context.

Cohen's suggestions echo, and have been echoed in, the work of epistemologists who argue that to know P, one must rule out all relevant alternatives to P.[45] The question is then what alternatives are relevant (or, in Cohen's terms, what 'all the relevant evidence' is)? Recently, contextualists have proposed that the answer to this question is determined by the context in which the question is asked. Thus, as we shall see in the next chapter, sceptical alternatives might be relevant in the context of sceptical challenges, but not in other contexts.[46]

While Cohen and other 'relevant alternatives' epistemological positions direct us to the reasoning out of error, they propose that the justification for belief (and

[44] ibid 319.

[45] GC Stine, 'Skepticism, Relevant Alternatives, and Deductive Closure' (1976) 29(4) *Philosophical Studies* 249; A Goldman, 'Discrimination and Perceptual Knowledge' (1976) 73 *The Journal of Philosophy* 771; F Dretske, *Knowledge and the Flow of Information* (Cambridge, MA, MIT Press, 1981).

[46] The clearest example is S Cohen, 'How to be a Fallibilist' (1988) 2 *Philosophical Perspectives* 91.

for some parts of legal and scientific proof) depends solely on the extent to which error is reasoned out. Justification does not depend first and foremost on the susceptibility of the evidence to full reasoning out of error, on the background of increase in mathematical (Bayesian) probability, as in error eliminability.

This leads to two related difficulties. First, it is not clear that Cohen succeeds in properly motivating his proposed transition from mathematical probability to inductive probability as a justification for belief. Cohen is concerned with methods, and his critique of mathematical probability is that it is blind to information that did not feed into the determination of these probabilities.[47] It is this fact, he suggests, that underlies the irrationality of believing based on such a method. Inductive probability, on the other hand, gives numerical expression to the extent to which all relevant information has been addressed and considered (assuming for the sake of the argument that we can estimate in an acceptable manner what all the relevant information comprises). The trouble is that only a naive account of mathematical probability would consider it blind to this missing information; as a statistically relevant method, mathematical probability would require that we feed as much information as possible into our statistics; and any full presentation of the statistics would clarify which information has and which has not fed into the statistics. Thus, if there is a problem, it is not with the method but with misleading presentation that might make us think that any quoted probability takes count of all possible relevant information. And if this is the difficulty, correcting any such misrepresentation would suffice. Once the statistics are properly presented, we can decide how strongly they support the relevant proposition: maybe a very high mathematical probability provides only a medium level of support to the proposition; still, it does support the proposition, and hence it does seem to provide a reason to believe that the proposition is true.

Second, even if we set the epistemic context aside, eliminative induction hardly receives any powerful practical motivation. As we saw, Cohen sees eliminative induction as a distinct logical form of inference that is appropriate in some practical contexts and in the epistemic context; yet he hardly provides a convincing explanation as to why these contexts and not others. After all, even some legal decisions are not based on eliminative induction; the decision whether an act is necessary (in the sense of the defence of necessity) is such. This question too is left to be resolved.

Accordingly, inductive probability remains lacking both in epistemic motivation and in practical motivation.

[47] Cohen notes 'The root of the trouble with mathematical probability, as the foundation for a rule of acceptance, is that … it does not measure the informativeness, completeness or "weight" of the premises. To be justified in accepting a prediction about tomorrow's weather we need to know most of the relevant facts, or at least the more important ones. It would be of very little value to have some small quantity of information, on which rain was highly probable, if additional information might radically change the picture.' Cohen (n 1) 318–19.

D. A Way Forward

Inductive probability thus seeks to provide some way of measuring hypothesis generation, or the extent to which possible errors have been negated; but this attempt is hard to motivate. A partial defence of eliminative induction would move away from the attempt to measure the scope of hypothesis generation to the possibility of doing so on the evidence. This defence would rely on the fact that eliminative induction incorporates error eliminability.

To motivate this defence of eliminative induction, we should examine the status of affirming propositions. The examination will show that in eliminative induction, the affirming propositions must be logically inferable from the premises. But requiring that the affirming propositions would be so inferable comes to requiring that error eliminability be met. As we have seen, error eliminability can be sufficiently motivated as a condition for rational belief; and as we shall see in the following chapters, it can also receive sound practical motivation.

i. Affirming Propositions in Eliminative Induction

Let us focus for a moment on the propositional structure of syllogisms based on eliminative induction. The process of eliminative induction is one of negating competing hypotheses, or of denying realities that are inconsistent with the main proposition. We infer that bees discriminate between different colours by negating the possibility that it is odour or another factor, or the combination thereof, that gives them clues about the location of their feeding-place.[48] Thus, in fact, in eliminative induction we infer the main proposition through negation of competing propositions or validation of its affirming propositions. In such an inference the negations and the validations have a logical status in a syllogism: first, the negations are the premises [P1O] from which [P2O] is derived; second, the validations or affirming propositions are then incidental parts of [P2O] that are logically derived from [P1O]. In Cohen's bees example, a full statement of [P2O] with all its incidental propositions would be [it is colours rather than odour, shape … or a combination thereof that bees discriminate between to navigate].

ii. Error Eliminability

Eliminative induction is thus a logical form of inference whereby not only the main proposition but also the affirming propositions are inferred from the premises. But as we shall see immediately, requiring that the affirming propositions be logically inferred from the premises essentially presumes that error in inferring the main proposition is logically eliminable. Thus, unsurprisingly, the logical

[48] ibid 130–31.

method of eliminative induction incorporates error eliminability. And the epistemic qualities of eliminative induction are to be found in error eliminability, yet without the difficulties associated with eliminative induction as outlined in the previous section.

To see all this, let us look at eliminative induction more closely. Remember that in eliminative induction, the process of inferring the main proposition begins with negations of competing propositions that are inconsistent with the main proposition. These negations then function as premises from which the main proposition, and incidentally also the affirming propositions, is inferred. At this point, the logical process ends.

Now, for the main proposition to be competently inferred from the premises by way of negation, error in its inference must be logically eliminable: error eliminability must be met. If error eliminability is not met, it remains possible on the evidence that there is at least one proposition that is inconsistent with the main proposition and that sometimes holds true. Since the possibility that such a proposition exists cannot be negated, the main proposition cannot be competently inferred from the premises by way of their negation. If it is so inferred, it is possible that it has been inferred together with the inconsistent proposition; and it is logically impossible to hold two inconsistent propositions true. Thus, for the main proposition to be competently inferred, it must be assumed that error is eliminable.

This might also be stated in the following terms: Cohen's epistemic suggestion is that the fact that competing propositions *have been negated* (i) makes it rational to believe that the main proposition is true; and (ii) relatedly, prevents us from falling into some of the traps of violating the principle of epistemic closure. Epistemic closure suggests that if one knows a proposition P, one knows all the propositions that are logically derived from P. This principle is violated if high mathematical probability allows knowing that the main proposition is true: high mathematical probability would then entail that we know that all similar propositions are true, but we also know that one (or some) of them might be untrue. Hence, we come to know a proposition and to also know that an inconsistent proposition might be true. The same does not happen if knowledge is based on the negation of competing propositions.

This is where both the insight and its limitation lie. The insight is that the rationality of belief and the irrationality of inconsistent beliefs are tied together and underly epistemological conditions. The limitation of Cohen's insight is that it does more than is required to avoid inconsistent beliefs. It conflates the (required) possibility of negating hypotheses on the evidence with the (unrequired) actual negation of hypotheses. And a requirement for actual negation of hypotheses is hard to motivate. But this conflation can be avoided. Focusing on error eliminability allows us to maintain and develop the insight while avoiding the difficulties.

2

The Challenge from Error and Error Eliminability

Error eliminability is the legal system's way of handling some of its concerns about erroneous judgments: complying with error eliminability ensures that it will have been rational to believe that facts were as determined, even if it turns out that they were not. The concern about error is clearly relevant for each specific legal judgment, as each such judgment includes assertions about facts. But in addition to that, the concern about error is relevant for the general ability of the legal system to make these judgments, and indeed for the general ability of any agent to make any epistemic judgement. The legal system has a clear interest in the ability to make the assertions it makes. It must have such interest because, as we shall see in the next chapters, it must be committed to the value of respect for persons that underlies these assertons.

This chapter first demonstrates that concern about error might threaten the ability to make legal judgments about facts, and indeed the ability to make any epistemic judgements. It does so by introducing sceptical challenges, one of which is the challenge about error. This challenge is of specific interest for the legal system. The chapter then demonstrates that error eliminability allows withstanding the sceptical challenge about error, and potentially also other sceptical challenges. Thus, error eliminability can neutralise the threat that concerns about error pose for the general ability to make (legal) epistemic judgements.

I. Sceptical Challenges

Sceptical challenges are directed at the concept of knowledge; they aim to demonstrate that knowledge is impossible. And if knowledge is impossible, legal judgments that seek to generate knowledge are impossible, much like any other epistemic judgements. Remember that knowledge is often defined as true justified belief; and there are also other accounts of knowledge. Such is Nozick's account, in which knowledge is defined as true justified belief that meets yet another condition ('sensitivity').[1] And Williamson understands knowledge as a

[1] R Nozick, *Philosophical Explanations* (Cambridge, MA, Harvard University Press, 1981) ch 3.

semantically un-analysable concept referring to the most general factive, stative attitude, which equals the totality of evidence in support of a proposition (thus, knowledge serves to justify belief rather than vice versa).[2] More will be said about this later.

Let us take knowledge to be a true justified belief. Knowledge is accordingly conditioned on the availability of justification for belief; and sceptical challenges then attack the idea that such a justification can exist. Error eliminability can thus provide a good justification for belief if it can withstand such sceptical challenges. Since error eliminability is the product of legal practice and its broader underlying aims, it is especially important that it withstands the challenge about the always-present possibility of error, which is of specific interest for the legal system. Let us introduce scepticism and consider to what extent error eliminability can withstand sceptical challenges.

A. Ancient Scepticism

In the ancient Greek world, Pyrrho gave scepticism its elaborate form. Sextus Empiricus has provided us with a detailed account of Pyrrho's scepticism. Sextus notes that the Pyrrhonian sceptic is characterised by an 'ability to set out oppositions among things which appear and are thought of in any way at all'.[3] Thus, the Pyrrhonian sceptic thinks through argument and count-arguments on specific matters. The arguments and the counter-arguments are similarly convincing, and hence the Pyrrhonian sceptic finds herself unable to determine the matter either way.[4] This inability to be convinced is structural; the structure of the available modes of argument produces it.[5] The Pyrrhonian 10 modes of argument were supposed to have fairly general applicability, and their application was presumed always to lead to an epistemological deadlock.[6]

[2] T Williamson, *Knowledge and Its Limits* (Oxford, Oxford University Press, 2000) esp sections 1.4 and 9.1–9.6.

[3] J Annas and J Barnes (eds), *Sextus Empiricus, Outlines of Scepticism*, 2nd edn (Cambridge, Cambridge University Press, 2000) (hereinafter *Outlines of Scepticism*) 1.8.

[4] For a good explanation of this position see M Williams, 'Scepticism Without Theory' (1988) 41(3) *The Review of Metaphysics* 547, esp 555.

[5] See SH Svavarsson, 'Two Kinds of Tranquility: Sextus Empiricus on *Ataraxia*' in DE Machuca (ed), *Pyrrhonism in Ancient, Modern, and Contemporary Philosophy* (Dordrecht, Springer, 2012) 19, 23.

[6] A summary of the modes of argument can be found in *Outlines of Scepticism* (n 3) book I, 36–38. For the role of the modes see KM Vogt, 'The Aims of Skeptical Investigation' in Machuca (ed) (n 5) 33, 47. For the structural nature of the deadlock, see Svavarsson (n 5) 23; M Burnyeat, 'Can the Sceptic Live His Scepticism?' in M Burnyeat (ed), *The Skeptical Tradition* (Berkeley and Los Angeles, CA, University of California Press, 1983) 117, 139. But compare with Massie, who argues that the deadlock is perceived by the sceptic as provisional rather than definitive (P Massie, 'Philosophy and *Ataraxia* in Sextus Empiricus' (2013) 1(4) *Peitho/Examina Antiqua* 211, 225–27).

The inability of the Pyrrhonian sceptic to determine matters produces anxiety. In a famous paragraph, Sextus notes:

> Men of noble nature, suffering anxiety (tarache) because of the anomaly in things and puzzled as to which of them they should rather assent to, came to investigate both what in things is true and what false, that they might become tranquil (ataraktesontes) by judging these things.[7]

In his interpretation of this paragraph, Svavarsson explains as follows:

> Sextus envisages a person who starts out holding beliefs ... But when confronted with a conflicting belief that challenges her own belief, the person grows anxious. This anxiety ... is general in scope. Call it epistemic anxiety ... Perhaps we should identify it with the state of intellectual perplexity (aporia), as Sextus suggests.[8]

Resolution comes with suspension of judgement. The epistemic anxiety of the Pyrrhoinan sceptic relaxes once she decides to adopt the sceptic position and suspend judgement:

> The great recommendation of Pyrrhonism is that suspension of judgement on all questions as to what is true and false, good and bad, results in tranquillity – the tranquillity of detachment from striving and ordinary human concerns ...[9]

Significantly, when the Pyrrhonian sceptic suspends judgement, she does so only because of her inability to be convinced, and without expressing the judgement that objectively the argument and counter-argument have equal force.[10] Accordingly, it has been argued that the aim of the Pyrrhonian investigation is to avoid falsehood rather than to discover the truth.[11] Suspension of judgement avoids falsehood.

The Pyrrhonian suspension of judgement might well come to intellectual paralysis. However, for the Pyrrhonian, this does not entail practical paralysis. Sextus's reply to the charge of practical paralysis that is often directed at scepticism is interesting, but this is not the place to present it in full.[12] The important point is that the Pyrrhoinan sceptic opts for non-philosophical practice rather than inactivity.

Thus, like courts, the Pyrrhonian sceptic is concerned with avoiding falsehoods; but unlike courts, the Pyrrhonian sceptic thinks that the risk of error is always logically ineliminable.

[7] *Outlines of Scepticism* (n 3) 1.12.
[8] Svavarsson (n 5) 23.
[9] M Burnyeat, 'The Sceptic in his Place and Time' in M Burnyeat and M Frede (eds), *The Original Sceptics: A Controversy* (Indianapolis, IN, Hackett Publishing Company, 1997) 92, 112. A different analysis of the way suspension of judgement leads to tranquillity can be found in Massie (n 6).
[10] See Williams (n 4) 555.
[11] Vogt (n 6).
[12] Much literature considers this charge and Sextus' reply. For a comprehensive account, see KM Vogt, 'Activity, Action, and Assent: On the Life of the Pyrrhonian Sceptic', draft, Princeton Colloquium in Ancient Philosophy 07 at www.katjavogt.com/pdf/katja_vogt_apraxia.pdf (last visited 13 April 2017).

B. Modern Scepticism

Like ancient scepticism, modern scepticism focuses on propositions that are inconsistent with a presumably known proposition P. The modern challenge would usually be that (i) had we known P, we would have known that the inconsistent proposition is untrue; (ii) however, we do not know that the inconsistent proposition is untrue; (iii) and, accordingly, we do not know P.

The challenges that follow this structure are of two types, depending on their construction of premise (ii). The first type assumes that all human beings might for ever be situated in a way that prevents them from knowing that the inconsistent proposition is untrue. If such is the case, we do not know that the inconsistent proposition is untrue because the information that would confirm that it is untrue finds no expression on any evidence that human beings can perceive; it transcends the human ability to observe evidence. The second type of challenge assumes that we do not know that the inconsistent proposition is untrue because the information that would confirm this is only evidence-transcendent for us now; however, it does find expression on evidence that can be accessible to us or to others at some point in time; the information thus does not transcend the human ability to observe evidence.

Let us consider some examples, starting with the first type of sceptical challenges. Decartes introduces the evil genius hypothesis, whereby he does not know that all his beliefs are not false and produced by a deception by an evil genius.[13] In this example it is assumed that no human being can ever access the information that distinguishes 'evil genius deceits' from 'true observations'. Accordingly, it is possible that all observations are fake. Once this hypothesis has been introduced, the challenge runs along the above-mentioned lines: had Decartes known that his beliefs were true, he would have known that his beliefs were not deceptively brought about by an evil genius; yet he does not know that his beliefs were not deceptively brought about; hence he does not know that his beliefs are true. For Decartes, the evil genius hypothesis provides reason to doubt that his propositions are true, and if there is such reason, one is not justified believing his propositions are true.

A more recent variation on evil genius is Brains in Vats (BIVs).[14] Here, the hypothesis that is inconsistent with any presumably known proposition P is that you are a brain in a vat held at a laboratory and wired to a computer that is feeding you all your current experiences, possibly under the control of a technician or a scientist. Here too, the information that might support the truth or untruth of the BIV proposition is presumed inaccessible to human beings. And here too,

[13] R Decartes, *Meditations of First Philosophy* (1641), ed and introduction by S Tweyman (London and New York, Routledge, 1993) First Meditation, 49–50.

[14] J Dancy, *Introduction to Contemporary Epistemology* (Oxford, Blackwell Publishing, 1985) 10–11; and see H Putnam, *Reason, Truth and History* (Cambridge, Cambridge University Press, 1981) ch 1.

had you known any of the propositions you think you know, you would also have known that you are not a BIV. However, you do not know that you are not a BIV (as nothing in your experience suggests or can suggest that you are not a BIV; the experiences of a BIV and a non-BIV are identical). Accordingly, you do not know all the propositions that you think you know.

Let us now consider an example of the second type of challenge, where the information that the inconsistent hypothesis is untrue is inaccessible only to us at this moment but it can be accessed by human beings. We can start with Decartes' dream hypothesis.[15] When a person dreams, the proposition the dreamer presumes she knows is that her experience is real, and the inconsistent proposition is that she is dreaming. Here, once she wakes up, she will know that she was dreaming; and others can tell that she has been dreaming. Thus, the information that she is (not) dreaming is evidence-transcendent for her right now, but it is observable on evidence that human beings can perceive. The challenge then runs along the above-mentioned lines: had she known that her experiences were real, she would have known that the proposition that she was dreaming was untrue; however, she does not know that the proposition that she is dreaming is untrue; hence she does not know that her experiences are real.

Another central example that further captures well the Pyrrhonian aim of avoiding falsehoods and the legal concern with error is the argument from error.[16] Here, the hypothesis that is inconsistent with a proposition P is simply no-P. The argument from error starts with the assumption that you have in fact erred in the past or might err in the future about various propositions. Your (possible) errors demonstrate that you do not always identify the truth, and when you do not identify the truth, you cannot tell that such is the case. This has several implications: first, it means that the information that had been evidence-transcendent for you when you erred was reflected on your evidence later when you realised that you erred, and it could have been reflected on others' evidence earlier. Thus, this information is not beyond human perception. Second, since you have erred before or might err at some point, you also have reason to believe that you might be erring about P now, and that no-P is in fact true. Once this is established, the challenge runs along the above-mentioned lines: in such conditions you do not know that no-P is false; and hence you do not know that P is true.

All these modern sceptical challenges have some common characteristics. First, if knowledge is true justified belief, all these examples attack the notion of justified belief as much as they attack the notion of knowledge.[17] They are based on lack of evidence that supports the proposition that the inconsistent hypothesis is untrue (and, in the argument from error also on the availability of evidence that indicates that it might be true). Thus, they target the rationality and justifiability of the belief that the inconsistent hypothesis is untrue and P is true.

[15] Decartes (n 13) 46–48.
[16] Dancy (n 14) 12–15.
[17] ibid 11.

In addition, the concern that all these challenges bring to surface is the same: it is the concern that the world is wholly or partly inaccessible to us, either by definition or contingently, and hence we can never know. We come to know the world with the mediation of evidence, but the evidence does not, or does not always, reflect the world as it is. Some or perhaps all the information about the true nature of the world is evidence-transcendent.

Furthermore, all these examples are based on the closure principle for knowledge. Remember that according to closure, if I know a proposition P, and I know that P entails another proposition Q, then I also know Q. Sceptical challenges use this principle to suggest as follows: proposition P entails that any proposition that is inconsistent with it is untrue; and hence had I known P, I would have known that the inconsistent proposition is untrue; however, I do not know that the inconsistent proposition is untrue; thus, I do not know P.

C. Withstanding Sceptical Challenges

Sceptical challenges are not merely theoretical puzzles. Legal practice constantly engages with the ability to know facts. If legal factfinders cannot know anything, the legal epistemic exercise is futile to begin with. This is a problem on its own merit, and it might also undermine the legitimacy of legal institutions that seek to resolve conflicts of truths.

So really how challenging are sceptical challenges, and how can the legal system deal with them? Note that sceptical challenges are less challenging for externalists like Williamson. Remember that for Williamson, knowledge is an attitude that equals the totality of evidence in support of a proposition. This opens the door for suggesting that we do not always know that we know, and that evidence equals knowledge. It is easy to see that under these assumptions, sceptical challenges are deflated.[18] This conception of knowledge might be attractive, but it would not necessarily alleviate the difficulty for the legal system. Being a system for the resolution of conflicts over truths, the legal system conceives its own role as one of establishing access to the truth deliberately and self-consciously; such deliberateness and self-consciousness support the system's legitimacy.

Sceptical challenges are particularly difficult for internalists. Remember that internalism is the thesis that knowledge and justified belief are generated by the agent's access to, and reliance on, reasons that can generate knowledge or justified belief.[19] Thus for the internalist, the justification for belief in a proposition requires that this belief be properly based on an evidential difference between this proposition and inconsistent propositions. And in sceptical examples this

[18] Williamson (n 2) ch 8.

[19] For the distinction between internalism and externalism, see L BonJour, *Epistemology: Classic Problems and Contemporary Responses*, 2nd edn (Plymouth, Rowman and Littlefield, 2010) 203–19.

evidential difference is inaccessible to the belief holder. Since the evidential difference is inaccessible, the belief holder cannot base her belief on this difference, and hence her belief is unjustifiable. And an unjustifiable belief cannot qualify as knowledge.

So how can internalists deal with sceptical challenges? This is where the distinction between the first and the second type of challenges enters the picture. The internalist has some ways available for dealing with challenges of the first type. Such challenges aim to show that human beings are wholly incapable of knowing a presumed external world. But it is possible to concede that information about the true nature of things might be human-transcendent, and still argue that this hardly matters. In coming to know, we can ignore all that is human-transcendent, and thereby reach human knowledge (rather than non-human knowledge). The devil is of course in the details, and more will be said about this towards the end of this chapter; but for our immediate purposes this brief account of the response is sufficient. Yet such a response is not available against challenges of the second type. Challenges of the second type assume that the relevant information is accessible to human beings; however, it is not accessible to the belief holder. These challenges thus cannot be set aside as concerning non-human knowledge while allowing space for a different, human knowledge. Accordingly, arguments of the second type, and specifically the argument from error, remain particularly persistent.

II. Error Eliminability and the Argument about Error

Out of all the different sceptical challenges, the argument about error is particularly troubling in the legal context. The argument about error concerns contingent error; it concerns error that is rooted in the tentative position of a specific observer rather than in the universal limitations of human perception. Thus the error is discernible and, accordingly, it matters for human beings; and, further, there is a point in trying to avoid it (such an attempt would not be futile). In the legal context, the argument about error would suggest that legal judgments that include factual assertions are impossible: the legal decision maker can never rationally believe that any facts are true, given the always present possibility that she might be misinterpreting the evidence or failing to observe some details. This is exactly the kind of error that legal practice seeks to rule out. Much of the legal fact-finding mechanism is aimed at ensuring that the possibility of such an error can indeed be ruled out. And an argument according to which error can never be ruled out is an argument that the law should be able to confront.

Error eliminability allows pushing back against the argument from error. The argument from error relies on the alleged lack of discernible differences between error cases and any case at hand. Jonathan Dancy captures the crux of this argument in the following paragraph:

> The argument from error holds that if your present cognitive state is, as far as you can tell, relevantly indistinguishable from another which was not a state of knowledge, you cannot now claim to know. And it's not just that you can't claim to know; you don't know, because your present state is relevantly indistinguishable from (similar in all relevant respects to) one in which you don't know.[20]

Error eliminability allows pushing back against this argument, because it presumes and requires that there would be discernible differences between error cases and the case at hand, and subsequently also between one's cognitive state when one errs and one's cognitive state when one knows. Where there are no such differences, belief would indeed be irrational. But in most cases, there would be discernible differences between my state when I err and my state when I do not err, and the argument from error loses its force.

To see this, let us observe the cognitive states of an agent who claims to know despite past or potential erroneous judgements. To do so accurately, it would be helpful to draw a distinction between two possible types of errors. This distinction is only meant to provide an analytical tool that will help in uncovering the cognitive states of our agent. The first type is error that originates in the limitations of the evidence: the evidence does not consist of all the information about differences between error cases and the case at hand, and subsequently we end up being led to error. The second type is error that originates in human fallibility. Here, the evidence does consist of all the relevant information about reality but the agent fails to discern some of this information.[21]

If errors are the outcome of human fallibility, there is a discernible difference between the cognitive state of the agent in error cases and her cognitive state in the case at hand. This difference goes not to the agent's state of belief, which is identical in all cases. Rather, it goes to a unique concession about the possibility of human error in each of the cases that accompanies the agent's beliefs. Whenever human fallibility is at play, the agent has 'information that there is more information' available on the evidence; and in each case where the agent then develops belief, she processes a limited amount of information out of all the information that is available on the evidence. Her reasons to think that error does not occur in that case

[20] Dancy (n 14) 240.

[21] Compare and contrast with Dancy (ibid 139), where he resorts to the suggestion that the argument from error is in fact only a very modest argument about human fallibility: '[T]he argument from error, although it is presented as depending on the belief that truth is evidence-transcendent, can in fact work on a much more mundane point that humans are never in so good a position that there is no room for error, no possibility, given the evidence, that our present belief is false. Even if there is no gap between the existence of the best possible evidence for P and the truth of P, there is always a gap for us between the evidence we have and the truth of P. How then can we tell whether we are in a situation in which P is true rather than one in which it is false? No matter how strong our antipathy to the existence of unverifiable differences, this sceptical question still has a bite.'

are thus of unique qualities and strengths. Subsequently, the agent concedes with a qualitatively unique risk of human error each time she develops her (rational and outright) belief. Such a concession essentially accompanies belief. The difference in concessions in different cases is discernible to the agent and indeed discerned by her. Thus, she can (and will) point to it as a reason supporting her belief that this time, unlike in past or hypothetical error cases, she is not erring. Indeed, this would be the mundane response to arguments about error: 'Back then when I erred, I was still a bit in the dark about the importance of looking into factors X, Y, Z; I have now accumulated experience and have subsequently considered factors X, Y, Z, and I have also exercised better care, and so I am more confident than ever that my judgement is sound.' Thus, if the argument about error collapses into an argument about human fallibility, it loses much of its force.

But things are different if errors are the outcome of limitations of the evidence; here, not only an agent's beliefs but also her accompanying concessions are the same in past erroneous cases and in the case at hand. Consider what happens if, when developing beliefs, all our evidence consists only of partial information about likelihoods of truth and of error. In such conditions, our cognitive states of (indeed irrational) beliefs + concessions are the same in a wide range of cases, where the likelihoods of error are similar. It is here that the argument about error bites. There is no difference between our cognitive state in error cases and our cognitive state in the current case; we therefore cannot know that we are not erring in the current case just as we did before or might do in the future; and hence we cannot know that our current proposition is true.

If this is correct, the concern about error because of limitations of evidence is the only worrying one that needs to be addressed. Yet to pull the carpet from underneath this concern, it is enough to suggest the following: first, that a distinction can be effectively drawn between evidence that consists of all the information that allows elimination of the risk of error, and evidence that does not consist of all this information; and, second, that the evidence on which I rely consists of all this information. Where such are the evidential conditions, the argument that there might be some evidence-transcendent information that leads to error in the current case is no longer valid. Any error would reflect mere human fallibility in uncovering the information comprised in the evidence; subsequently, as we saw, there are discernible differences between erroneous and knowledgeable cognitive states, and the argument about error is undermined.

As might be clear by now, error eliminability presumes and requires just that. Error eliminability requires that it would be logically possible to eliminate the risk of error when forming a belief based on evidence. Error eliminability is thus based on the assumption that a distinction can be effectively drawn between evidence that consists of all the information needed to eliminate the risk of error, and evidence that consists only of partial information. It further requires that belief only be based on the first type of evidence. If this condition is met, any error that nevertheless occurs can only be the result of human fallibility. The argument about error is thus undermined.

III. Error Eliminability and Other Sceptical Arguments

What about sceptical arguments of the first above-mentioned type, namely, such that concern information that can find no expression on humanly perceivable evidence? At first sight error eliminability does not seem to deal all that well with such challenges, like BIV. Remember that a BIV argument runs as follows: it is possible that 'presumably-persons' are in fact BIVs; if I am a BIV, this would not be reflected in any of my perceivable evidence; accordingly, I would not be able to exclude the BIVs from my reference class of persons; and hence I cannot know that I am not erring when I judge in the case at hand that I am not a BIV. This move is directed at forcing us to accept that we can never preclude the possibility of evidence-transcendent information; we can always envision some information that would not be reflected on any type of perceivable evidence.

Such challenges are stronger than the argument about error, but they are also weaker: the evidence-transcendent information on which they rely must be such that it cannot be (and hence has never been and never will be) reflected on any perceivable evidence; it must be such that can only belong in the imaginary realm. This might be why such sceptical challenges are sometimes met by a shrug of the shoulders. And unlike the argument from error, they would fail to impress the legal system: the law would happily ignore any propositions that by definition can only find expression in the imagination, even if this would logically entail forgoing belief in and knowledge of all other propositions, and instead adopting belief(*) in and knowledge(*) of all other propositions. Such a move seems plausible enough, but it has a conceptual cost, namely, sacrificing the principle of closure. It forces us to accept that while I know(*) that there is a table in front of me, I do not know(*) an inconsistent proposition, namely, that I am not a BIV. Indeed, one of the costs of Nozick's account of knowledge is that it similarly sacrifices Closure.[22]

But it is also possible that error eliminability offers a way out of the trap of sceptical challenges like BIV. These challenges presume and seek to convince us that there can be information that transcends all possible evidence (and that will thus lead to error that can never be discerned). We can call this information evidence-transcendent information*, or ETI*. But the rationality of this assumption can be questioned. It can be suggested that it is rational to make an a priori assumption that there can be no ETI*; that if we are BIVs, this would find some expression in evidence, even if, because of our human fallibility, we are still not familiar with this specific expression and cannot envision what it might be. And if we can make such an a priori assumption, belief on error eliminability becomes rational and justifiable. Let us examine how such an argument might run.

[22] See S Roush, *Tracking Truth: Knowledge, Evidence, and Science* (Oxford, Oxford University Press, 2005) esp section 2(3).

Logically, the assumption that there is ETI* is refutable with evidence, but the assumption that there is no ETI* cannot be so refuted; and since the only way to refute either assumption is with evidence, only the assumption that there is no ETI* is irrefutable. When it comes to ETI*, there are two exhaustive, competing and mutually exclusive hypotheses: (1) there is no ETI*; and (2) there is ETI*. Logically, there can be (evidence-based) reasons available in support of (1): if, for example, the scientist who controls the BIVs has given us as yet undiscovered signs of her existence and of her control of BIVs, this would support the hypothesis that there is no ETI*. Yet logically, there can be no reasons in support of (2): such presumed reasons would be evidence supporting the existence of evidence-transcendent information*, and the information would then no longer be evidence-transcendent information*. This has implications for the refutability of the two hypotheses: it means that logically, (1) and only (1) cannot be refuted. There can be no (evidence-based) reasons refuting (1) and thus essentially supporting (2). Yet the same does not go the other way round. Logically, there can be (evidence-based) reasons refuting (2) and supporting (1). Accordingly, it is rational to take (1) as an a priori assumption.

And if we can rationally hold an a priori assumption that there is no ETI*, sceptical arguments like BIV lose their force, and belief can be justified on error eliminability as noted before. Error eliminability merely requires that the evidence consists of all the information that is needed to eliminate the possibility of error. Clearly, the assumption underlying error eliminability is that there is no ETI*, and hence the risk of error can logically be eliminated on evidence. But this is not problematic, as we have shown that it is rational to take this as an a priori assumption. If this is the case then all error is eliminable on our perceived evidence, and we can thereby even know that we are not BIVs.

Error eliminability can thus help in withstanding sceptical arguments. Notably, the focus on the evidence rather than on the exact way in which they feature in determining one's belief is what error eliminability has in common with externalists. And as we saw, externalists can similarly withstand sceptical challenges. Externalists withstand sceptical challenges by suggesting that the justification for belief, and the state of knowledge, depends directly on the truth and the reasons to which it gives rise. Yet unlike externalists, error eliminability focuses on *our reliance* on the fact that there are reasons available that support belief in the proposition, rather than on the mere existence of such reasons.

Now that we have seen the full epistemological potential of error eliminability, it might be a good time to confess that I do not think it was necessary to reach so far. For me, the realm of the truth is the realm of the knowable truth, which is accessible to us because we have a part in determining (or, if one wishes, in 'constructing') it. Accordingly, our inability to reach that which we cannot reach does not matter for our ability to know the truth. Subsequently, the principle of epistemic closure can only sensibly apply to the knowable truth, not to all that is beyond it. And the only sceptical challenge that bites is the challenge from error. As we have seen, error eliminability withstands it. Accordingly, legal judgments remain possible.

3

Between the Epistemic and the Practical: Pushing against a Persisting Difficulty

We have seen that error eliminability is a condition of legal fact finding. We have also seen that error eliminability can justify belief and hence allow the generation of knowledge. But why should the law care about knowledge? Whatever the law's aims are, they do not include increasing our knowledge of the world. The aims of the law are practical in nature. Hence, we should expect the law to be governed solely by considerations of accuracy; and if probabilism provides maximum accuracy, we should expect the law to be governed by probabilism. Unless, that is, it is shown that there is some deeper connection between the epistemic and the practical.

The fact that error eliminability regulates these two domains (the legal and the epistemological) can be accounted for in different ways. One possibility is that knowledge is in some way legally valuable, or that practical reasons are in some way epistemically valuable. Another possibility is that error eliminability is a method that allows for non-probabilistic inferences wherever these are appropriate, be it in epistemology, in the law or in other domains. Yet another possibility is that there is one value that overarches the epistemological, the legal and, possibly, other practical domains; this value calls for non-probabilistic inference based on error eliminability; and subsequently, the domains intersect – knowledge is valuable in a range of other domains because it reflects a value that overarches them all.

This chapter considers these possibilities, focusing on the first and opening the door to fuller examination of the second and third. It begins by introducing the contentious discussions about the practical value of epistemological concepts and the epistemological value of practical concepts. It then looks at one attempt to suggest that methods used in epistemology are of wider application, before considering literature that might point to a shared overarching value.

The presentation aims to be simple and brief, even though it includes some critical comment. Readers who are familiar with the philosophical discussions on the connection between knowledge and practical justification, and who are still convinced that such a connection is insufficiently established, may wish to skip to the next chapter.

I. Does Knowledge Have Practical Value?

Investigations of the practical value of the justification for belief are usually conducted as part of investigations of the value of knowledge. The question started with Socrates, who questioned the hypothesis that knowledge is practically valuable by demonstrating that true belief is just as practically valuable even if it does not qualify as knowledge: if one wants to go to Larissa, truly believing which way leads to Larissa, albeit without possessing knowledge, is just as valuable as knowing which way leads to Larissa. In both instances, one will arrive at Larissa.[1] Socrates' assumption here is that knowledge consists of true justified belief. The Socratic discussion demonstrates that true belief has practical value, and thus the remaining question is whether the justification and its combination with true belief has any independent practical value at all.

It is not easy to see the practical value that the justification for belief might have, or indeed the practical value that knowledge might have. In fact, one view is that neither the justification for belief nor knowledge has any practical value. David Papineau has gone as far as suggesting that knowledge has practical disvalue. Focusing on the legal context as his prime example, he notes 'We are being seduced by archaic ways of thinking into procedures that positively hinder our attempts to punish the guilty and save the innocent. We need to stop thinking in terms of knowledge.'[2] Papineau then extends his analysis to all practical contexts, including personal relationships and assertorical communication.

This position is forceful. If practical value is outcome-oriented, it is not clear how anything except accuracy in reaching outcomes might be practically valuable. The rejection of a practical reference to epistemological concepts thus draws much of its force from a normative analysis of action. Action is analysed as aiming solely at achieving its practical goal; accordingly, even when an action is merely likely to achieve its goal, it is justified and will be pursued. Neither knowledge nor epistemic justification is relevant for action.

Still, there is a troubling tension between this normative analysis and our practices. In various contexts, we do act only based on knowledge (or justified belief). It is possible that this is just an irrationality that is explicable in evolutionary terms, as Papineau suggests.[3] But one must admit that if such practices are widely common, and if, as Cohen has shown, they characterise the experimental sciences as much as they characterise the law, an explanation in this spirit would be hard to accept. Let us thus observe the practices of human action and examine the extent of the connection they manifest between the epistemological and the practical.

[1] Plato, *Meno*, tr B Jowett (Champaign, IL, Infomotions Inc, 2000) 29.
[2] D Papineau, 'The Disvalue of Knowledge' (2021) 198 *Synthese* 5311, 5313.
[3] ibid 5311–12.

The difficulty with the assumption that the epistemic is irrelevant for the practical goes to the basic observation that there are any actions at all for which the epistemic is irrelevant. Observation of action demonstrates that this is not the case. The justification of all action includes some assumptions about the possibility that epistemic conditions would be met. For all action, likelihood of success is a necessary but insufficient condition for justification. In addition to likelihood, the proposition that the action achieves its goal must be knowable, or at least justifiably believable.

Let us consider a broad spectrum of actions, including moral and non-moral ones. Observation of a broad spectrum of actions demonstrates that while knowledge is not always required for action, the possibility of knowledge or at least of justified belief is required. We act when we have reason to think that knowledge or justified belief is either possible or might be possible at a later stage when further evidence unfolds.

To see this, think first of non-moral action such as financial investment. One chooses how to invest even though the available evidence does not yet generate knowledge that this investment will pay off, neither does it justify belief that this investment will pay off. All the evidence allows is believing that the investment will probably pay off. Still, further evidence is expected to emerge (this is the default assumption: we act based on our rational evaluation of how future evidence will unfold); and this evidence is expected to support knowledge of, or justify belief in, the proposition that the investment has either paid off or has not paid off. Had we thought that the answer to the question whether the investment has paid off would never be known or justifiably believed, and that the only thing we would ever know or justifiably believe is that the investment has probably paid off, we might not have bothered to make an investment. In any case, as a descriptive matter, one's expectation when investing is that evidence will unfold that will allow knowing if the investment has paid off.

Now think of moral action. Generally, one takes moral action only where the available evidence already generates knowledge, or at least epistemic justification for the belief that the action is moral. One would condemn a person heard making a racist slare; but one would not condemn a person where the evidence is that this person was present in a house where most of the people present made racist slares. One does not decide to condemn another based on high probability of desert, only with the expectation that the decision will 'prove right' or come to be known or justifiably believed once further evidence unfolds at some point in the future. Yet there are some moral actions where the attainability of knowledge or justified belief includes future attainability. In such cases moral action is similar to non-moral action: it is taken even absent knowledge or justified belief, but with the expectation that knowledge or justified belief will be generated at a later stage. This is the case of action in conditions of necessity, where only the future will tell if the action was indeed necessary.

If all this is correct, moral and non-moral action is only taken where knowledge or justified belief is attainable; the attainability of likelihood of success is not enough. Yet in the moral context, knowledge or justified belief often needs to be attainable at the time of the action rather than in the future.

That action is not taken where knowledge or at least justified belief is unattainable means that action is not motivated in such conditions. Thus, one way in which epistemic justification might be practically relevant concerns motivation: the prospect of epistemic justification, and hence of knowability, provides motivation for action. We saw in the previous chapter that the Pyrrhonian sceptic faced the possibility of regression to passivity and inaction. We have not, however, paused to consider why. And it is possible that where belief cannot be justified and knowledge is beyond reach, action cannot be motivated.

Unfolding this argument requires a detailed theory of motivation that goes beyond the scope of this book. The following brief comments will suffice here. A relevant theory of motivation would suggest that what motivates action is the expectation that a wish (a desire or a want) would be satisfied; and satisfaction requires knowledge or justified belief that that which is aimed at has occurred. Moral action is meant to satisfy a wish that morality will ensue; and it is arguable and consistent with evidential practice that such satisfaction can only be achieved through knowledge or justified belief that morality has ensued. If one condemns another whom one justifiably believes is only very likely to have made a racist slare, a sense of satisfaction will not be brought about. Accordingly, one cannot be motivated to moral action where knowledge is unattainable. Similarly, an action like investing one's financial excess is directed at satisfying a desire for financial gain. And it is arguable and consistent with evidential practice that the desire for financial gain can only be satisfied by knowledge or justified belief that the investment had indeed been fruitful. Accordingly, the existing prospect of gaining such knowledge or justified belief with the help of further evidence that is expected to unfold can motivate action. Such motivation can sometimes develop even without the immediate availability of knowledge-generating evidence, based on the possibility of gaining knowledge when further evidence emerges.

Note that this brief suggestion says nothing about the force of epistemic facts to motivate the formation of belief or to motivate epistemic practices such as searching for more evidence.[4] This account addresses only the motivational force of the desire to know the aimed for outcomes of actions.

Why does the prospect of knowledge or epistemic justification bring satisfaction and motivate action? Why does doubt paralyse? There can be different ways of answering these questions, but for current purposes we can leave them without an answer. The important thing to note is that as a descriptive matter, there is a strong, possibly causal, connection between epistemic warrant and virtually all practical action. Considering the breadth and strength of this connection, the suggestion

[4] For a critical discussion, see C Boult and S Kohler, 'Epistemic Judgement and Motivation' (2020) 70 *The Philosophical Quarterly* 738.

that epistemic warrant lacks practical value (and indeed that it might be practically disvaluable) might be hasty.

II. The Practical Value of Epistemic Reasons: Stability of Belief and Successful Action

The thought that knowledge might have practical value has a long history. Socrates' response to his Larissa example is to try to identify the value that knowledge might nevertheless have. The Platonic dialogue suggests that knowledge is a true belief that is tethered to the truth, and hence it stays with us. The Platonic view that a true belief that qualifies as knowledge is more stable than a true belief that fails in this regard is defended by Williamson. Williamson thinks of knowledge as precluding the materialisation of human fallibility, whereby one does not know when one relies on good evidence inappropriately. He notes:

> One can lose a mere true belief by discovering the falsity of further beliefs on which it had been essentially based; quite often, the truth will out. One cannot lose knowledge that way, because a true belief essentially based on false beliefs does not constitute knowledge. For example, I might derive the true belief that this road goes to Larissa from the two false (but perhaps justified) beliefs that Larissa is due north and that this road goes due north; when dawn breaks in an unexpected quarter and I realize that this road goes south, without having been given any reason to doubt that Larissa is due north, I abandon the belief that this road goes to Larissa. Since that true belief was essentially based on false beliefs, it did not constitute knowledge. The case is an obvious variation on Gettier's counterexamples to the analysis of knowledge as justified true belief.[5]

Thus, when we rely on the evidence appropriately and know, our true belief is stable, we will act on it and our action will achieve its practical goal. But we can believe truly even when we rely on evidence inappropriately, namely, when our intellectual fallibility materialises (but the belief is nevertheless accidentally true). Yet when we rely on evidence inappropriately and nevertheless end up with a true belief, we will later discover that we relied on the evidence inappropriately, as further evidence that indicates this will show up. In such a case, we will desert our true belief and act on a different false belief. Therefore, our action will fail to achieve its practical goal.

For Williamson, knowledge is a primary concept. Note, however, that if knowledge is analysed as a secondary concept that is composed of several elements (as Williamson would object that it can be), his anaysis in fact highlights the

[5] T Williamson, *Knowledge and Its Limits* (Oxford, Oxford University Press, 2000) 78. By 'Gettier's counterexamples' Williamson is referring to examples seeking to demonstrate that a true justified belief might not constitute knowledge if it is based on reasons that turn out to be false. Such examples were introduced in E Gettier, 'Is Justified True Belief Knowledge?' (1963) 23 *Analysis* 121.

practical value of meeting error eliminability. Williamson presumes with Gettier that on a 'true justified belief' conception of knowledge, the relevant unstable beliefs are justified. And they are indeed justified on various accounts of epistemic justification (such as Nozick's). But as we saw in chapter 1, these beliefs are not justified on error eliminability. They are not justified where misleading evidence is accidentally interpreted as indicating the truth; and they are surely not justified where the evidence is merely statistical. Yet if this is the case, then Williamson's analysis demonstrates that unstable beliefs are irrational and unjustified ones. This, in turn, might indicate that it is epistemic justification (error eliminability) that makes true beliefs stable.

Still, Williamson's argument that knowledge has practical value can be put under pressure. His assumption is that there is practical value in the stability of true beliefs, because true beliefs guide successful action. There are three difficulties with this assumption. First, it is not clear that we will hold more steadily to knowledge than to true beliefs. Even when we know, further misleading evidence that seems to contradict that which we know might later appear, and given human fallibility we might well be convinced by this new evidence and avoid successful action. Second, it is not clear that the appearance of new evidence that contradicts true beliefs will interrupt successful action. This will essentially depend on the timing of action over the timeline of the evidential examination. It is possible that one has chosen to act before the new evidence has become available. If this is not the case, it is also possible *and indeed probable* that one's response to the new contradicting evidence would be to desert one's belief but to withhold action and search for further evidence. Once more evidence appears, one would adopt the true belief yet again and act. If true belief has lesser practical value at all, it is then only in delaying action, not in producing unsuccessful action. And the answer to the question whether delaying successful action reduces its practical value would depend on contingent circumstances. Third, even if true beliefs are deserted in the face of new evidence, this might be practically valuable in the long run. We can only maximise our overall knowledge by fallibly examining whatever evidence is or becomes available; thus, maximising knowledge comes with the cost of possible errors (adopting some false beliefs or rejecting some true beliefs). The instability of true beliefs is thus part of an essential mechanism for maximising knowledge. Once it is acknowledged that the instability of true beliefs is essential for maximisation of knowledge in an imperfect world, it becomes apparent that, overall, this instability is practically valuable.

III. Pragmatism: The Epistemic Value of Practical Reasons

Pragmatism is the view that there are some essential, non-contingent relations between epistemic reasons and practical reasons. There is a wide variety of pragmatists. They offer varied views about the nature of the truth, the nature of epistemic warrant and the nature of other possible conditions of knowledge. Not all of them can be considered here. I would like to focus on two branches of pragmatism that have been dominant in the discussion of the practical value of knowledge. The first branch considers the role of practical considerations in either justifying belief or meeting any additional condition of knowledge. This version of pragmatism is considered in this section. The second branch conceptualises epistemic practices as social practices governed by semantic norms.[6] We will return to some of its suggestions in chapter 7 when considering the responsibility of assertors.

Pragmatic encroachment theorists have suggested that the question about the practical value of knowledge should be reversed: it is not that knowledge is first established on pure epistemic grounds and then its practical value should be revealed; rather, practical reasons have epistemic value: they either affect the justification for belief,[7] or they affect the generation of knowledge.[8] Thus, when the stakes in a practical decision are high, the epistemic threshold for justifying belief or generating knowledge of the relevant facts will be high. If this is correct, epistemic judgements are subject to pragmatic encroachment. Pragmatic encroachment theorists introduce various examples to demonstrate their claim. To take one such example, when it is not particularly important that you deposit your pay cheque any time soon, you might postpone depositing until Saturday, explaining that you know the bank is open on Saturday as you were there on Saturday two weeks ago; but when there is a bill pending and little money in your account, and it is therefore very important that you make the deposit by Saturday, you will deposit on Friday, conceding that even though you were at the bank on Saturday two weeks ago, you do not know that it would be open on Saturday again, as banks often change their hours.[9] To take another example, you will take back your claim that you know that there is no chocolate in the cake because you have never encountered a lemon cake with chocolate in it, once you learn that one of the children who will be eating the cake suffers a very severe allergy to chocolate.[10]

Philosophers have sought to apply these suggestions about pragmatic encroachment to the legal context. Sarah Moss, for example, has suggested that the criminal standard of 'beyond reasonable doubt' sets a knowledge threshold for conviction; that knowledge is subject to pragmatic encroachment; and that accordingly, there might be at least an a priori reason to provide juries with sentencing information

[6] This is Brandom's view as stated, amongst other places, in RB Brandom, *Perspectives on Pragmatism: Classical, Recent and Contemporary* (Cambridge, MA, Harvard University Press, 2011) (see, eg, ibid 129–30).

[7] J Fantl and M McGrath, *Knowledge in an Uncertain World* (New York, Oxford University Press, 2009).

[8] J Stanley, *Knowledge and Practical Interests* (New York, Oxford University Press, 2005).

[9] ibid 3–4.

[10] Compare with S Moss, 'Pragmatic Encroachment and Legal Proof' (2021) 31 *Philosophical Issue* 258, 259.

before they decide whether the knowledge standard has been met. Moss has further suggested that the civil standard sets a threshold of probabilistic knowledge for civil judgment; that being justified in believing 'more likely than not' is not yet knowing that 'more likely than not'; and that to know that 'more likely than not', the relevant stakes for the parties need to be considered.[11]

Moss's suggestions give rise to difficulties that highlight the more general difficulties with pragmatic encroachment. As for criminal law, the proposal seems to indicate that there is an a priori reason to provide juries with information about the consequences of sentencing for the specific defendant. Might juries be right in principle to acquit a prodigy pianist who would otherwise be sentenced to life imprisonment based on evidence that would have led the jurors to convict a homeless person with low prospects in life? As for the civil standard of proof, more difficulties are added by the notion of probabilistic knowledge. It is far from clear that I am justified in believing that John rather than Sarah probably stole my mobile phone based on the statistical evidence that more men than women steal mobile phones.[12] Even if that were the case, the question would rise again: does the jury need to further consider John's financial situation and the implications of a compensation judgment on him before it judges that it knows that John probably stole my phone?

But a more general objection to pragmatic encroachment can be proposed. Pragmatic encroachment theorists make much of our tendency to backtrack on a claim of knowledge once the stakes rise. If I am asked if I know whether there is chocolate in the cake, I might answer 'Yes, I do, there is no chocolate in this cake.' If I am then alerted to the fact that one of the children who will be eating the cake has severe allergy to chocolate, I will backtrack and say 'No, actually I'm not sure; you'd better check this.'[13] But it is not clear that much can be made of this backtracking. This backtracking is not necessarily from a claim of knowledge to a claim of lack of knowledge. It is more plausible that the backtracking is from an unqualified claim of knowledge to the qualified claim that Sandy Goldberg has captured in the expression 'to the best of one's knowledge'.[14] Once stakes are increased, we would qualify a claim that we know with 'to the best of my knowledge', and concede that before action is taken more evidence needs to be sought. Even when we say 'actually I don't know', it is hard to suppose that we would reject the use of 'to the best of my knowledge' in the circumstances. And if this is correct, the rise in stakes does not impact any epistemic statuses or standards; it does not negate or diminish the justification for belief, neither does it prevent knowledge. All it does is signify that

[11] ibid, esp section 3.

[12] See B Salow, 'Probabilistic Knowledge, by Sarah Moss. Oxford: Oxford University Press, 2018' (2020) 129 *Mind* 515. See also D Enoch and L Spectre, 'Statistical Resentment, or: What's Wrong with Acting, Blaming, and Believing on the Basis of Statistics Alone' (2021) 199 *Synthese* 5687, suggesting at 5694 that it might not even be justified to believe that the members of a certain group are more likely, say, to be criminals. More will be said about this in ch 9.

[13] Compare again with Moss (n 10).

[14] S Goldberg, *To the Best of Our Knowledge: Social Expectations and Epistemic Normativity* (Oxford, Oxford University Press, 2018).

there might be a gap between meeting epistemic conditions and the availability of practical reasons for action.

Qualified knowledge claims where stakes are high can also explain the different legal burdens of proof and their relation to epistemic and practical standards. The law does not shift between a standard of propositional knowledge in criminal law and a standard of probabilistic knowledge in civil law. Rather, the law requires that unified epistemic standards are met before a court makes a judgment, namely, that to the best of the court's knowledge such and such is the truth. Different standards of proof then determine at what evidential point the court's knowledge converges with additional practical aims, namely, that the knowledge is good enough to make practical decisions based on it. This is where stakes matter: more evidence would be needed before the court's knowledge can justify a criminal conviction; less evidence would be needed before the court's knowledge can justify a civil ruling of compensation.

This suggestion should be distinguished from that of Sandy Goldberg in *To the Best of Our Knowledge: Social Expectations and Epistemic Normativity*.[15] Goldberg considers assertions, which will be discussed in the next chapter. He suggests that assertions are governed by a norm of epistemic warrant, and the evidential threshold that provides epistemic warrant is determined by the context: a person who makes a statement (an assertion) is responsible to satisfy expectations that others are entitled to have regarding his epistemic position.[16] Goldberg therefore speaks of the entitlements of others, and he explains that some of these entitlements are connected to specific professional or other roles of the person making the statement, and others are more general entitlements shared by all members of the epistemic community as such.[17] What makes others entitled to hold these expectations is the social-institutional context and its underlying rationale: we would not have exchanged information and practised as we do (generally or in specific contexts) if it were not for these mutual expectations. Thus, the source and conditions of epistemic norms are in social practice and in its constitutive rationale.[18]

[15] ibid. See also SC Goldberg, 'Should Have Known' (2017) 194 *Synthese* 2863; SC Goldberg, *Assertion: On the Philosophical Significance of Assertoric Speech* (Oxford, Oxford University Press, 2015) 1.1; and see his discussion of ethics ibid section 7.

[16] A concise statement of this position can be found in Goldberg (n 14) 127: 'My claim is that epistemic responsibility in the broader sense … is simply a matter of satisfying all of the legitimate epistemic expectations on one.'

[17] For elaboration see ibid ch 5.

[18] Goldberg writes (ibid 106–07) 'But we might ask: what *entitles* us to have such epistemic expectations of one another? My answer is that these epistemic expectations reflect a number of presuppositions that inform our engagements with one another. These engagements are of two main types: information-exchanging engagements (where the aim is to share information), and practical engagements (where the aim is to act together or in coordination with one another).' And further (ibid 110) '[O]ur practices of information-exchange and practical engagement with one another have a rationale supporting them – that is, participation in these practices avoids practical irrationality – only if we are entitled to expect certain things of other epistemic subjects; but these engagements *do* have a rationale supporting them (one can deny this only at the cost of a profound distortion of our lives as fundamentally social creatures); so we are entitled to have the expectations.'

Such a position is similar to Moss's, namely, it suggests that the practical context affects epistemic rationality. Yet unlike Moss, Goldberg might be capable of avoiding the objection regarding inappropriate individuation of the epistemic standard. For him, it is the rationale of the social practice, rather than the impact on specific individuals, that determines the epistemic standard.

Still, it is not clear what such a proposal means for unjustifiable social practices: they might give rise to epistemic standards that are justified in their context but cannot be justified in principle. Furthermore, Goldberg's suggestion can also be objected to on the ground that it hardly fits normal usage of knowledge claims. It is perfectly natural to say 'to the best of my knowledge, this is how things are, but if I were you I'd check further before acting', or 'to the best of my knowledge this medicine should work well for you, but it might be wise if I raise this in an end-of-day consultation before I prescribe it to you'. Such usage of knowledge claims implies what has been suggested here: that the epistemic threshold is fixed, but it does not always converge with the practical threshold.

If this is correct, pragmatic encroachment and theories in its surroundings can hardly provide a satisfactory account of the relation between the epistemic and the practical. The search must continue.

IV. A Shared Method of Reasoning for the Epistemic and the Practical

Another possible connection between epistemic and practical reasons might be found not in the content of the reasons but in their structure. Enoch, Fisher and Spectre have noted that some epistemological reasons and some practical reasons have the structure of counterfactuals; and that this reliance on counterfactuals leads to the same evidence having epistemological value and practical value. In epistemology, the authors focused on Nozick's sensitivity condition. Remember that the sensitivity condition uses counterfactuals to identify knowledge; it requires examining whether and how a belief that P, which is developed based on E, would change or would undergo qualification if in reality P were false. In the practical context, the authors focused on incentives. Relying on Sanchirico's account of 'bad character evidence',[19] they noted that evidential reasons relating to incentives for positive conduct rely on counterfactuals: they require examining if and how the conduct of potential defendants might change if the evidence is admissible in law. Thus, the authors note,

> though the epistemological story is not itself of legal value, and though the instrumental story that is of legal value is not itself epistemologically respectable, both of them still

[19] CW Sanchirico, 'Character Evidence and the Object of Trial' (2001) 101 *Columbia Law Review* 1227.

> stem from the same source, Sensitivity-style counterfactuals. These are needed both for knowledge (or are in some other closely related way epistemically relevant) and for a reasonably efficient incentive structure.[20]

In highlighting the possibility that there is a common structure to epistemological and practical reasons, this account is fundamentally important. Yet the identification of this alleged common structure gives rise to difficulties. First, it is eclectic, focusing on one epistemological account and on one highly specific type of practical reasons. Second, as Fisher notes in a later article,[21] the authors' account of incentives can be criticised for being partial. A more comprehensive account that also considers the increase in punishment expectancy for guilty defendants following admission of naked statistical evidence could lead to different conclusions: it could indicate that admitting naked statistical evidence actually creates incentives for refraining from crime, thus supporting admission. And if this is true, the epistemological story and the instrumental story actually diverge rather than coincide. Third, it is not at all clear that counterfactuals indeed play the instrumental role the authors suggest they play.[22] The assertion that potential defendants actually consider evidential rules and apply counterfactuals when deliberating whether to commit crime, and the related conclusion that admission of naked statistical evidence works to diminish their motivation to commit crime, seem to stretch reality when presented without empirical support. Fourth, as the authors acknowledge, even if the instrumental story were valid, their analysis would still fail to provide any deep explanation of a seemingly surprising state of affairs; it would fail to provide any deep explanation of the fact that counterfactuals seem to play a similar role and lead to similar conclusions in two allegedly different and unrelated contexts.

For an account about a common structure of epistemic and practical reasons to succeed, it thus needs to apply convincingly and sufficiently broadly to epistemic and practical reasons; and it further needs to be explicable: what is it about a structure that makes it suitable for both contexts? And is there a shared value that underlies this suitability? As the book progresses, such an account will gradually unfold. According to this account, epistemic reasons and practical reasons of respect share one structure, namely, error eliminability. This common structure is explicable with reference to the underlying rationale of epistemic reasons and reasons of respect: because of their uncompromising nature, epistemic reasons and practical reasons of respect admit no probabilistic structure; rather, they require that reasons be available to think that the risk of error has been eliminated. It will

[20] D Enoch, L Spectre and T Fisher, 'Statistical Evidence, Sensitivity, and the Legal Value of Knowledge' (2012) 40 *Philosophy and Public Affairs* 197, 220.

[21] T Fisher, 'The Theoretical Foundations of Evidence Law' (2015/16) 39 *Tel Aviv Law Review* 107, 126–27 [in Hebrew].

[22] I thank Andrew Lang for this point.

further be suggested that at a deeper level, the rationale underlying epistemological reasons is, at least in part, a rationale of respect.

To open the door for this argument, it would be useful to observe another account of epistemic reasons that indicates that they are in some way connected to reasons of respect. While this account too will not yet give us the answers we are after, it provides an appropriate prelude.

V. An Overarching Value: Introducing Respect

Some accounts of knowledge focus on the value of the intellectual activity involved in knowledge generation rather than on the practical value of knowledge for (other) action. Virtue epistemologists suggest that the acquisition of knowledge involves the exercise of intellectual virtues; and the exercise of intellectual virtues endows knowledge with value.[23] Virtue epistemology presumes that knowledge consists of a true justified belief, and that the knower appropriately relies on the justification, so that human fallibility that is side-lined by good luck is ruled out. It has, accordingly, been associated with 'anti-luck epistemology.'

Regardless of the question whether and to what extent the claims of virtue epistemology are successful, these claims do not seek to demonstrate any convergence of epistemic and practical reasons. Thus it is not surprising that virtue epistemology can hardly explain legal practice, and for fairly trivial reasons. First, an account that attributes at least some value to avoiding human fallibility is not suitable for explaining legal practice. Legal practice accepts human fallibility and does not attribute special significance to it. Second, accounts that focus on the virtue displayed by knowledge generation can hardly explain the legal deference to justified belief: the legal system hardly aims to produce valuable intellectual activities by decision makers; it aims to produce valuable legal action.

But while virtue epistemology does not seek to demonstrate convergence of epistemic and practical reasons, it does insightfully shift the focus of the discussion about the value of knowledge. The discussion is no longer about the value of knowledge but about the value of gaining knowledge; and from here, the way is short to a discussion of the value of persons who are capable of gaining knowledge. Enter respect for persons. Respect for persons, it will be shown, requires that when we make some judgements about persons, we comply with error eliminability.

To demonstrate this, the next chapter outlines an account of respect, and shows that it demands meeting error eliminability; hence, all expressions of respect

[23] See, eg, E Sosa, *A Virtue Epistemology: Apt Belief and Reflective Knowledge* (Oxford, Oxford University Press, 2007); D Pritchard, 'Anti-luck Virtue Epistemology' (2012) 109 *The Journal of Philosophy* 347.

converge with justified beliefs. Furthermore, some beliefs are directly required by reasons of respect. The convergence of respect and justified belief, or the shared condition of error eliminability, is then accounted for as follows: the concept of respect for persons is prior to the justification for belief. Respect for persons is one of the foundations of the epistemological project as much as it is one of the foundations of the moral project; and hence the justification for belief receive the structure of the justification from respect (error eliminability).

PART II

The Practicality of Legal Fact Finding

4

Respecting, Asserting and Error Eliminability*

Legal fact finding is the process of establishing and subsequently asserting that a legal wrong has (or has not) taken place. Finding and asserting facts are some of the core functions of the law. Assertions, in turn, are regulated by an epistemic norm: they are to be made only when some epistemic conditions are met. But why should it be so? After all, fact finding is, allegedly, merely the basis for practical steps, such as the imposition of punishment or of duties to compensate. Why, then, not use decision-theoretic principles to decide whether such steps should be taken given existing uncertainties? Decision theory would not require that facts be found and asserted but only that their probabilities be estimated. So why fact finding?

This chapter is the first out of four chapters that unfold the relation between the epistemic and the practical in legal practice. It begins by defending the claim, thus far taken for granted, that legal judgments include assertions of fact. It then considers why legal judgments include such epistemically warranted assertions. To answer this question, first, respect for persons is introduced. It is shown that the practical norm of respect, like the epistemic norm of justified belief, is error eliminability; and further, that practical reasons of respect also regulate beliefs and assertions. Next, it is demonstrated that respect for wronged persons requires asserting that wrongdoing has been committed; such assertions need to be epistemically warranted, or based on error eliminability. Furthermore, respect for wrongdoers requires that when the state decides to burden them, the decision should comply with error eliminability. Subsequently, the decision should be founded on epistemically warranted assertions.

I. Legal Assertions

Legal judgments usually include two analytical components. The first component is an account of the facts as these have been found by the court. The court might, for example, find that a defendant bought a knife or made a bank transfer. The second derivative component is an account of the legal implications of these

* Parts of this chapter were published previously in L Levanon, 'Statistical Evidence, Assertions and Responsibility' (2019) 82 *MLR* 269.

facts and of their legal consequences. The court might, for example, find that the defendant was in possession of illegal weapons and should serve time in prison, or that the defendant was in breach of contract and should pay compensation.

The two analytical components thus take the form of public assertions about what the court has found. Assertions should be taken here to have their common, immediate meaning; the use of the term should not imply any of the heavy philosophical load it carries among linguists. As the chapter progresses, it will become clear which (narrow, mainly epistemic) characteristics legal assertions possess.

While it seems fairly uncontroversial that legal decisions include assertions of facts, an objection should nevertheless be examined. According to this objection, there exists a familiar distinction between the truth and the 'legal truth'.[1] The 'legal truth' is defined as meaning findings of facts and of liabilities made by the court based on legal rules of evidence, procedure and substantive law.[2] Allegedly, since these rules often reflect considerations that are inconsistent with the objective of truth finding, the 'legal truth' can diverge from the truth. Accordingly, legal findings are not really meant to represent the truth. And as they do not present propositions as true,[3] they do not include assertions.

There are several responses to this objection. First, the objection assumes that the court's findings are made in the context of some 'make-believe' game about reality. This assumption is unattractive: it is implausible that when a court finds that a defendant committed a crime, all it finds is that it has been legally proved that the defendant committed a crime, and the parties and members of the public should not understand this finding as a claim that the defendant actually committed a crime.[4]

Second and relatedly, the distinction between the truth and the 'legal truth' is not fundamental as far as it refers to factual findings. A fundamental distinction between the truth and the 'legal truth' sometimes refers to findings of liability; here, it reflects an alleged gap between legal liability and moral responsibility, or between substantive legal definitions and moral definitions (for example, 'for the law she is a thief, but she is not "really" a thief'). Alternatively, sometimes the distinction between the truth and the 'legal truth' does refer to factual findings, but in this context it is not fundamental: it merely reflects the gap between absolute certainty and higher levels of risk of error, all within the framework of commitment

[1] For some of the discussions of this distinction, see RS Summers, 'Formal Legal Truth and Substantive Truth in Judicial Fact-Finding – Their Justified Divergence in Some Particular Cases' (1999) 18 *Law and Philosophy* 497; MS Moore, 'The Plain Truth about Legal Truth' (2003) 26 *Harvard Journal of Law and Public Policy* 23. See also L Laudan, *Truth, Error and Criminal Law: An Essay in Legal Epistemology* (Cambridge, Cambridge University Press, 2006).

[2] For current purposes, the relevant part of this definition concerns findings of fact made based on legal rules of evidence and procedure.

[3] Laudan (n 1).

[4] It can further be noted that the reference to 'truth' (legal or otherwise) expresses commitment to a certain fit between all of the court's determinations and reality, and it reflects understanding that the parties and the public take the determinations as claims about the reality.

to a search for the truth.[5] As we have seen, the epistemic search for the truth does not demand absolute certainty. It demands that the evidence increase the probability that a proposition is true given the evidence, so that it is higher than 0.5; and further that reasons be available on the evidence to think that error does not occur. Acknowledging that it is always possible that we have misidentified the reasons to think that error does not occur, and hence absolute certainty is practically beyond reach, is consistent with such commitment.

Third, to the extent that the distinction between the truth and the 'legal truth' is more fundamental even in the context of factual findings, it is valid only for negative findings of lack of liability. It is possible that when the law makes a negative finding, it does not make any assertions about the truth; rather, it only declares that there is no ground for making assertions that would, amongst other things, have the power to alter whatever beliefs the public is otherwise expected rationally to hold.[6] But this is not the case when the law makes a positive finding and thereby declares that there is ground for the public to alter its beliefs about the truth. Such declarations are nothing but assertions about the truth. In the context of criminal law, such a view might associate the willingness to increase the risk of 'false negatives' for the sake of avoiding 'false positives' and for the sake of other interests with the fact that (only) negative findings do not include assertions about the truth anyway.[7]

Thus, much legal decision making involves presenting factual propositions as true, and accordingly it involves assertions. Indeed, as already noted, courts decide more than just the facts, and accordingly their decisions involve more than assertions of facts. Courts also make practical decisions based on these facts; and in

[5] The civil standard of proof is an example: when a court finds that a fact has been proved to this standard, it remains committed to the truth despite acknowledging a relatively high risk of error. Another example is the law's decision to put limits on proof of collateral facts: despite allowing some risk of error for the sake of efficiency, this decision does not reflect a break up with the truth.

[6] Compare with some of the arguments made in F Picinali, 'The Presumption of Innocence: A Deflationary Account' (2021) 84 *MLR* 708.

[7] The stringent criminal standard of proof (beyond reasonable doubt) works to minimise the number of false convictions at the cost of increasing the number of false acquittals. See A Stein, *Foundations of Evidence Law* (Oxford, Oxford University Press, 2005) 172. Furthermore, relevant prosecution evidence aimed at proving facts that establish guilt is often excluded. A few examples include the regulation of admission of confessional evidence in ss 82(1) and 76 of the Police and Criminal Evidence Act (PACE) 1984; the discretion given to the court in PACE 1984, s 78(1) to exclude probative prosecution evidence where admission would be unfair to the accused; or the *Turnbull* warning laid down in *R v Turnbull* [1977] QB 224, which concerns the special caution required when convicting based on identification evidence introduced by the prosecution. Such evidence might be excluded on the basis of considerations that have nothing to do with the truth, like considerations of human rights, legitimacy or the need to maintain public trust in the integrity of the legal system. See Laudan (n 1). By contrast, relevant defence evidence aimed at refuting guilt is hardly ever excluded. If defence evidence is excluded at all, the exclusionary rule is significantly narrower than the equivalent rule for prosecution evidence. See, for example, the broad admissibility of defence evidence of a co-accused's bad character in s 101(e) of the Criminal Justice Act 2003, and the substantial possibility for a co-accused to disprove a claim that confessional evidence has been extracted by torture or in other conditions that draw mandatory exclusion in s 76A(2) of PACE 1984.

principle, the norm of practical reasoning is not necessarily identical to the norm of assertion.[8] However, given that the court's practical decisions are based on the decided facts rather than directly on the evidence, the norm of (legal) assertion and the norm of (legal) practical reasoning cannot diverge. In the legal context, the norm of assertion and the norm of practical reasoning merge.

The concept of assertion will be considered in further detail in section IV, but the following should already be noted: assertions are sayings governed by an epistemic norm, which can be a norm of belief, of warrant, of knowledge or of truth.[9] Some accounts further add requirements of intention, such as the intention that the hearer will believe that the proposition is true.[10] Yet other accounts define assertions as sayings that involve certain commitments[11] that are at least partly epistemic. These commitments can include the commitment to justify the assertion if and when challenged, or the commitment to withdraw the assertion if and when shown erroneous, or the commitment (to be discussed further later in this book) to be held accountable for errors and their practical outcomes.

Why do courts make assertions about the truth? Why can they not just decide what to do? Whom to punish and whom to compensate? And if courts do make assertions about the truth, what is the epistemic norm that should govern them? To start answering these questions, let us consider the reasons which are in operation for those who possess evidence of wrongdoing.

II. Informing of Wrongdoing

We can start with reasons to inform of wrongdoing that exist for those who have clear evidence of wrongdoing, like the evidence provided by observation of wrongdoing. Upon observation of wrongdoing, the observer has a moral reason to inform the wrongdoer, the victim (if there is such), and members of the public that a wrong has been committed. Consider the following example: you see a child stealing a bike; you have a reason to respond by saying 'That's wrong, it should

[8] For discussion of this question, see R McKenna, 'Why Assertion and Practical Reasoning are Possibly Not Governed by the Same Epistemic Norm' (2013) 4 *Logos & Episteme* 457; M Montminy, 'Why Assertion and Practical Reasoning Must Be Governed by the Same Epistemic Norm' (2013) 94 *Pacific Philosophical Quarterly* 57; and J Stanley in his earlier writing, for example, *Knowledge and Practical Interest* (Oxford, Oxford University Press, 2005).

[9] A useful brief overview can be found in M Gerken and E Nedenskov Petersen, 'Epistemic norms of assertion and action' in S Goldberg (ed), *The Oxford Handbook of Assertion* (Oxford, Oxford University Press, 2020) 683.

[10] K Bach and R Harnish, *Linguistic Communication and Speech Acts* (Cambridge, MA, MIT Press, 1979).

[11] A detailed account is found in RB Brandom, *Making it Explicit* (Cambridge, MA, Harvard University Press, 1994). See also RB Brandom, *Perspectives on Pragmatism: Classical, Recent & Contemporary* (Cambridge, MA, Harvard University Press, 2011).

not be (or should not have been) done.' Or, to remove the harm element, consider a different example: you hear racist slurs on a homogeneously populated island with no minorities living on it; the slurs might be made by blameless children or by blameworthy adults. Either way, you have a moral reason to say such conduct is wrong. In both examples, the relevant reason supports merely conveyance of information; any additional practical responses, such as holding the perpetrator to account, might or might not be morally required but there is no need to consider them here.[12]

Such a reason to inform of wrongdoing has been partly recognised in what has come to be known as survivor's right to know the past.[13] This individual and public 'right to the truth' and the corresponding duty of states to investigate, reveal and inform of the truth has not yet gained formal status in public international law, but it has found various expressions in international practice and in case law.[14] For the time being, we can suspend consideration of the question whether there is indeed such a right and a corresponding duty, or whether there is only a reason to let survivors and the general public know the past. Furthermore, we can for now suspend consideration of the question whether the reason is to generate knowledge, and focus on a reason to inform. Setting these issues aside, a moral reason has been acknowledged that supports transmitting information about wrongdoing to those who are wronged (if any), and to the general public. Thus, we can consider the moral reason to inform moral agents about wrongful acts.

III. Reasons to Inform as Reasons to Assert: Respect for Persons

That there is a reason to inform of wrongdoing is intuitive, but the grounding of such a reason still requires elucidation. After all, it is not clear that merely transmitting moral information is morally valuable. This is easy to see if we think of moral information as information regarding a procedure, like the Kantian categorical imperative: merely transmitting the information that one should avoid action if the imperative to perform it cannot be universalised is hardly morally valuable in itself, ignoring any educational value that such transfer of information might have. Furthermore, it is doubtful if transmitting information

[12] The integration of these practices in a communicative theory of punishment is proposed in RA Duff, *Punishment, Communication and Community* (Oxford, Oxford University Press, 2003).

[13] See Y Naqvi, 'The right to truth in international law, fact or fiction?' (2006) 88 *IRRC* 245.

[14] For a comprehensive overview, see AM Panepinto, 'The right to the truth in international law: The significance of Strasbourg's contributions' (2017) 37 *Legal Studies* 739.

about the content of a specific moral reason or even moral duty is practically valuable: there might be epistemic value in transmitting the information that it is wrong to kill dinosaurs, but such information has no moral, practical value. And the same can be said about killing humans, if we consider the mere transmission of information (say as part of a descriptive essay written by an alien on the morality of persons) rather than any separate practical impact it might have. But might it be morally valuable to transmit to moral agents the information that a specific action that was in fact taken is wrongful? And if so, should the information be epistemically warranted? The answer to both questions is 'yes', and it is grounded in the notion of respect. Once wrongdoing is committed, reasons of respect support transmitting epistemically warranted information that grounds belief about this wrongdoing. And once a person is wronged by another, reasons of respect for persons support transmitting epistemically warranted information that grounds belief about this wrongdoing.

The argument will unfold as follows. First, respect will be introduced, and the relation between the conditions of respect and the conditions of rational belief will be considered. It will be shown that reasons of respect are reasons to treat things consistently with their value. Accordingly, it is impossible to 'probably respect'. 'Probably respecting' is an oxymoron, as treatment that 'probably respects' projects value that is lower than the value of whatever merits respect. Thus, the determination of whether conduct would comply with reasons of respect needs to be made based on the non-probabilistic ground; such ground is provided by error eliminability. The conditions of respectful conduct and the conditions of rational belief thus converge. Furthermore, holding the belief that valuable things have properties that demand respect is itself a form of respectful treatment in thought.

Next, it will be demonstrated that reasons of respect for wronged persons call for assertions about wrongdoing. These reasons apply to all, including legal institutions. Wrongdoing poses a twofold challenge for respect for persons. Practically, it engages with the wronged person in a way that fails to follow the demands of respect. Epistemically, it challenges the rationality of the belief that the wronged person has properties that demand respect. This epistemic challenge has independent moral implications. The twofold challenge needs to be met. Meeting it requires a twofold response that, first, demonstrates the rationality of the belief that the wronged person has properties that give reasons to respect her; and, second, demonstrates the practical effectiveness of reasons to respect the wronged person. And such demonstrations can be made by way of transmitting epistemically warranted information about wrongdoing.

Last, it will be shown that reasons of respect for wrongdoers entail that legal judgments should include assertions. When the state imposes burdens on wrongdoers, reasons of respect require that it should not decide these burdens on probabilistic grounds; rather, burdens should be decided based on error eliminability. This has epistemic implications: legal judgments should accordingly be founded on epistemically warranted assertions.

A. An Account of Respect for Persons

Let us consider respect for persons and what it requires. Raz's Kantian account is instructive.[15] Raz notes that for Kant, respect is a feeling rather than a moral status or a practical demand. This feeling is spontaneously produced when we observe exemplifications of the moral law, and it plays the role of a motivator for obeying the moral law. Raz builds on this account to construct his own notion of respect, which comes to treatment of things of value in ways that are consistent with their value. Like in the Kantian account, respect does not add new reasons beyond those that already exist. Unlike in the Kantian account, respect captures appropriate forms of treatment rather than a feeling that motivates them. Furthermore, on Raz's account respect is owed to all that is of intrinsic value rather than only to persons who are of value (as ends) in themselves. Raz's account is consistent with current use of the term 'respect', so I shall follow it here.

What do reasons of respect require? Respect for persons is a form of treatment of persons in one's mind and in one's conduct. Raz unfolds three forms of respect: thinking and talking about the valuable in ways that are consistent with its value (when we do); preserving that which is valuable; and engaging with the valuable in ways that are consistent with its value (when we do).[16] Furthermore, Raz notes that the flouting of reasons of respect when they predominate is wrong.[17] Clearly, what specific types of conduct or thoughts would or would not form respectful treatment requires unfolding.

Significantly, Raz emphasises that there are reasons to respect persons (as ends) in themselves; and that these reasons are complete and unconditional. They are complete in the sense that they are the consequence solely of an intrinsic property of persons: 'the ground for the reason involves nothing else … its intelligibility can be established without reference to anything else'.[18] Raz does acknowledge that there might be some exceptions: possibly we do not owe a duty of respect to the terminally comatose, or to psychotic murderers.[19] But these exceptions will be at the margins. In general, reasons of respect are complete. And they are unconditional in the sense that their existence depends on nothing else but the property of persons; they would persist 'however much the rest of the world changes'.[20]

Let us now consider the human property that commands respect. Raz proposes that what Kant refers to as 'respect for persons' is in fact an extension of respect for something else: for exemplifications of the moral law (for Kant).[21] For Raz, what commands respect is the capacity of being a valuer: 'the status of being someone of

[15] J Raz, *Value, Respect and Attachment* (Cambridge, Cambridge University Press, 2001).
[16] ibid 161–62 and 164.
[17] ibid 168.
[18] ibid 139.
[19] ibid 159.
[20] ibid 159.
[21] ibid 134–35.

value in oneself marks a potential in one, the potential to engage with value in the right way'.[22] Accordingly, the reason to respect persons as valuable in themselves (or as ends) comes to this: that the capacity of persons to respond to intrinsic value provides, in Raz's terms, an unconditional and complete reason for respect. It always exists regardless of any other reasons, and it depends only and fully on human capacities.

As for the force of reasons to respect persons, Raz first chooses to postpone the discussion for another opportunity, and he seems to imply that potentially, the reasons to respect persons (as ends) in themselves can be defeated by other reasons.[23] Later, Raz seems to at least make room for an absolute reason to refrain from some forms of conduct that disrespect persons (as ends) in themselves. He notes:

> People have much that is good and much that is bad about them, and we have reason to respect them for whatever is good, and lack respect for them for whatever is bad. But there is one reason for respect that they all share: they are all persons … And as persons, they all deserve the same respect, that which is due to persons … The respect due to them is among the foundations of morality.[24]

B. Respect and Belief

Respect and belief are connected in two main ways: the conditions of respectful conduct partly overlap or converge with the conditions of rational belief; and rational beliefs can themselves manifest respect.

We can start with the partial overlap or convergence of the conditions of respectful conduct and the conditions of rational belief. Respect is uncompromising; it is impossible to abide by reasons of respect by 'probably respecting'. It is impossible, because when we 'probably respect', our conduct projects less value than would be consistent with the full value of that which merits respect.[25] Accordingly, for conduct to be respectful, reasons must first be available for thinking that error in the form of disrespect does not occur; error eliminability must first be met. Error eliminability is thus not only a necessary and sufficient condition of rational belief, but also and more fundamentally a necessary condition of respectful conduct.

To see this, let us consider the two situations in which error eliminability is not met and subsequently an agent's conduct 'probably respects' rather than respects another person. First, an agent's conduct might 'probably respect' another person when this conduct imposes an ineliminable risk of disrespect, even where the agent hopes that the risk will not materialise. In such a case, the agent concedes

[22] ibid 157.
[23] This seems to be his position in *Value, Respect and Attachment* (n 15).
[24] J Raz, 'On Respect, Authority and Neutrality: A Response' (2010) 120 *Ethics* 279, 284–85.
[25] This claim is further unpacked in ch 5.

that her conduct should disrespect the person in some unlucky circumstances; or that her conduct should be inconsistent with the person's value in some unlucky circumstances. Such a concession is itself a disrespectful thought, or a thought that is inconsistent with the person's value. Furthermore, this disrespectful concession is a premise that underlies the agent's conduct as one of its reasons. It therefore changes the meaning and value of the conduct, turning it into conduct that is inconsistent with the value of the person and hence disrespectful.

Second, an agent's conduct might 'probably respect' another person when, for the agent, there remains some ineliminable likelihood that the conduct's target is not a person who is valuable (as an end) in himself but rather, say, only an object that is not valuable in itself. Where such a likelihood is present, the conduct is again disrespectful, and for similar reasons. It is disrespectful because its underlying reasons compel disrespect. The agent who acts based on the premise that her target might not be a valuable person thinks of someone who is in fact a valuable person either as valuable in herself or as an object lacking in such value. This thought is itself inconsistent with the person's value, and it is thus disrespectful. Such a thought might further be translated into an assertion of the reasons for further action; and the assertion is then disrespectful. Last, as the content of this thought or assertion underlies subsequent action as one of its reasons, it changes the meaning and value of the action itself: it turns it into an action that is inconsistent with the value of a person, or to a disrespectful action.[26]

In the next chapter, we shall see that 'probably respecting' is connected with disrespect in another way: when the evidential conditions only allow 'probably respecting', it is not necessarily irrational to bring about further disastrous consequences for individuals for the sake of other social goals. No reasons are available that guarantee that such a choice would be irrational. In other words, only well-identified reasons of respect can preclude the bringing about of such disastrous consequences from the scope of rational action. There might indeed be other reasons (which are not reasons of respect) to refrain from bringing about disastrous consequences for individuals, but none of them can guarantee that it is always irrational to do so. Thus, 'probably respecting' is not only immediately disrespectful; the evidential conditions that underly it also open the door for the imposition of further harmful and disastrous consequences on individuals for the sake of others. As a principle of action, it is therefore unjust.

Since 'probably respecting' amounts to disrespecting, reasons of respect rule out probabilistic reasoning about the value that our conduct in fact projects and about the value that our conduct should project. Accordingly, conduct is respectful when reasons are available to think that the risk that it is does not project the correct value (and is thus disrespectful) has been eliminated. Such reasons would support the proposition that there is no error in identifying the value of

[26] More will be said about this in the next chapter, where the reasons underlying such an action will be unfolded.

that which merits respect, and they would further support the proposition that there is no error in identifying the value projected by the conduct. Respect thus requires that error eliminability be met, both with regard to the value of that which merits respect and with regard to the value projected by the conduct. And this, as is by now clear, has epistemic implications: first, it means that respect presupposes rational belief in the value of a person whom we treat in thought or action. Second, it means that respect further requires rational belief in the proposition that our conduct projects this value.[27]

Notably, this also means that the value of probability is similar in the context of respect and in the context of belief. The fact that conduct is probably respectful is valuable; it is surely better to 'probably respect' than it is to 'less-probably respect'. Yet this is not because the conduct is then 'more respectful' or projects value that is closer to that which should be projected. Action that reflects 90 per cent likelihood that the targeted person is not subhuman is not 'more respectful' of that person than a different action that reflects 70 per cent likelihood that this person is not subhuman. Both these actions are plainly disrespectful, as respect is not a matter of degree. Rather, the first action is better because it demonstrates general regard to reasons of respect even when they cannot be met, and it is thus less (or not) blameworthy. In the same way, the fact that a proposition one holds is probably true is valuable; other things being equal, it is better to hold propositions that are probably true than propositions that are less likely to be true. Yet this is not because the holding of such propositions is 'more knowledgeable' than the holding of propositions that are less likely to be true. Knowledge (and rational belief as an element of which) is not a matter of degree. Rather, holding a proposition that is probably true is better because it demonstrates regard to the acquisition of knowledge even when a true justified belief cannot be held, and accordingly it is a less (or not) faulty epistemic practice.

In addition to this convergence of justifications, beliefs are value-projectors, and accordingly they can themselves be respectful or disrespectful, and so can be the failure to rationally develop them. As Raz notes, beliefs are one type of thought, and as such, they are guided not only by epistemic reasons but also by practical reasons of respect.[28] A justified belief that the person we engage with is valuable in herself is an independent manifestation of respect in thought. To see this, let us consider the implications of failing to hold such a rational belief when engaging with persons. If an agent fails to rationally believe that a person is valuable in herself, the agent would be doing one of the following: the agent might be holding such a belief based on bad reasons or no reasons, but the agent then is not responsive to the reasons provided by personhood, thus failing to respect. Alternatively,

[27] More will be said about this connection between respectful action and rational belief in the next chapter.

[28] Raz (n 15) 161.

the agent does not hold such a belief. In this case, the agent either thinks that the specific person he engages with is not valuable in herself, or she thinks this person is either valuable in herself or she is not. If the first (the agent thinks the person is not valuable in herself), the agent thinks of the person in a way that is inconsistent with her value. If the second – say, the agent thinks that the person is likely to be valuable in herself, but she might also not be valuable in herself – the agent similarly thinks of the person in a way that is inconsistent with her value (the thought that a person might not be valuable in herself is inconsistent with the real value of the person). Thus, the belief that the person engaged with is valuable in herself must be presupposed whenever we think of any specific person, if the demands of respect in thought are to be met. It is this connection between belief and respect that will be at the centre of attention later in this chapter.

Notably, Raz emphasises that respect does not demand that we believe that whatever is of value is of value:

> There is no general reason to know, or believe, that what is of value is of value, any more than there is a general reason to know or believe in all true propositions. No reason for me to believe that there is in Kazakhstan a good statute of the Buddha, even though there is such a statute there. But there is a general reason that if we think of an object which is of value, we should think of it in ways consistent with its value. This applies … [t]o our plain beliefs.[29]

Raz thus denies that we should believe or know that people are of value in themselves (as a general truth), but he suggests that we should believe or know that the person we engage with is of such value.

It can be added that the presupposition of a belief that at least the persons we are engaging with are valuable in themselves is not unique to Raz's account of respect; rather, it is a general characteristic of accounts of respect. Consider, for example, Darwall's famous account of respect, in which to respect something is 'to regard it as requiring restrictions on the moral acceptability of actions connected with it'.[30] According to this view, respect involves not only restricting our actions (for whatever reason, be it fear of sanction, expectation of reward or any other reason); it involves restricting our action because we recognise or, presumably, believe that the value of an object demands that we restrict it. Belief in value is thus presupposed.

These connections between rational belief and respect are not accidental. As already implied, respect for persons is one of the values that underly the anti-sceptical epistemological project. Scepticism forms an attack on the notion of respect. It suggests that any proposition we hold comes with an ineliminable risk of error. Respect, however, takes no ineliminable risk of error. If the risk of error is

[29] ibid.
[30] SL Darwall, 'Two Kinds of Respect' (1977) 88 *Ethics* 36, 40.

ineliminable, we cannot rationally believe anything at all, nor indeed the proposition that persons are valuable (as ends) in themselves. Our set of rational beliefs must thus be disrespectful. In addition, we cannot rationally act on the premise that persons are valuable (as ends) in themselves; rather, acting rationally is acting on disrespectful premises, like the premise that persons might not be valuable in themselves. And in such conditions, bringing about disrespectful consequences for the sake of other goals (like general utility) would sometimes be within the scope of rational action. Accordingly, if respect is to be upheld, the sceptical suggestion about an ineliminable risk of error needs to be countered. This is achieved as epistemology successfully incorporates the condition of respect, namely error eliminability.

C. Respect for Wronged Persons

We are now ready to consider why reasons of respect ground reasons to transmit epistemically warranted beliefs about wrongdoing. Our interest is mainly in legal judgments, but we can begin by demonstrating that reasons of respect might require that anyone who encounters wrongdoing against persons assert that wrongdoing has been committed; these assertions are to be directed at the wrongdoer, the wronged person and others. The relevant reasons are reasons to respect wronged persons.

To advance this argument, let us focus on one type of reasons of respect, namely, reasons to preserve value. Raz refers to such reasons mainly as reasons to preserve that which is of value. Yet it seems that if there is a reason to preserve value, there is also a reason to preserve the effective practical power of such value, or its transition from potentiality to actuality. If, as Raz suggests, having value marks having the potential to be engaged with in certain ways, this potential must include the effective power to be actualised; if the potential has no power to actualise, it is no longer a potential. If this is correct, the reason to preserve value is also a reason to preserve the effective power of value, or the effective power of the reasons to respect that which is of value.

Raz notes that the reason to preserve that which is of value can be defeated by other reasons.[31] Apart from anything else, an undefeatable reason to preserve things of value would tie us into constant and relentless engagement with preservation. Furthermore, as Raz notes, it is easy to see that often there are good reasons for us to just 'mind our own business'.[32] Still, reasons to preserve that which is of value do exist.

[31] Raz (n 15) 162, esp fnn 43 and 44.

[32] Raz's example concerns a person speaking rudely to his child: Raz (n 24) 295. It could be asked whether we have such reasons to mind our own business in clearer cases of wrongdoing, such as exploitation or violation of trust.

What does the reason to preserve value and its effective power require upon encounter with wrongdoing? Wrongdoing challenges the effective power of moral reasons; and when directed towards other persons, it thereby challenges the effective power of the reason to respect these persons. Clearly, this challenge is first practical and moral. By engaging with a person inappropriately, wrongdoing demonstrates that if there is a reason to respect this person at all, it is practically ineffective; this would come to demonstrating that there is no such practical reason at all, or that the wronged person is not valuable in herself.

In addition, wrongdoing launches an epistemic challenge directed at the belief that the wronged person possesses a property that makes her valuable in herself (thus giving effective reasons to respect her). Wrongdoing implies that the wronged person might not possess such a property. Wrongdoing indicates that the wrongdoer holds, either explicitly or implicitly, the belief that the wronged person might not be valuable in herself (or that the value of the wronged person has no effect in some circumstances, which comes to the same thing). Thus, wrongdoing indicates that there are no grounds for believing that the wronged person is valuable in herself. As we have seen, this epistemic challenge has moral implications: it is a premise or a thought that is inconsistent with the real value of the person.

If there is a reason to preserve the effective power of the value of persons, the practical challenge and the epistemic challenge need to be countered. For this purpose, the reasons that were challenged need to be effectively acted on and believed. And they need to be effectively acted on and believed upon in connection with the wrongful conduct, so that their demand in connection with that conduct remains operative even in the shadow of a violation.[33] And this can be done by transmitting epistemically warranted information about the commission of wrongdoing.

First, when we make an epistemically warranted assertion that wrongdoing was committed, we respond appropriately to the very reasons of respect that wrongdoing challenged as ineffective. We take action in the context of the wrongful conduct as these reasons require that we do, if they are to remain effective in that context; and we take this action based on error eliminability as these reasons require. In making epistemically warranted assertions, we thus turn reasons of respect into effective reasons grounded in the value of the wronged person; and we ensure that their effective power operates in the context of the wrongful conduct. By so engaging, we counter the moral challenge directed at the effective power of these reasons.

In addition and relatedly, since the transmission of information meets error eliminability (as reasons of respect require that it would), it also counters the

[33] Note in this respect Raz's grounding of reasons of respect in the good that respecting people brings to those who respect. He notes (Raz, n 15, at 158–59) 'respecting people is good for those who respect them. That means that in being of value in themselves people are also intrinsically good, that is good for other people.'

epistemic challenge of wrongdoing: it reflects a warranted belief that the wronged person is valuable in herself, thus demonstrating that there are grounds for holding such a belief. As we have seen, countering the epistemic challenge is both epistemically and morally valuable.

Before moving on, it can be noted that in a similar spirit, Frowe and Parry have argued that mere observation of wrongdoing can give rise to practical duties such as a duty to compensate. Their argument is narrower than the argument advanced here, as it is limited to what they call 'degrading wrongs'. Their suggestion is that not all wrongdoing involves disrespect, which they think is equivalent to degradation. It is hard to see how wronging persons might not involve disrespect for persons (in the sense of treating persons in ways that are inconsistent with their value). But it possible that Frowe and Parry wish to limit their argument to humiliating or degrading wrongdoing, where the wrongdoer benefits from the disrespect rather than from something else, such as property, that was achieved in a disrespectful manner. Their argument is also different from that advanced here, as it concerns purely practical rather than informational duties that also have epistemic significance. Accordingly, they seek to identify a distinct wrong that is associated with observation of wrongdoing and that does not consist of merely leaving the challenge to respect unmet. Still, that observers might have moral reasons to act is something that the two accounts have in common.

D. A Derivative Reason to Investigate Evidence of Wrongdoing

If there is a reason for whoever encounters wrongdoing to make assertions about wrongdoing, there is also a derivative reason to follow on initial evidence and establish if a person has been wronged. Establishing and asserting are two ways of preserving that which is of value. Rather than being an observer of wrongdoing, one is then an observer of initial evidence of wrongdoing. This evidence provides reason to think that wrongdoing might have been committed. This thought then provides reason to establish if a person has been wronged and, if so, to counter the challenge that such wrongdoing poses.

There is, however, no general duty to investigate where evidence of wrongdoing is available; the reason to follow on initial evidence is not exclusionary in Raz's sense, at least not in all circumstances. If, while taking a walk, one thinks that one hears a couple of children shouting neo-Nazi slogans at another child, it is possible that one has an exclusionary reason to make a reasonable effort to establish if such is the case, so that, if needed, the challenge this conduct poses can be countered by oneself or by someone else who is better situated to counter it. In many other cases, the reason will not be exclusionary: considerations of personal convenience would be legitimately weighed when deciding whether to investigate further. Moreover, often other reasons will predominate; as far as private citizens are concerned, there are strong obvious reasons against interfering in another's business or intruding into another's privacy in search for further evidence of wrongdoing.

Beyond what is needed for the purposes of the current discussion, it can be briefly emphasised that there is no reason to seek for evidence of wrongdoing in the absence of initial evidence. Searching for such evidence without having any basis to think that they are committed where and when we look would be irrational.

E. Respect for Wrongdoers

We can now move on to the specific context of legal judgments. Here, reasons of respect for wrongdoers straightforwardly require that judgments be based on error eliminability; they thus entail that judgments should include epistemically warranted assertions. These reasons of respect for wrongdoers operate in addition to the general reasons of respect for wronged persons that were considered in sections III.C and III.E.

To see this, a distinction should first be drawn between illegal wrongdoing and legal wrongdoing. Remember that we seek to justify legal fact finding and not substantive legal rules. Thus, we can assume that the scope of the law has already been determined based on all the relevant reasons, including reasons of respect, reasons related to the liberty of citizens, reasons related to the availability of enforcement resources, etc. The scope of the law might well have been delineated based on the need for a response that goes beyond merely asserting that a wrong has been committed; it is possible that the reasons to merely assert are not strong enough to justify the operation of the legal apparatus, and only reasons to decide on compensation, punishment of wrongdoers, etc can provide such justification. But once it has been determined that the law should respond in some way, it is justified to require that this response include establishing and asserting that a wrong has been committed.

In the case of illegal wrongs, the state decides to engage with the persons involved through its legal apparatus. Accordingly, in the case of illegal wrongs reasons of respect are reasons to engage with persons, when we do, in ways that are consistent with their value. They are no longer (only) reasons to preserve the value of persons. When the state does decide to engage with persons, it is obliged to engage with persons respectfully; and this reason is weighty if not absolute. Thus, once it has been decided that a wrong is illegal and hence the state will be engaging with the persons involved, the engagement needs to be consistent with the value of these persons. Let us examine what this entails for the state's engagement with defendants.

If the state decides to merely take some practical steps against a defendant on probabilistic grounds, those steps would be inconsistent with the intrinsic value of the defendant. Such practical steps would be based on the premise that they should in some unlucky circumstances be inconsistent with the value of the defendant's conduct. This premise is itself inconsistent with the value of the defendant (as an end) in himself: that persons are valuable in themselves entails, among other things, that we should not treat them in ways that are inconsistent with the value of their conduct. At least when imposing legal burdens, this requirement is stringent. Alternatively, probabilistically grounded practical steps would be based on the premise that it is possible (even if unlikely) that the defendant does not merit respect at all. Either way, the practical steps would only 'probably respect' the defendant, thus disrespect him. Accordingly, practical legal steps should not be based on probabilistic grounds; rather, reasons of respect require that they should be based on error eliminability. And as we have seen, this has epistemic implications: as error eliminability is also the norm of warranted belief, respect for wrongdoers entails that legal judgments should include epistemically warranted assertions.

There is no need for us to determine what the scope of substantive law should be, or when the state should respond by means of law or indeed by any other means to instances of wrongdoing by individuals. It can be briefly noted that the easier cases are of wrongdoing that involves violations of basic rights; and cases of wrongdoing that disrupts the broader apparatus of justice. This is because, as we shall see in the next chapter, failure to respond to those would be an instance of political injustice; and it is plausible that the state has conclusive political and moral reasons to avoid such instances. Thus, the state has a conclusive duty to assert that wrongdoing has been committed. Such would usually be the case in the context of core criminal law offences. But there would be other types of wrongdoing to which the law – perhaps in its non-criminal branches – should respond. And whenever the law should respond to such wrongdoing, it should establish and assert that wrongdoing has been committed.

IV. Respect and the Norm of (Legal) Assertion

The analysis of reasons to investigate, establish and assert can explain the place of assertions in the legal process. When the court makes assertions, it responds to reasons to respect the wrongdoer and the wronged person. We can now take a moment to reflect on the norm of (legal) assertion. This norm is not just a norm of epistemic warrant (ie error eliminability); it is, arguably, a norm of epistemically warranted belief. To see why, we should return to respect for wronged persons.

An assertion that wrongdoing has been committed should counter the challenges posed by wrongdoing. If it cannot do so, it engages with the wronged persons without meeting reasons of respect. As we have seen, the challenge is not only moral; it is also directly epistemic (and subsequently moral). The question is which epistemic norm assertions should comply with if they are to counter this dual challenge with its moral and epistemic components. We have already seen that to counter the challenge, assertions would need to comply at least with a norm of epistemic warrant, and we have briefly considered why this is so. We can now consider this question in more detail, with reference to different possible norms and their expected impact.

The first possible norm of assertion is a norm of belief ('one must: assert P only if one believes that P'). This norm can be motivated if speech acts are defined by the attitudes they express, and assertions are speech acts that express belief.[34] In such a framework, assertions are regarded merely as expressive tools. A norm of belief would address the epistemic challenge as one of subjective belief that need not be rational. But this would affirm the challenge rather than counter it: it would confirm that the question whether persons are valuable in themselves is a matter of subjective belief, or that there is no objective answer to the question whether this person is valuable in herself. It would thus confirm that whatever 'value' the person has, it does not provide any effective reasons to respond well to this value. As a result, an assertion that is based on a norm of belief would not counter the practical moral challenge posed by wrongdoing but rather affirm it.

Another possible norm of assertion is a truth norm ('one must: assert P only if P is true'). This norm has been proposed in combination with conversational norms about the point of assertions (to add content), and about the reasonable expectations from assertors (to clarify if their warrant is not of the kind hearers expect).[35] It is not clear if such a truth norm remains wholly independent of a knowledge norm. But be that as it may, a truth norm has limited guiding power for assertors; it only provides a basis for the evaluation of assertions, assuming that we have come to know the truth. Accordingly, it does not provide a helpful tool for countering the challenge of wrongdoing upon observation. Such would also be the case with respect to a knowledge norm ('one must: assert P only if one knows P'). The knowledge norm is discussed below, but it can be noted here that without further development, it can hardly guide assertors, as one of the elements of knowledge is the truth of the known proposition.

Yet another possible norm of assertion is a warrant norm ('one must: assert P only if one has warrant to believe that P'). Such a norm does not require that

[34] Note that while such an account can be offered with reference to the semantics of assertions, it has been argued that it is pragmatic in nature. See K Bach, 'Applying Pragmatics to Epistemology' (2008) 18 *Philosophical Issues* 68.

[35] M Weiner, 'Must We Know What We Say?' (2005) 114 *The Philosophical Review* 227.

one believe that the asserted proposition is true, but only that one has warrant to so believe.[36] A lively discussion has emerged in the context of assertions regarding the nature of such warrant, and whether it is fixed or 'sliding' depending on the social context in which the assertion is made.[37] Those offering sliding norms propose that in some social contexts, the degree of warrant required for assertions need not be as high as the degree of warrant required for knowledge. The question of what warrants belief has been considered in previous chapters; so have the suggestions that epistemic warrant changes based on pragmatic considerations and social context. We have seen that epistemic warrant is fixed and determined by the conditions of error eliminability; and that this warrant does not always converge with practical justification for action.

While a warrant norm does not yet allow for countering the challenge posed by wrongdoing, when combined with a norm of belief it becomes potent. A norm of warranted belief ('one must: assert P only if one holds a warranted belief that P') can counter the moral and epistemic challenge posed by wrongdoing. Assertions guided by such a norm are nothing but the transmission of epistemically warranted information that is also appropriately believed. And we have seen that such transmission can counter the moral and epistemic challenge. It responds to reasons that have been disregarded as ineffective; and it responds appropriately: it reflects warranted belief that the wronged person is valuable as a person (belief that has epistemic and also independent moral value). Thanks to the rationality of belief that is based on error eliminability, the assertion can effectively counter the unsupported epistemic challenge posed by wrongdoing; and as it is a conduct that is premised on such actual respectful beliefs, the assertions further counter the moral challenge.

As is clear by now, assertions cannot be governed by a norm of maximal accuracy. They cannot be based on, say, the proposition that persons are mammals and virtually all mammals are valuers and hence valuable in themselves. Assertions based on a norm of maximal accuracy would lack the power to counter the challenge posed by wrongdoing: if such assertions are based on grounds that can only lead to irrational belief, they cannot counter the epistemic aspect of this challenge. Furthermore, assertion based on a norm of accuracy can only suggest that is it highly likely that a person has been wronged. In such conditions, even if assertions are made, they do not properly respond to the value of persons.

[36] See J Lackey, 'The Norms of Assertion' (2007) 41 *Noûs* 594, esp 608; J Kvanvig, 'Assertion, Knowledge, and Lotteries' in D Pritchard and P Greenough (eds), *Williamson on Knowledge* (Oxford, Oxford University Press, 2009) 140.

[37] Norms that take account of the conversational and pragmatic context have been offered, for example, in M Gerken, 'Discursive Justification and Skepticism' (2012) 189 *Synthese* 373; R McKinnon, 'The Supportive Reasons Norm of Assertion' (2013) 50 *American Philosophical Quarterly* 121; S Goldberg, *Assertion: On the Philosophical Significance of Assertoric Speech* (Oxford, Oxford University Press,

What about a knowledge norm of assertion ('one must: assert P only if one knows that P')? The knowledge norm of assertion was proposed by Unger,[38] famously defended by Williamson, and has since been widely accepted.[39] Williamson suggests that this is a constitutive norm of assertion, analogous to the rules of a game, whose violation calls for non-moral criticism.[40] In some cases an assertor has good grounds for believing that she knows P when in fact she does not know P because P is not true. In such cases, Williamson suggests, the assertion is reasonable even though the assertor in fact lacks warrant to assert.[41] In these cases, asserting constitutes a violation of the rules of the game about which we are relaxed, as it does not undermine the game. Williamson's norm can thus be seen as a qualified knowledge norm.

Recall that Williamson thinks of knowledge as a primary concept that captures a mental state of acquaintance with a true proposition, and not as a concept that can be broken down into components such as true belief that has warrant. Within this framework, a norm of warranted belief in the sense considered here is not an option; belief is not justified where not based on knowledge. Accordingly, only knowledge can warrant assertion, with the implication that some assertions are unwarranted but still reasonable or perhaps excusable.[42] But if we set to one side these reasonable yet unwarranted assertions, Williamson's inappropriate assertions are ones made when the assertor does not have good grounds for believing that she knows, in the sense proposed here. Williamson's discussion of lottery paradoxes in his account of the knowledge norm of assertion confirms this.[43] Thus, in the end, such a qualified knowledge norm is not significantly different from a norm of warranted belief in terms of its ability to counter the challenges for respect for persons that are posed by wrongdoing.

V. Conclusions

Respect provides reasons for the state to follow on initial evidence of illegal wrongdoing, to establish if illegal wrongdoing has taken place and to assert that it has. The assertion is to be based on a norm of belief warranted by error

2015); and S Goldberg, *To the Best of Our Knowledge: Social Expectations and Epistemic Normativity* (Oxford, Oxford University Press, 2018).

[38] P Unger, *Ignorance: A Case for Scepticism* (Oxford, Oxford University Press, 1975).

[39] See, eg, J Hawthorne, *Knowledge and Lotteries* (Oxford, Oxford University Press, 2004); and J Stanley in his earlier writing, eg, *Knowledge and Practical Interest* (Oxford, Oxford University Press, 2005).

[40] T Williamson, 'Knowing and Asserting' (1996) 105 *Philosophical Review* 489, 489–92.

[41] ibid 509.

[42] On the possibility of epistemic excuse, see C Littlejohn, 'A Plea for Epistemic Excuses' in J Dutant (ed), *The New Evil Demon Problem* (Oxford, Oxford University Press, forthcoming).

[43] T Williamson, *Knowledge and Its Limits* (Oxford, Oxford University Press, 2002) section 11.3.

eliminability. Such assertions are value-projectors; accordingly, they counter the dual moral and the epistemic challenge to respect for persons that is posed by wrongdoing. Furthermore, such assertions provide basis for legal judgments that respect defendants and are consistent with the value of their actions. Asserting thus complies with predominating reasons to respect persons and their actions, and it meets any duties of respect (and, as we shall see immediately, of justice) for persons that the state might have.

5

Respecting, Doing Justice and Error Eliminability

Legal practice demonstrates that if it is irrational to believe that a legal judgment is not erroneous, it is unjust to make such a judgment. The norm of justice and the norm of rational belief in the truth of propositions are one and the same: it is the norm that demands that we be as uncompromising in our judgements about what is true and what is just as the human condition allows. Error eliminability guarantees this; it is thus the principle of reasoning that governs judgements about the uncompromising; it governs judgements about the truth and judgements about justice. The basic notion that underlies these judgements and that resists compromise and entails error eliminability is respect for persons. If justice, like rational belief, is founded on respect for persons, identifying what is just requires that error eliminability be applied in evidential conditions that allow for its application. This chapter unpacks these claims.

The argument that justice presumes and requires adherence with error eliminability will involve an evidential reconstruction of Rawls's Justice as Fairness. It will be suggested that Rawls's principles of justice demand elimination of the risk of some disastrous outcomes that are inconsistent with the value of persons and are accordingly disrespectful. Furthermore, Rawls's procedures of fairness involve modification of the evidential conditions in the public sphere, so that it can be established decisively, or without ineliminable risk of error, that such outcomes would indeed disrespect persons. Once this is established, it becomes irrational to adopt any principles that fail to allow and indeed demand ruling out entirely the risk of such consequences. In other words, it becomes irrational to adopt any principles that do not incorporate error eliminability.

This evidential reconstruction makes Rawls's procedures of fairness relevant both for distributive contexts (where the relevant disastrous outcomes are a failure to distribute to persons that which they deserve as persons) and for retributive contexts (where the relevant disastrous outcomes are a failure to give persons that which they deserve based on their right or wrongdoing). This evidential reconstruction further makes Rawls's procedures of fairness relevant both for the generation of substantive principles of distribution and retribution, and for the generation of evidential principles across the board in distributive and retributive contexts. All such evidential principles must incorporate error eliminability.

If this is correct, the principles of justice and the conditions of rational belief at least partly overlap or even converge. The argument that this convergence is not accidental, but rather stems from the value of respect, will be unfolded as follows: respect for persons is one of the values underlying both the epistemological project and the practical project. In the epistemological context, the uncompromising nature of error eliminability allows the withstanding of scepticism about all premises, including the premise that people are valuable (as ends) in themselves; this, in turn, allows for the respecting of persons in thought and in subsequent action. In the context of justice, the uncompromising nature of error eliminability allows establishing that all those who might be affected by public policy merit respect; and this guarantees that disastrous outcomes would not be imposed on persons for the sake of other social goals, in a way that would have disrespected them.

I. Justice as Fairness and Justified Belief: The Convergence of Justifications

> Justice is the first virtue of social institutions, as truth is of systems of thought. A theory however elegant and economical must be rejected or revised if it is untrue; likewise, laws and institutions no matter how efficient and well-arranged must be reformed or abolished if they are unjust. Each person possesses an inviolability founded on justice that even the welfare of society as a whole cannot override … The only thing that permits us to acquiesce in an erroneous theory is the lack of a better one; analogously, an injustice is tolerable only when it is necessary to avoid an even greater injustice. Being first virtues of human activities, truth and justice are uncompromising.[1]

Because the discussion of justice and fairness has developed especially in the context of distribution, this is where the examination will begin. In a Rawlsian theory of justice,[2] a principle is just only if it has been chosen from behind a 'veil of ignorance' that ensures fairness. This 'veil of ignorance' conceals our current contingencies such as social class, wealth, gender, etc. In the 'original position' that prevails behind the veil of ignorance, we are not yet characterised by any such contingencies; and we do not know which contingencies we will possess once the veil is lifted. Equipped with such ignorance, we should decide our principles of justice. In such conditions, Rawls proposes that the principles of justice that would be chosen are as follows: first, each person is to have an equal right to the most extensive system of equal basic liberties, which is compatible with a similar system of liberties for all. Second, social and economic inequalities are to satisfy two conditions: (i) they are to be attached to offices and positions that are

[1] J Rawls, *A Theory of Justice*, 2nd edn (Cambridge, MA, Belknap Press, 1999) 3–4.

[2] I will be relying here mainly on Rawls's statements of the conditions of fairness and of the principles of justice in *A Theory of Justice*.

accessible to all; and (ii) they are to the greatest benefit of the least advantaged.[3] These principles are termed the Priority of Liberty Principle and the Difference Principle.

Rawls justifies the choice of these principles of justice with the help of an analogy to decision theory. Decision theory provides practical rules for optimal decision making based on the utility value of each possible decision. The two main parameters that guide optimal decision making are the utility of each possible outcome and its probability. The conditions in Rawls's original position are those of deep ignorance: the probabilities of different outcomes of any adopted principle are unknown. If we know the probabilities of possible good and bad outcomes, it is rational to decide based on the prospects of value that attach to each candidate principle. Justice as fairness, however, requires that we move to a domain where we do not know the probabilities of good and bad outcomes, and identify the rational decision in such conditions. So, what would be the principles of decision making in such conditions, and how do they stand in relation to Rawls's principles of justice in conditions of fairness?

Rawls notes that decision theory would refer to the maximin rule for decision making in conditions of deep ignorance; and that maximin is analogous to his identified principles of justice.[4] Maximin requires that in conditions of deep ignorance we should maximise the minimal level of value obtainable with each decision. Accordingly, maximin works where we can discern one potential decision whose worst outcome has more value than that of the worst outcome of other potential decisions. If this is not the case, and the minimal obtainable value is identical for all potential decisions, the lexical maximin rule comes to play: if the worst outcomes are equal, we should maximise the value of the second worst outcome; if the second worst outcomes are equal, we should maximise the value of the third worst outcome; and so on.

Rawls describes the relation between his principles of justice and maximin in the following terms:

> There is an analogy between the two principles [of justice] and the maximin rule for choice under uncertainty. This is evident from the fact that the two principles are those a person would choose for the design of a society in which his enemy is to assign him his place. The maximin rule tells us to rank alternatives by their worst possible outcomes: we are to adopt the alternative the worst outcome of which is superior to the worst outcomes of the others … [T]hat *the two principles of justice would be chosen if the parties were forced to protect themselves against such a contingency explains the sense in which this conception is the maximin solution.* And this analogy suggests that if the original position has been described so that it is rational for the parties to adopt the conservative attitude expressed by this rule, a conclusive argument can indeed be constructed for these principles.[5]

[3] See Rawls (n 1) 60, 83.
[4] ibid 152–53.
[5] ibid.

Several conclusions can be drawn from this account. First, Rawls suggests that the principles of justice are analogous to maximin in ruling out the worst possible outcomes. It is also possible, however, to refer directly to maximin as the principle that requires the adoption of the principles of justice: Rawls notes that his conception of justice as exemplified by the two principles of justice is the maximin solution; it will be adopted where choice is guided by maximin. Rawls's analogy is then between the principle that governs the identification of the two principles of justice (I will call this principle 'Justice as Fairness') and maximin. Like maximin, Justice as Fairness seeks to rule out the worst possible outcomes; this is achieved by adopting principles that would prohibit any distributive rule that allows for the worst possible outcomes.

Second, the materialisation of the worst possible outcome can be conceptualised as an error outcome. In the domain of justice, the error is one of injustice. Thus, once all possible outcomes of the set of all possible principles of Justice and their subsequent sets of permissible distributional rules are identified, justice as Fairness requires ruling out any principle (and subsequent rule) whose possible outcomes are worst/erroneous/unjust. Once we have done so, we will be rationally led to Rawls's principles of justice.

Third, it is of course the case that even if we follow Rawls's principles of justice, errors or instances of injustice are still possible, for example where we competently try but nevertheless fail to correctly identify the set of possible outcomes of a specific rule, or when we apply a rule incorrectly. Such errors or instances of injustice would reflect human fallibility. In such circumstances the choice that led to error would be considered unjust.

Fourth, Rawls's conception of justice as fairness is blind to the probability of error; it is only sensitive to the possibility of error, and it requires that it be eliminated as far as possible. This sensitivity to the possibility of error in the form of the worst possible outcomes reflects the deontological nature of justice as fairness: it rules out certain outcomes to the extent that they can be ruled out, regardless of the possible utility of allowing them in small quantities.

Fifth and relatedly, since the worst possible outcomes are identified from behind a veil of ignorance, their possibility is logical rather than actual. From behind the veil of ignorance, it is unknown whether and which outcomes would in fact come about once the veil is lifted. Thus, from behind the veil of ignorance all the logically possible outcomes can be and are indeed identified, and the worst one is signalled out as unjust or erroneous. Justice as fairness is thus sensitive to the worst logically possible outcome and insensitive to the question if it will indeed come about (and accordingly no further evidence is needed or expected to unfold that would indicate if the error might come about at all).

Accordingly, Justice as Fairness works prospectively as a practical justification in the same way that error eliminability works prospectively as an epistemological justification. Justice as Fairness is based on the logical eliminability of an error in the form of the worst possible outcome; error eliminability is based on the logical eliminability of an error in the form of false belief. And both Justice as Fairness and error eliminability would lead to similar results when applied correctly: Justice as Fairness requires rejecting principles and subsequent rules that make error logically ineliminable in at least one of its applications; and error eliminability requires rejecting evidential principles and subsequent practices that make error logically ineliminable in some of its applications. In both contexts, the unavailability of reasons to think error would not come about in any specific application removes justification.

Justice as Fairness and error eliminability thus at least partly converge. This partial convergence allows for the following restatement of Rawls's account: Rawls's Justice as Fairness requires moving from the domain of practical justification to the domain of epistemic justification through a veil of ignorance, before the veil of ignorance is lifted again, and the epistemic justification gains practical force. Justice as Fairness thus requires nothing more than this: that it would be rational to believe that the principles we are opting for do not lead to error (the worst possible outcome) when applied to any random member of the relevant reference class. The role of the veil of ignorance is then to extend the relevant reference class, so that it includes all members of society and therefore also ourselves.

This is hardly surprising. From behind the veil of ignorance, where an error in the form of the worst possible outcomes might mean a catastrophe, and thus the stakes are so high, it is rational to rule out the possibility of error (barring unavoidable human error in application). It is rational to be as uncompromising as we can be, given the human condition. This is the practical rationale behind maximin. Yet when we rule out error, it is also rational to believe that error does not occur. One entails the other.

Accordingly, we can justify the choice of the principles of justice by saying 'in such conditions, I would like to ensure that an error does not occur in my case'; and we could also justify this choice by saying 'in such conditions, I would like to know that an error will not occur in my case'. And knowledge depends on the truth of the proposition (which is ensured as far as possible) and on availability of justification for belief that the proposition is true, or on meeting error eliminability.

It remains to be explained why, out of all the descriptions to which this convergence of justifications can give rise, it makes sense to choose the one that identifies a transition from the practical domain to the epistemological domain. Perhaps the two domains simply have the same justificatory structures, because they both require reasoning out error; but none involves any 'transition' to the other. Yet as Rawls's suggested cognitive exercise clearly demonstrates, in the context of Justice as Fairness a cognitive transition does occur. The operation of political institutions is part of the practical domain; and in this domain, justification usually has a structure that is different from that of epistemological justification: it takes account of existing contingencies and of the subsequent different prospects associated with error, and accordingly it is sensitive to actual outcomes and to their probabilities. The discussion of fairness thus begins with the assumption that contingencies are practically relevant; and Rawls then calls us to nevertheless change our default justificatory structure and ignore them. Rawls invites us to move to an imaginary domain in which contingencies have not yet been distributed, and hence the prospects associated with error are the same for all.

But what is this imaginary domain? In the real world, the only domain in which contingencies have no impact and the prospects associated with error are the same for all is the epistemological domain. When it comes to knowledge of mundane facts, only our basic and common cognitive abilities matter, and hence no one has any advantage over another. Indeed, the legal jury system, where facts are determined by randomly chosen 'lay persons', reflects this premise. Contingencies matter only in rare cases (for example when a person's perception is limited). Hence, error is usually relevant for all and to the same extent. Rawls thus invites us to transition from the practical domain to a domain that has the exact same characteristics of the epistemological domain. Notably, this feature of Rawls's theory has been interpreted as recourse to the Kantian conception of the person as pure mental capacities, rather than as a cluster of contingencies that also determine mental capacities.[6]

An initial objection might be that there is only partial and accidental convergence between the justifications. In fact, the epistemological motivation of error eliminability is different from the practical motivation of Rawls's principles of justice: error eliminability is motivated by the need to allow error elimination, while the principles of justice are motivated by the need to ensure error elimination. Accordingly, belief can still be justified even if erroneous, while a distribution is unjust and unjustified whenever erroneous. Thus, any partial convergence of the justifications is merely accidental.

We shall see later that the convergence of the two justifications is not accidental. Yet for now, the following can be noted: the two justifications are motivated by the need to allow meeting of the goals of their respective domains, and they are designed accordingly. In the domain of justice but not in the epistemological domain, subsequent failure to meet the goal also negates justification.

To see this, consider the goals of the reasoning exercises that take place in the epistemological domain and in the domain of justice. The goal of the two exercises is one and the same: to reason out all error entirely in specific cases. If error is reasoned out entirely, knowledge is generated and justice ensues. But no

[6] See MJ Sandel, *Liberalism and the Limits of Justice*, 2nd edn (Cambridge, Cambridge University Press, 2010); RS Taylor, *Reconstructing Rawls: The Kantian Foundations of Justice as Fairness* (Pennsylvania, PA, Penn State University Press, 2015).

prescriptive justificatory principle can effectively guarantee that error is reasoned out entirely in all cases. Prescriptive norms can only allow us to reason out error entirely in all cases by instructing us on the right way to do so, but they cannot guarantee that agents will not then err in the reasoning-out process. Human fallibility means that no matter how much we reason, some errors will there be. Thus, Justice as Fairness and error eliminability prescribe 'avoid principles that logically bar reasoning out error'.[7] It remains possible that such principles are avoided and yet an error will nevertheless fail to be reasoned out (a subsequent distributive rule would fail to identify the worst possible outcomes; or a subsequent evidential practice would fail to identify that the reference class was not sufficiently narrowed down to include only true propositions). The question is then how to treat such human fallibility when it materialises: should it or should it not affect the availability of a justification? In other words, should the justificatory principle include an additional uninstructive yet not insensible norm that further prescribes 'reason error out successfully'?

In the epistemological domain, this is where the difference between internalists and externalists comes to play. Internalists would usually say that human fallibility should not affect justification; one can be justified even where human fallibility has materialised and, possibly, error has occurred. Human fallibility then only disrupts the generation of knowledge, not the justification for belief. Thus, for a belief to be justified, error merely needs to be eliminable through reasoning; it need not have been eliminated. Externalists would say that human fallibility undermines justification: if one's belief fails to rightly correspond with all the evidence, this belief is unjustified.

In the domain of justice, there is hardly space for a parallel disagreement. Since justice is a property of institutions that captures only impact on others (or outcomes for others), there is hardly any point in differentiating between the justification of just action and the characterisation of its outcome as just or unjust. Where the outcome is unjust, the action was unjustified. Thus, the justificatory principle prescribes both 'avoid principles that bar reasoning out error' and 'reason out error successfully'; it prescribes 'reason out error successfully based on principles that do not logically bar success'.

If this is correct, the objection that the basic justificatory principles are differently motivated and hence cannot converge is not valid. The immediate motivation of a practical justification from fairness is the same as the immediate motivation of an epistemic justification from error eliminability: allowing elimination of error, which is the only thing that a prescriptive norm can effectively do. Any remaining differences between the justifications go to yet additional justificatory norms. They

[7] In the context of justice, maximin amounts to 'avoid principles of justice that permit irrationality on the evidence available to you behind the veil of ignorance'. In epistemology, error eliminability amounts to 'avoid evidential principles that permit irrationality on the evidence available to you'.

go to the question whether in each of these domains there is a complementary justificatory norm that further prescribes 'reason error out successfully'; or alternatively whether error elimination is not part of the justification but merely an element of the ultimate goal of the reasoning practice.

II. The Context of a Legal Trial

We have thus established that a practical justification from fairness partly converges with an epistemological justification from error eliminability. The context of a trial requires and fits both justifications; accordingly, its structural characteristics illuminate different aspects of this partial convergence.

Before we move on to observing these, it should be noted that in the context of a trial, factual and practical determinations are singular, but their applicability is wider and rule-like. A determination that a legal party who is evidentially situated in a certain way should bear legal consequences applies logically to all potential parties who are similarly situated. In this, such a determination is analogous to general rules of distribution that allocate a burden to a class.

The first characteristic of legal practice that makes it a suitable domain for justice and for knowledge is the irrelevance of luck and lucky contingencies. Legal practice emphasises the irrelevance of contingencies for its epistemic judgments in four related procedural ways. First, the members of the jury who draw legal inferences are randomly selected. No contingency of a potential juror can be relevant for the way in which she draws epistemic inferences. Second, the same fact-finding procedure applies to all parties regardless of their contingencies; no contingency is relevant for the way in which one's evidence is evaluated. Third, if a party suggests that due to her unlucky situation an error occurs, reasons must be available to show that this is not the case. Even if a suggestion about error is not explicitly made by a party but it is possible on the evidence, legal practice often requires that reasons be available for rejecting it.[8] And fourth, error is the business of all rather than only of the parties who carry its practical implications.

As might be clear by now, all these luck-defeating characteristics of legal procedures are associated with the justice of legal judgments as much as they are associated with their epistemic validity. That defeating contingencies is associated with fairness and with justice is hardly surprising. The main motivation for Rawls's Justice as Fairness is the thought that no one deserves any benefit or

[8] See, eg, the Forensic Science Regulator Codes of Practice and Conduct: Development of Evaluation Opinions (FSR-C-118, Issue 1) (Crown Copyright, 2021) paras 8.2.8–8.2.12 for cases in which the defendant remains silent. The guidance requires that the expert witness would generate propositions about error, as required by scientific method. Notably, in jury systems, the requirement that reasons to think that error does not occur be available would take the form of jury directions; and in non-jury systems they would have to be stated in the judgment. This way or the other, the law formally requires that any claim about mere bad situational luck be refutable with reasons.

detriment based on their lucky or unlucky situation. The conditions of the original position are accordingly designed to neutralise the impact of lucky contingencies in decision making. They are designed so that error would have the same likelihood and the same impact for all. As such, they converge with the conditions of the epistemic domain: contingencies do not matter for the development of belief on evidence.

The second characteristic of legal practice that makes it a suitable domain for knowledge and justice is its interest in withstanding challenges about error. As Rawls notes, truth and justice are both uncompromising; hence, the availability of equally good or better judgements that can motivate a challenge about error is undermining. Legal practice requires that reasons in refutation of challenges about error be available. As we saw in chapters 1 and 2, the requirement that the challenge from error be met is associated with the epistemic validity of legal judgments. Yet the requirement that such reasons be available is also associated with the fairness and justice of legal judgments.[9] This requirement is one element of the rule of law and the legal principle of non-arbitrariness, both of which are associated with fairness.[10] This seems obvious enough, and it too can be explained with reference to Rawls's analysis. As we saw, the transition to the original position is meant to make us see ourselves as the possible bearers of error at an unknowable likelihood, and hence to make it rational for us to protect ourselves by protecting everyone from error. This comes to ensuring that reasons are available that support the proposition that an error would not occur in our case as much as in any other random case. And this, in turn, means that Justice as Fairness is motivated by the need to ensure the same immunity to challenges about error that characterises the epistemic domain.

Before moving on, it can be noted that the context of a legal trial further partly dismantles at least one possible general objection to the Rawlsian notion of Justice as Fairness that converges with epistemic justification. According to this objection, the practical domain is essentially governed by the actual rather than the logical. The objection is targeted at the fact that the veil of ignorance requires that decisions be made based on worst possible outcomes that might never come about. From behind the veil of ignorance one is to imagine not only that one should be assigned the most disadvantageous position in society, but also that the rules adopted by this society would further disadvantage one; this is the 'worst possible outcome' from which one needs protect oneself. It is however possible, for example, that no one is assigned such a disadvantageous position, or that the rules adopted are not ones that might further disadvantage those who are already worst off. It is thus hard to see why, when making any practical decisions (even decisions about justice), we should address

[9] For the requirement to provide reasons in English law and its connection to fairness and due process, see *Flannery v Halifax Estate Agencies Ltd* [2000] 1 All ER 373.

[10] See M Krygier, 'The Rule of Law: Pasts, Presents, and Two Possible Futures' (2016) 12 *Annual Review of Law and Social Science* 199, esp 203–05.

logically possible outcomes at all, rather than addressing only actual outcomes. It is hard to see why there should be any practical reason to protect anyone from outcomes that are imagined from behind a veil of ignorance, rather than only from outcomes that are in fact threatening actual people.

We shall see later that the answer is rooted in the notion of respect: any viable practical notion of respect for persons that can be successfully applied in the public sphere requires a cognitive procedure like the one Rawls suggests. But setting respect aside for now, it is notable that at least in the context of a trial, this objection is dismantled. In the context of a trial, logically possible errors are not merely logically possible. They are actual. Where the legal system decides liability on evidence that is equally probative with respect to all existing members of a reference class (including those who have not been brought to justice), it signals to the public that there is reason to believe all members of the reference class should be held liable and socially treated as such. In such circumstances the innocent members, if there are such, might not suffer the full-blown consequences of a false legal judgment, but they would suffer at least some of them. An error is thus not only imaginable or logically possible; it actually occurs.

This discussion of legal practice can be generalised. The legal trial can be viewed as one example of a competition between propositions that is determined according to the rules of fair games. Accordingly, all the above-mentioned characteristics can also be viewed in the context of other 'fair games'. In sports games, for example, the determination that this season, a specific team or player is the nationally most virtuous one in game X is epistemically valid and fair if and only if it passes a 'competition test' that confirms it. The competition is a process whereby the determination is examined repetitively in conditions that confirm that there are no instances in which it is erroneous. Since the determination in sports games is a single judgement that is not generalisable (it concerns a specific time and is made in relation to specific competitors only), the possible competitors are the actual competitors, and error eliminability and error elimination converge. Such competition rules out the possibility that mere situational luck would affect the determination of which team is the strongest at a particular time, as least to the extent that situational luck is not designed to be a component of the game. Competition further ensures that reasons are available in refutation of arguments about error.

III. Accounting for the Convergence and Taking it Forward: Respect, Evidential Conditions and 'Disaster Prevention'

It was noted earlier that the convergence between Rawls' Justice as Fairness and error eliminability is not accidental: it is rooted in the notion of respect for persons. This argument will now be unpacked as follows: As we have seen, respect requires at first instance that reasons be available to think (i) that error in the form of failing to identify a conduct as disrespectful does not occur; and (ii) that error in the form of failing to identify reasons of respect does not occur. Justice as Fairness guarantees just that; it allows identification of such reasons in the public domain, where they are hard to identify. Subsequently, it is guaranteed that potentially disrespectful disastrous outcomes would not be rationally imposed on individuals for the sake of other social goals. As demonstrated in chapter 1, in such conditions the identified reasons also make it rational for us to believe that reasons of respect exist and that our conduct is respectful. This is hardly surprising, as respect for persons underlies not only the moral project but also the epistemological one.

We can begin by unfolding the claim that the public sphere is not conducive to respect and hence to justice: in the public sphere, the reasons that need to guide action for it to be respectful can hardly be identified. Note that this claim does not presume that people are necessarily egoistic and tend to prefer their own interests over those of others when they act rationally. Rather, this claim merely presumes that people are not always capable of identifying well the reasons that are in fact in operation: the further away other people are from us, the more difficult it is for us to identify that they merit respect. And in the public sphere, targeted people are indeed far from the eyes of decision makers. What the claim then comes to is that while it is possible to act rationally in the public sphere, it is often impossible to act respectfully. Rational action in the public sphere is not respectful action.

The first premise to be examined is as follows: in some imperfect evidential conditions, rational action would not be respectful. Consider first the conditions for respectful action. Remember that respect for persons is based on their human capacities (Raz would say: their capacities as valuers); where a person possesses these capacities, respect demands that any engagement with this person would be consistent with the value of her capacities. Note further that derivatively, respect demands that any engagement with persons would not risk being inconsistent with the value of these capacities. Conduct that might end up disrespecting a person who deserves respect should not be pursued. Such conduct only 'probably respects' this person, and hence, as already noted, it projects less value than it should. Respect thus requires ruling out the possibility of error in the form of disrespect; it further requires doing it successfully in the sense that any conduct would be unjustified in cases of failure.

Now consider the conditions for rational action. I take conduct to be rational when an agent responds appropriately to the reasons that are available to her, namely, those which she has competently identified. Conduct can thus be rational for the agent to pursue but disrespectful all things considered. Such will be the case when reasons of respect are hard to identify. In such conditions, the reasons that the agent has competently identified as operative might not be all the reasons that are in operation; rather, they might be only reasons that leave her the choice between disrespecting and 'probably respecting' (which would come to disrespecting if reasons of respect are indeed in operation). In such a situation, 'probably respecting' might be rational but it would be disrespectful.

Let us zoom in further. To see clearly why 'probably respecting' would be rational, and why it would be disrespectful, let us examine more closely the situation in which the agent's choice is between disrespecting and 'probably respecting'. In this situation, the agent is incapable of identifying reasons of respect decisively, or without a remaining ineliminable possibility that reasons of respect are not in operation at all. As we saw in chapter 4, the agent would then entertain this ineliminable possibility, and she might decide nevertheless to pursue the conduct that reasons of respect seem to require (if they are in operation). She might do so because the likelihood that reasons of respect are not in operation is sufficiently low, so she reasons that the value prospect of complying is sufficiently high and outweighs the value prospect of not complying for the sake of a different goal; or she might do so because she believes that reasons of respect would predominate or trump the other reasons that are at stake, and hence she prefers not to show general disregard for reasons of respect by knowingly risking disrespect. This way or the other, let us assume, her choice is rational in the situation.

Yet on a closer look it transpires that in such conditions, her conduct cannot meet reasons of respect. The conduct cannot meet reasons of respect because the reasons that have guided it already compel disrespect. The agent has thought about persons as either valuable in themselves or lacking such value. Her choice is then a choice to benefit them with the (rationally ineliminable) qualification, 'even if they do not merit the benefit'. This qualification is itself disrespectful, and it further changes the meaning and the value of the action.

The meaning of the action changes from respectful action to a different kind of action. A distributive action is then, at best, merciful: it projects a sympathetic willingness to let someone enjoy despite the ineliminable possibility that they might not merit it based on their capacities alone.[11] Perhaps there is something good about allowing them to enjoy to some undefined extent, based on the general fact that all imperfections deserve sympathetic understanding and treatment. But this good is not that of responding appropriately to their human capacities. Mercy is indeed a good where appropriate, but it is not the good of respect for persons (as ends) in themselves.[12]

At worst, the action reflects instrumentalisation of persons for the sake of an attempt to maximise respect across society; it reflects willingness to benefit with a qualification, because this would, allegedly, work in the long run to prevent

[11] Compare with M Nussbaum, 'Equity and Mercy' (1993) 22 *Philosophy and Public Affairs* 83; and with the discussion of the notions of mercy and love in the context of punishment in J Tasioulas, 'Where is Love? – The Topography of Mercy' in R Cruft, M Kramer and M Reiff (eds), *Crimes, Punishments and Responsibility: The Jurisprudence of Antony Duff* (Oxford, Oxford University Press, 2011) ch 3.

[12] A ruler who thinks that many of his subjects might well be subhuman, but who further reasons that he might as well give them a portion of wealth out of mercy, does not thereby treat his subjects in a way that is consistent with their human value. Note, however, that giving more than one deserves as a person based on other additional foundations for desert would not include the 'even if they do not deserve it' qualification, and accordingly would still be consistent with the value of persons as ends in themselves.

disrespect of those who do merit the benefit. In this case, the attempt to maximise respect is futile. Given the qualification that underlies the action, it cannot respond appropriately to reasons of respect for any of the persons it targets. Accordingly, the action might be reflecting a cost analysis, where the withholding of benefits from individuals is taken to be very costly. And cost analysis might be a good, but it too is not the good of respect.

Alternatively, since the agent is acting in conditions where respect is impossible, her action might then be a demonstration of her general regard for reasons of respect. It is a token that demonstrates that had she been able to identify reasons of respect and comply with them, she would have done so. Such a demonstration is also a good, but it too does not make the action respectful.

Thus, in such conditions, rational action is possible based on the reasons available for the agent, but respectful and hence just action can hardly be rationally attained. No rational action will project the value of persons (as ends) in themselves.

The next premise to be examined is that disrespectful action would be unjust. It could be argued that while it is true that in such a situation rational conduct cannot be respectful, this still says nothing much about the possibility of justice. In fact, this demonstrates that justice cannot be about respect. According to this argument, while respect depends not only on the action but also on the thoughts and attitudes that accompany this action, justice does not and should not give any regard to such thoughts and attitudes. As long as a state provides the relevant protection to those who in fact merit such protection, it is a just state; it does not matter if protection is provided for reasons of respect, for reasons of mercy or for reasons that involve instrumentalisation.

I think I am content to bite the bullet and insist that justice is about respect. Further, I doubt that in the context of state action, the above-mentioned disrespectful premises indeed take the form of mere thoughts and attitudes rather than of express or implied assertions that accompany state action and which all would agree might affect the justice of this action. Last, if Rawls is right in suggesting that justice requires precluding from the scope of rational action any action that risks certain disastrous consequences for individuals, then decisively identified reasons of respect are the only ones that can achieve this outcome.

Let us take each of these arguments in turn. First, while the view that justice is not affected by thoughts or attitudes is the more commonly held one, it seems to conflate the question when injustice occurs with the question when it provides grounds for state intervention. There are indeed no grounds of justice for the state to interfere where a citizen, say, refrains from harming another despite despising her and purely on instrumental reasons. But this does not mean that the citizen is acting justly (assuming that justice is a property of individuals as well as institutions). In addition, it is plausible that there are grounds for the state to conduct itself respectfully, and these grounds are of respect and justice at the same time. It seems safe to assume that a member of a racial or religious minority will not think she lives in a just state if this state protects her from disastrous outcomes 'notwithstanding the fact that she might be subhuman and hence might not merit such protection'. And I tend to think such a minority member would be correct to identify the state not only as disrespectful but also as unjust. It is hard to see how a state whose institutions systematically treat some of its citizens disrespectfully can nevertheless be considered a just state.

Second and relatedly, when a state provides protection subject to an ineliminable reservation about the value of targeted persons, this reservation is not only the thought of an individual decision maker. Rather, it is an assertion by an institution that would find explicit or implicit expression in the official or unofficial statement of reasons that must accompany any state action. Such an assertion would concern a possibility: it would reflect the thought or indeed the belief that it is not impossible that the targeted persons do not merit respect. And assertions are 'speech acts' that are governed by both epistemic and practical reasons. Accordingly, in the context of state action, the reservation about the value of targeted persons takes a practical form. Since it is then impossible to separate the reservation from the relevant state action, the suggestion that the action can be just notwithstanding the reservation, because the reservation is a mere thought, is no longer valid.

Last and perhaps most importantly, if Rawls is right in suggesting that justice requires precluding certain forms of treatment (call them 'withdrawal of protection') from the scope of rational decision making, then decisively (non probabilistically) identified reasons of respect are the only ones that can achieve this result. We have seen that a state can decide to refrain from withdrawing protection from individuals based on considerations of mercy or as an instrument for achieving maximal protection for those who deserve it. The state can also refrain from withdrawing protection as a way of showing general regard for reasons of respect, even when they cannot be met. Yet none of these considerations precludes withdrawal of protection from the scope of rational action. Mercy is based on sympathetic understanding, and it guarantees nothing concrete except general commitment to leniency.[13] Instrumentalisation as part of cost analysis is contingent on the circumstances: blanket protection of all creatures that are more likely than not to merit respect might prove unattainably costly (thus rationally compelling prioritisation of those who are more likely to merit protection). And demonstration of general regard for reasons of respect even when they cannot be met is desirable, but it can be achieved to various extents in more than one way. It can, for example, be achieved by way of sincere assertions that demonstrate such regard. Accordingly, sometimes such considerations might make it rational to avoid withdrawal of protection from individuals; but at other times they might not. Where the map of reasons is such, withdrawal of protection for the sake of other competing goals remains a rational option, at least in some circumstances.

This is not the case where reasons of respect are at play and are decisively identified. Reasons of respect are neither flexible nor contingent; they present a stable and concrete demand for protection. Thus, when in operation and predominating,

[13] Compare with Nussbaum (n 11).

they preclude withdrawal of protection from the scope of rational action that responds appropriately to reasons. And in this way, reasons of respect facilitate justice. It is true that reasons of respect arguably achieve more than this: they further preclude from the scope of rationality disrespectful thoughts and assertions; and some might regard these additions as going beyond the requisites of justice. But even if this is so, these additions are part of the pact that makes justice possible. Justice thus depends on respect.

So far we have seen that justice is about respect; and that in certain conditions, it is rational to act disrespectfully and unjustly: when reasons of respect are hard to identify and the choice is between disrespecting and 'probably respecting', rational action cannot be respectful and just (because of the ineliminable reservation about the value of the targeted persons, and the subsequent rationality of bringing about further disrespectful consequences). The question is then how to deal with such conditions; how to align rationality with respect and justice, or how the evidential conditions should be adjusted to make it possible for an agent or for the state to act rationally and respectfully. The answer, as might be clear by now, is that the evidential conditions should allow for eliminating the possibility that reasons of respect are in fact not in operation; reasons of respect should be decisively identifiable. When reasons of respect are decisively identifiable, the rational course of action is also the respectful one.

We can now move on to considering the last premise, namely that the evidential conditions of the public sphere are such that rational action would be disrespectful; accordingly, the evidential conditions of the public sphere need to be adjusted. Outside the public sphere, the conditions are such that rationality and respect usually align. Since reasons of respect for persons are complete and unconditional, they are usually decisively identifiable: they are directly and exclusively associated with basic human capacities that are easily demonstrable. When engaging with any specific person who demonstrates such capacities, it is rational to take reasons of respect to exist and to have a set stringency. There is no need to attend to likelihoods that such reasons do not exist or are not as stringent. Clearly, it is always good that people can easily and decisively identify the relevant reasons that are in operation; but since, as Raz notes, the reason to respect persons is one of the foundations of morality,[14] it is especially good that it can be identified easily and decisively.

Yet what Rawls's analysis captures is that, given some evidential characteristics of the public sphere, the complete and unconditional reasons to respect persons are deprived of this powerful normative potential: they cannot be decisively identified, and hence they cannot rationally guide conduct in a way that is uncompromising. In such conditions, rational action would be disrespectful.[15]

[14] J Raz, 'On Respect, Authority and Neutrality: A Response' (2010) 120 *Ethics* 279, 285.

[15] As might be clear by now, this has nothing to do with the availability of countering reasons to maximise our own good (egoism) or to maximise the overall public good (unrestrained utilitarianism). While it is surely the case that the Rawlsian procedure of fairness constrains the dictates of egoism and of unrestrained utilitarianism, and that this is one of its main attractions, it is not the case that rationality requires prioritising such reasons.

Rules adopted in the public sphere target individuals to whom the decision maker has no direct access; hence, the only available evidence about their capacities is semi-statistical (ie, it is based on a generalisation that is presumed to be statistically valid): the decision maker would assume that at least the majority of persons possess the full relevant capacities, and accordingly it is likely that the impacted individuals do too. As we saw in chapter 1, where this is the only evidence at hand, no reasons are available that support the proposition that error does not occur; no reasons are available to support the proposition that the targeted individuals do not belong in a potential class of persons with diminished capacities who do not give rise to the same normative demands as others. Indeed, in large and impersonal societies, the proposition that the criminal, the homeless, the mentally disabled, or the 'other' and the Rawlsian 'worst off' more generally might not possess the full capacities that give rise to a complete and unconditional reason to respect them is (too) easy to entertain. That such propositions are in fact entertained and feed into decision making is evident in prevalent institutional biases against minorities.[16]

In such conditions, the rational decision maker is likely to do either of two things: first, she might try in vain to prioritise respect (but as we have seen, her conduct would still project lower value than that required by reasons of respect). Second, in such conditions, the decision maker has another (sometimes more) rational route: since she cannot act respectfully anyway, she might as well act beneficially, notwithstanding even a high risk of disrespect. She might, for example, withdraw all financial support for unemployed convicted criminals with low likelihood of rehabilitation, and use the funds for other social purposes. The difficult outcome is that rational action in the public sphere might well be disrespectful.

This is where Rawls's notion of fairness comes to play. The Rawlsian procedure of fairness changes the evidential conditions in the public sphere. Rawls presents a cognitive procedure whereby, from behind the veil of ignorance, individuals to whom we have no access are replaced by ourselves. From behind the veil of ignorance we consider the possible outcomes that a principle of distribution might have for us if we were to end up in the position of these other individuals to whom we have no direct access. Thus, the situation changes in two ways.

First, when it comes to us, the evidence that we have about our capacities and about our value is non-statistical; it is evidence based on our direct mental access to ourselves and on our direct perception of the way others treat us. Such evidence provides reasons to think we do not belong with a class of persons whose capacities are diminished so that they do not give rise to stringent reasons of respect for persons. Second, once reasons of respect are decisively identified, it becomes irrational to opt for a distributive principle that fails to respond to these reasons by not ruling out disrespect. Post fairness procedures, it is decisively established

[16] Institutional biases are widely acknowledged and discussed. The discussions usually focus on specific institutional contexts, like police bias or bias in the health system. One example of an attempt to generalise with reference to the role of lobbying is SD Ehrlich, *Access Points: An Institutional Theory of Policy Bias and Policy Complexity* (Oxford, Oxford University Press, 2011).

that reasons of respect are in operation in relation to the targeted persons; and distributive principles should respond appropriately to these reasons by closing the door on disastrous distributive outcomes. If respect for persons predominates or trumps whatever other values are at play, it would rule out any distribution that would be inconsistent with reasons of respect for persons that, we now have decisive reason to think, are in operation. Rawls's principles of justice are reflect such ruling out.

Notably, this evidential reconstruction of the Rawlsian veil of ignorance sidelines the Rawlsian idea of an overlapping consensus over principles of justice, and instead focuses on reasons and their effective identification. It is a modest reconstruction or re-rationalisation of the veil of ignorance, which does not seek to elaborate in any great detail what distributive principles of justice are required by the reason to respect persons in themselves (later, something will be said about requirements in the context of retributive ethics).

Furthermore, this reconstruction means that the judgements we make behind the veil of ignorance are not necessarily guided by maximin, unless there is full equivalence between the worst possible outcome of a set of possible rules and disrespect (which might not be the case). This last point might seem troubling if we take maximin to be the cornerstone of Rawls's account. But while Rawls indeed supports the principles of justice with reference to maximin, we saw that he merely cautiously speaks of an analogy to maximin that is based on the idea of insuring from disaster. He is careful not to claim that the principles of justice are nothing but maximin. Furthermore, it is at least arguable that Rawls's maximin move is problematic, as indicated by the various suggestions that different principles would be more rational, or at least as rational, to adopt from behind the veil of ignorance.[17]

We are now ready to examine the epistemological aspect of this reconstruction. As might be clear by now, the change in the evidential conditions provided by the veil of ignorance is also an epistemological change. It is a transition from evidential conditions that do not justify belief to evidential conditions that justify belief; or from evidence that does not meet error eliminability to evidence that does meet error eliminability. Accordingly, reasons to think that there is no error in identifying the value of targeted individuals justify both belief that these individuals deserve the same respect that virtually all persons deserve, and action that respects them.

This is hardly surprising. As already noted, it is plausible that respect is one of the values underlying both the epistemological project and the practical project. If we can never know (have reasons to think that our true proposition is indeed not erroneous), or if the contingent evidential conditions are such that we cannot know, our true reasons to respect persons can never be decisively identified in

[17] See Taylor (n 6).

a way that would make them practically viable. Epistemology enlists rationality to save us from general scepticism and from the general question mark it poses over the value of persons. Procedures of fairness enlist rationality to save us from contingent epistemic positions that exist in the public sphere, and which might similarly undermine our ability to identify viable reasons to respect persons in the public sphere. The two domains are intertwined: our general epistemology and our specific evidential conditions determine our effective practical reasons.

Respect for persons thus demands ruling out some epistemic and subsequently practical 'disaster outcomes' that are inconsistent with it. The discussion that follows briefly reorients previous discussions, emphasising the role of epistemic norms and norms of justice in ruling out disrespect for persons in various contexts. It demonstrates that respect requires ruling out the epistemological disaster of scepticism; the distributional disaster of scarifying some basic interests of individuals for the sake of external goals; and then also the retributive disaster of false imposition of liability on individuals in a way that fails to respond appropriately to their value.

A. Respect and 'Disaster Epistemology'

Scepticism is not only an epistemic disaster. It is also a moral disaster. It is a moral disaster because, first, it pulls the carpet out from under a viable reason to respect persons as such. The sceptical argument is that even if there is such a reason, we cannot access it; and if this is the case, it might be rational to act in ways that are in fact inconsistent with this reason. Reasons of respect then lose their potency.

Furthermore, scepticism is a moral disaster because rational belief that a person is valuable in herself is itself respectful, and indeed it is presupposed by the notion of respect for persons. If we do not hold such a belief, and instead think that persons might or might not be valuable in themselves, this thought is already inconsistent with an obligation to think of persons in ways that are consistent with their value: the thought that people might not be of value in themselves is inconsistent with the thought that they are of value in themselves.

As we have seen, error eliminability allows withstanding scepticism, thus preventing not only an epistemological disaster but also a related moral disaster of the collapse of a viable notion of respect for persons.

B. Respect and Distributive Disasters

As distributive disasters have been unpacked in this chapter, the following is only a brief summary. If we follow Rawls, the distributive disaster that should be ruled out successfully is imposing the worst possible distributional outcomes on the worst off. Maximin as operated in the Rawlsian original position is a barring condition that rules out such distributional policies. Yet for it to be rational for agents to apply maximin or indeed any 'disaster-preventing' norm in the public sphere, and for such a 'disaster-preventing' norm to be truly disaster-preventing, the evidential conditions need to be altered as we have seen. The alteration allows decisively identifying reasons of respect, whose implication is that ruling out 'disaster distributions' becomes the only rational course of action. As we have further seen, it is possible that the worst possible outcomes imposed on the worst off are not necessarily disrespectful, or that there can be additional distributions that are disrespectful. But be that as it may, the identification of reasons of respect guarantees that it is irrational to allow the bringing about of disrespectful distributions.

Note that so far, we have not considered the application of just distributional policies in specific cases. More is said about this in the next section and in chapter 9; yet it can already be noted that respect requires that in addition to the reasoning out of 'disaster policies', those policies that have been identified as just would be applied justly. Consider, for example, a tax change that is beneficial for the worst off. If some of the worst off fail to be identified as such because of reliance on inappropriate evidence, a distributional disaster will occur regardless of the justness of the policy. Thus, reasons of respect further require the reasoning out of disastrous applications. They require that error eliminability be adopted as the evidential rule for the application of just policies.

C. Respect and Retributive Disasters: Introducing Fairness in Retribution

We are now able to take the analysis a step forward to consider what respect requires in the retributive domain. I use 'retributive' in a loose manner to capture the appropriate imposition of burdens in response to conduct for which one is responsible. Note that this is closely connected to distribution, which seeks the appropriate response to some valuable human characteristics.[18] The discussion will focus on imposition of legal liability for wrongdoing.

[18] Rawls would trace the difference in responsibility: he would attribute wrongful conduct to agents, but unproductive conduct to bad luck (and accordingly his principles of justice focus on illegitimate responses to unproductive conduct). This distinction between wrongful conduct and unproductive conduct is arguably difficult. Still, the important point for us is that reasons of respect are relevant when it comes to human capacities and when it comes to all forms of conduct for which one is responsible. The question what reasons of respect would call for in the face of unproductive conduct goes beyond the scope of this book. It is arguable that unproductive conduct is indeed conduct for which the person is responsible, yet it reflects an inappropriate response to reasons that are entirely different from moral reasons (or a failure that is very different from a moral failure). Accordingly, respect does not require asserting that the conduct is unproductive; and further, it requires letting the unproductive person carry only some of the consequences of her unproductiveness (so allowing some burdens, but preventing unjustified 'distributional disasters').

Respect requires that false impositions of liability be decisively ruled out, as they fail to respond appropriately to exercises of moral capacities. Moral action (or inaction) is an exercise of the capacity for rationality; it exemplifies and actualises this capacity. Thus, treating moral action or inaction in a way that is inconsistent with its value (for example by falsely imposing liability) is inconsistent not only with the value of this action or inaction, but also with the value of that which it exemplifies and actualises, namely, the capacity for rationality.

Accordingly, respect for persons (as ends) in themselves requires (i) decisively ruling out the possibility that the relevant persons do not possess full capacities and thus do not demand refraining from false impositions of liability; and (ii) decisively ruling out the possibility of false imposition of liability in each case.

We can take each in turn, starting with ruling out the possibility that the relevant persons do not possess full capacities. Public imposition of liability for wrongdoing usually impacts a person to whom the decision maker has direct access. The evidential realities can thus rationally support the proposition that this person does not belong with a class that possesses only diminished value. And indeed, courts do not tend to fail to acknowledge reasons of respect. Rather, the difficulty is with proposals for reform made from armchairs, and with legislated retributive regimes. When it comes to these, it cannot be ensured that reasons of respect would be correctly identified without altering the evidential conditions by a transition to a Rawlsian 'original position'. Only following such a transition does it become clear that reasons of respect apply in full force, and thus it is rational to respond to them by adopting the appropriate retributive regimes.

As for decisively ruling out the possibility of false impositions in each case, this requires that evidential regimes that do not allow ruling out the possibility of false imposition of liability should themselves be ruled out. Such regimes would be rejected from behind a veil of ignorance. Respect thus has evidential implications: respect requires evidential regimes that allow decision makers to rule out the possibility of error through reasoning.

Now, such evidential regimes need not address the reasoning out of human error. As we have seen when discussing the argument about error in chapter 2, the possibility of human error can always be decisively reasoned out by decision makers: evidence is always available for the decision maker about the conditions of her decision making, and this evidence would provide reasons to think that error does not occur in this case. For example, evidence would be available for the decision maker that she was not tired, went over relevant materials, received good advice, etc. Since this is always the case, the possibility of human error does not need to be addressed by evidential regimes.

We are left with the possibility of error that is imposed by the evidence (because the evidence might be capturing some error cases). If it is to allow reasoning out erroneous false impositions, the evidential regime needs to deal effectively with the possibility of error imposed by the evidence. Accordingly, the evidential regime needs to guarantee that the evidence allows narrowing down of the reference class it captures until it includes no cases of perpetrators who are not liable. Only then does the evidential regime allow reasoning out false impositions of liability. If this is correct, respect requires that the evidential regime be one of error eliminability. And this means that respect requires an evidential regime that also grounds belief in the proposition that the relevant person deserves to carry the relevant burden.

Alternatively, retributive rules can be analysed as analogous to distributive rules; if distributive rules concern the distribution of resources, retributive rules involve the distribution of burdens when the evidence indicates that they are deserved. Thus, what respect requires is ruling out certain distributions of such burdens. We have seen that Rawls's suggestion is that risking the imposition of the worst consequences on the worst off would be distributionally unfair and unjust. A different view is that failing to ensure a certain threshold of welfare would be distributionally unjust. An evidential regime that imposes burdens based on evidence that does not meet error eliminability would be unjust according to both views. It risks imposing the worst consequences on the worst off, and it further fails to ensure a threshold of well-being. For this reason too, it would be rejected from behind a veil of ignorance; an evidential regime that allows justified belief would be adopted. Let us see why, taking each view in turn.

Worst consequences for the worst off: note that rejecting error eliminability risks erroneous imposition of burdens based on a person's contingencies. As we have seen, forgoing error eliminability allows judgment based on statistical evidence indicating a high likelihood of commission in a defendant's contingent reference class. Now, defendants who contingently belong in such a reference class are the worst off in the relevant (retributive) respect. High likelihood of commission in the reference class reflects the strong incentives or pressures on members to commit criminal or immoral acts. And in retributive contexts, being 'worst off' is having the strongest incentives to act wrongfully (thus having to summon great powers to resist commission). A rule that allows deciding solely on contingencies risks false impositions of liability on those who are situated in this most difficult position. It thus risks imposing the worst on the worst off. When it comes to criminal convictions, this is even more pronounced, as there is supposedly some correlation between low socio-economic status and high crime rates. Those who will suffer error because of their contingencies will thus often be the worst off in other respects too. Furthermore, we shall see in chapter 7 that in the criminal context, such errors are profoundly tragic and potentially morally worse than errors in other contexts. From behind a veil of ignorance, we would avoid such a policy.

It could be objected that in the retributive context, increasing accuracy by forgoing error eliminability would improve the position of the worst off. After all, accuracy prospectively reduces the prospect of erroneous burdens even for those who end up carrying them. The objection fails. The retributive context is not different in this respect from the distributive one; there too, a policy is to be rejected if it increases prospects for everyone but does not guarantee that, unless a human error occurs, the worst possible outcomes will not fall upon anyone because she happens to be badly situated. Such a distributive policy would be inconsistent with respect, as it accepts the (retrospective) worst outcomes for the worst off. The same is true in the retributive context. Justice requires ruling out the possibility that the worst consequences will fall on some people because they happen to be badly situated.

If there is a difference between the distributive and the retributive context, it comes only to this: that in the distributive context, everyone who is badly situated will be negatively affected because of their contingencies, while in the retributive context, only some who are badly situated will be as negatively affected because of these contingencies. This practical difference makes no moral difference. As we have seen, reasons of respect for individuals require (successfully) ruling out some outcomes, rather than merely minimising their prevalence.

Threshold: the threshold of well-being that needs to be guaranteed must be taken to be affected by considerations of just desert, or else criminal sanction would be illegitimate. Accordingly, the legal regime should not take anyone under the threshold determined in this way. Yet an error might still take one below the threshold as determined with reference to one's lack of liability (so, a higher threshold than that of the liable). An error would not take all defendants below the threshold, but it will take some below it: the worse off the defendant is to start with, and the heavier the imposition, the more likely it is to take the defendant below the threshold. Accordingly, an evidential regime that does not allow for (successfully) reasoning out such error would be rejected from behind a veil of ignorance; an evidential regime that adopts error eliminability and allows justified belief would be preferred.

IV. A More Rigid Account: Epistemic Value as a Source of Moral Value

We are making progress in revealing the connection between the epistemic and the practical. This might be a good point to highlight an even deeper possible connection. Arguably, our epistemic capacities are the source of our moral value; they are the capacities that demand respect.

As already noted, one persisting critique of Rawls's theory of justice is that, for better or worse, it cannot escape the Kantian conception of a person: the Rawlsian person who adopts principles behind a veil of ignorance is, like the Kantian one, pure intellectual capacities and nothing else.[19] As we have seen, this person is well equipped for epistemic and moral judgements; her epistemic judgements allow her to identify moral reasons given by persons, or to value persons in themselves. Yet the (critical) suggestion is that this is all that Rawlsian persons are, and hence this must also be why they are valuable. Persons are pure mental capacities; hence

[19] See Sandel (n 6).

these capacities must be the source of moral value. The connection between the epistemic and the practical is accordingly fundamental: epistemic capacities might be a source of moral value.

Hints for such a line of argument can already be traced in the literature that explores the value of knowledge. Haddock, for example, relies on Socrates' metaphor of knowledge as involving beliefs that are tethered to the truth to argue as follows:

> [W]e value knowledge because knowledgeable beliefs are rationally immune to doubt. Independent of the fact that knowledge thereby enables us better to attain our goals, knowledge also serves to manifest our rationality in a distinctive way, by ensuring that a certain kind of behaviour we engage in (as it happens, that of disregarding apparent reasons to abandon our beliefs) is justified.[20]

Setting the details of the argument aside, the suggestion is that holding on to knowledge is rational, and exercises of rational capacities are valuable. Note, however, that this does not yet imply that persons are pure rational capacities and, significantly for our purposes, that persons are valuable as pure rational capacities.

A more far-reaching suggestion would be that knowledge is access to all truths (factual and normative) through our mental capacities or our reason. Consider, for example, Putnam's (later deserted) 'internalist realism', which comes very close to what is often described as Kantian constructivism. Putnam notes:

> [T]ruth is an idealization of rational acceptability. We speak as if there were such things as epistemically ideal condition, and we call a statement 'true' if it would be justified under such conditions. 'Epistemically ideal conditions' are, of course, like 'frictionless planes': we cannot really attain epistemically ideal conditions, or even be absolutely certain that we have come sufficiently close to them. But frictionless planes cannot be attained either, and yet talk of 'frictionless planes' has cash-value because we can approximate them to a very high degree of approximation.[21]

[20] A Haddock, 'Knowledge and Justification' in D Pritchard, A Millar and A Haddock, *The Nature and Value of Knowledge: Three Investigation* (Oxford, Oxford University Press, 2010) 195, 210.

[21] H Putman, *Reason, Truth and History* (Cambridge, Cambridge University Press, 1981) 55. Christopher Norris commented as follows on this position: 'Much better, Putnam thought, to give up that inherently self-defeating and scepticism-inducing idea in favour of a conception of knowledge as being *framework-relative* and an idea of truth – or, more aptly, of veridical warrant – that brought it back within the scope of what could be achieved. Such an outlook could be saved from wholesale relativism by invoking some limit-point notion such as "idealised rational acceptability", truth "at the end of enquiry", or that upon which our investigations are destined to converge when all the evidence has been gathered and evaluated under optimal conditions. This now seemed to Putnam the only hope of heading off the kinds of epistemological doubt that have plagued philosophers ever since Descartes. Otherwise there will always be room for the opponent to insert his sceptical wedge and remark that we can *either* have objective (recognition-transcendent) truth *or* knowledge within the bounds of present-best human cognitive grasp but surely not both.' C Norris, 'Hilary Putnam on Realism, Truth and Reason' (2004) *Philosophy Now: A Magazine of Ideas* at https://philosophynow.org/issues/49/Hilary_Putnam_on_Realism_Truth_and_Reason.

Thus, the intellectual exercise of eliminating contingencies and coming close to these idealised conditions is what constitutes the only truth that can matter to us. The access that we gain to the truth through reason, in turn, constitutes us as subjects in the world. The implication of the fact that we access truths through reason is that the world is what human reason says it is. And this means that human reason conditions the world just as much as it is conditioned by it. Such a relation comes to this: persons are subjects in the world; their epistemic capacities condition facts and values. And this is why the epistemic capacities of persons are themselves distinctly valuable; they are valuable because there are no facts without them. Epistemic capacities are thus the source of all value, and hence the capacities that make persons morally valuable. Epistemic capacities constitute respect and at the same time make us worthy of it, thus motivating both the anti-sceptical epistemological project and the moral project.

V. Conclusions

Justice and respect are closely connected. This has implications for the choice of just evidential principles in retributive contexts. This choice should be based on reasons of respect for persons. Respect for persons requires successfully reasoning out false impositions of liability that are inconsistent with the value of persons. Thus, where reasons of respect are decisively identified, they require ruling out evidential principles and rules that do not allow for successfully reasoning out these outcomes. Respect thus requires the adoption of error eliminability, or of evidential principles and rules that allow the generation of justified belief that a person deserves to carry a retributive burden.

The trouble is that in the public sphere, reasons of respect cannot be decisively identified. Error eliminability is not met with respect to the value of persons to whom we have no direct access, and thus the possibility that there are no reasons to respect them cannot be rationally ruled out. In such evidential conditions, reasons of respect lose much of their normative power: no rational choice of principles would demonstrate respect, and it is further not irrational to adopt (evidential) principles that would risk additional disrespect in their application. The Rawlsian veil of ignorance changes the evidential conditions to allow identifying reasons of respect in the public sphere.

If all that has been suggested so far is correct, whenever we adopt principles that involve a risk of undeserved burden (or whenever a distribution that might detract from the deserved welfare of another is similarly on the cards), reasons need to be available in support of the proposition that disrespect would not be brought about. These include reasons to think that two types of error do not occur: error in the form of failing to accurately identify reasons of respect, and error in the form of failing to identify that any imposition is undeserved. The first type of reason is available behind a veil of ignorance; the second is subsequently made available when the adopted evidential principles and rules meet error eliminability. In such conditions, the principles, rules and subsequent decisions in specific cases would be consistent with the complete and unconditional reason to respect persons; and they would further allow the generation of rational beliefs (which are themselves respectful). Accordingly, decisions would be both just and epistemically solid.

6

Resolution

The law understands itself as a mechanism for resolution of conflicts over truth and justice. The interest of the law in knowing the truth and doing justice is thus inherent in its interest in resolving such conflicts. This has two implications for evidential principles. First, opting for an evidential principle such as error eliminability can be justified not only based on its epistemic and moral values, but also based on its resolutive properties. Second, error eliminability should be complemented by procedures that allow for the exhausting of these resolutive properties.

This chapter focuses on the resolutive properties of error eliminability and the procedures associated with it. It begins by showing that parties to a conflict over truth and justice seek a binding determination of truth and justice by a third party that would have the power to resolve their conflict and would allow them to move on. For this to be the case, the determination must not give rise to fresh conflict. And there is a danger that it might: a resolution can always fail to reflect truth and justice, and in such a case it might undermine the losing party's ability to direct her life intentionally. But this danger can be deflated if parties exercise agency in the generation of the resolution. Error eliminability allows for such exercise of agency; and in the legal system, relevant procedures guarantee that this potential of error eliminability is exhausted. Thus, resolutions based on error eliminability cannot give rise to fresh conflict over agency, and they can bring the parties' conflict to an end. Because they can bring conflicts to their end, such resolutions are likely to be accepted by the parties and the public; and further, they are legitimate resolutions produced by institutions that themselves enjoy legitimacy.

I. Conflict Resolution Outside and Inside Legal Discourse

Thus far we have seen that legal assertions about the truth are regulated by a norm of error eliminability, and that such assertions are required by reasons of respect for those who suffer from wrongdoing and for those accused of wrongdoing. In the legal context, assertions based on error eliminability can be further justified on the practical grounds of conflict resolution.

To see this, let us observe conflict resolution. The concept of 'conflict resolution' has received considerable attention in the literature in recent decades.[1] Some foundational texts claimed to have identified a gulf between the legal assertion of the truth and conflict resolution.[2] In these texts, conflict resolution is conceived as thoroughly addressing the roots of the conflict or its underlying causes; these include struggles for primordial and universal needs like the needs for security, identity, recognition and development.[3] Such a needs-based approach suggests that every conflict begins with an original deprivation of basic needs that is then channelled to conflicts over interests. Accordingly, a resolution that upholds the relevant basic needs while possibly compromising some interests is a good resolution that would also be acceptable to, and accepted by, the parties. This conception of conflict resolution is contrasted with coercive legal processes that are conceived merely as pragmatic means of temporarily settling a dispute by supressing it.[4]

While focusing attention on the causes of conflict has its appeal, it is not always appropriate or useful for resolution. Other approaches to conflict resolution have cast doubt on the viability of an exclusive 'basic needs' or 'causes' approach, noting that it might be artificial, unsuitable and disproportionate where conflicts are conceptualised by the parties as conflicts over factual truths and over values.[5] In such cases, an all-or-nothing resolution by a third party is the appropriate resolution. This is the resolution that the parties seek. The parties who require resolution do not seek to negotiate the truth and to compromise. Neither do they necessarily suggest that their truth is more probable; indeed, they might concede that it is less probable and yet insist that it is the truth. What they seek is a third party who will determine the truth, as probable or improbable as it might be.

Various accounts have considered deeper resolutive properties of outright determination of the truth by a third party. Jacob Bercovitch and Richard Jackson explain that such determination of the truth forms one element of a more comprehensive theory of reconciliation: both conceptually and psychologically, official

[1] The literature is vast. While much of it focuses on conflict resolution in specific contexts and settings (such as international conflicts, conflicts in the family, or conflicts in the workplace), there are also attempts to generalise. One of these early attempts is JW Burton, 'Conflict Resolution as a Political System', *Center for Conflict Analysis and Resolution, George Mason University, Working Paper* 1/1993. Later examples include JA Schellenberg, *Conflict Resolution: Theory, Research and Practice* (Albany, NY, State University of New York Press, 1982); PT Coleman, M Deutsch and E Marcus, *The Handbook of Conflict Resolution: Theory and Practice*, 3rd edn (San Francisco, CA, Jossey-Bass, 2014); J Bercovitch, *Social Conflict and Third Parties: Strategies of Conflict Resolution* (New York, Routledge, 2019).

[2] Burton (n 1) is a central example.

[3] ibid 3. For a recent critical analysis of Burton's human needs theory, see T Väyrynen, *Culture and International Conflict Resolution: A Critical Analysis of the Work of John Burton* (Manchester, Manchester University Press, 2018).

[4] Burton (n 1) 6.

[5] V Aubert, 'Competition and Dissensus: Two Types of Conflict and of Conflict Resolution' (1963) VII *Conflict Resolution* 26, 37–38.

assertion of the truth by a third party opens the door for humanisation of all parties and for forgiveness. In this way, official assertions facilitate deep and comprehensive conflict resolution.[6] And Nadim Rouhana explains that the reconciliation approach to conflict resolution seeks an enduring end of conflict; this requires, amongst other things, asymmetrically revealing (rather than negotiating) historical truths. Uncovering the truth transforms the relationship between the parties and guarantees mutual recognition.[7]

The suggestion that assertions of the truth by a third party can provide resolution has been taken on board in the context of transitional justice.[8] Following the success of the South African Truth and Reconciliation Commission, 'truth commissions' have become a common component of resolution. They are considered appropriate especially where the populations involved in conflict remain in close proximity to one another and need to carry on living together. Truth commissions are different from courts in many respects: they lack authority to sanction, and indeed sometimes they are based on amnesty; their focus is on wide social patterns rather than on the accountability of individual perpetrators; and they often make recommendations for the future. Yet historically, truth commissions developed in response to the partly contingent inability of courts to deal with conflict in times of transition; and as the term suggests, their core role is still shared with that of courts, namely, investigating and subsequently asserting the truth.

This connection between asserting the truth and resolving conflict has been recognised to some extent in legal literature, especially in the context of criminal jurisprudence. Legal theorists often regard the legal system as a system of conflict resolution;[9] and different theorists have proposed different accounts of the role of truth finding in facilitating conflict resolution. Most of these accounts do not demonstrate awareness of the difference between accurately revealing the truth and asserting the truth, and they thus do not engage directly with the role of assertions. Still, some conclusions can be drawn about the possible role of assertions in resolving the legal conflict.

[6] J Bercovitch and R Jackson, *Conflict Resolution in the Twenty-first Century: Principles, Methods, and Approaches* (Ann Arbor, MI, University of Michigan Press, 2009) 153.

[7] NN Rouhana, 'Key Issues in Reconciliation: Challenging Traditional Assumptions on Conflict Resolution and Power Dynamics' in D Bar Tal (ed), *Intergroup Conflicts and Their Resolution: A Social Psychological Perspective* (New York and London, Psychology Press, Taylor and Francis Group, 2011) 291, 295–96.

[8] See PB Hayner, 'Past Truths, Present Dangers: The Role of Official Truth Seeking' in PC Stern and D Druckman (eds), *International Conflict after the Cold War* (Washington, DC, National Academy Press, 2000) 338.

[9] I Dennis, *The Law of Evidence*, 6th edn (London, Sweet & Maxwell, 2017) 52–60. For adjudication as resolution, see ibid 27. Dennis takes this to be the starting point of a discussion of the aims of evidence law, referring to the more general discussions of adjudication in HLA Hart, *The Concept of Law* (Oxford, Clarendon Press, 1961) 94–95, and J Finnis, *Natural Law and Natural Rights* (Oxford, Clarendon Press, 1980) 266 ff. See also T Weigend, 'Is the Criminal Process about Truth? A German Perspective' (2003) 26 *Harvard Journal of Law and Public Policy* 157.

In his descriptive account of the adversarial system, Thomas Weigend has gone as far as suggesting that conflict resolution is an overarching objective to which truth finding is merely instrumental:[10] 'The public will accept whatever is presented as "justice" only if justice is perceived to be based on an honest effort to find the "truth."'[11] It therefore seems that courts might 'assert' non-truths if this would resolve conflict. This suggestion is descriptively interesting, yet there is something highly perplexing about it, as it equates resolution with subjective psychological contentment; no space is allowed for a conceptually objective notion of resolution.

Ian Dennis has proposed a more nuanced account that aims to be normative. For Dennis, the aim of adjudication is conflict resolution; conflict resolution requires legitimacy; truth finding is one central foundation of legitimacy; there are other foundations for legitimacy with which truth finding might be in competition, such as respect for defendants' procedural rights, as well as for the rights of other participants in the legal process; and the competition needs to be settled in a way that would work best to ensure the legitimacy of legal decisions.[12]

While attractive, this account leaves some open questions. It does not consider the uncompromising nature of the search for the truth and, relatedly, it does not consider the role of rational ways to reason about the truth. For this reason, it is not clear whether Dennis sees the courts as bound by an epistemic norm of assertion and, if so, why (is epistemic warrant a foundation of legitimacy?). Furthermore, Dennis hardly suggests any substantive justification for many of his claims about legitimacy and its conditions; he makes do with general reference to moral, political and legal sources.[13] It is therefore not clear if and how exactly the reference to the legitimacy of resolutions gives rise to any concrete and well-delineated claims that need to be met, including claims that relate to the truth or its assertion.[14] To the extent that the theory collapses to the idea that legitimate resolutions must reflect commitment to justice, it does

[10] Weigend (n 9).

[11] ibid section VI. See also earlier in that section, where Weigend explicitly refers to the alleged efforts to cling to a theory or indeed a fiction of truth in the following terms: 'These efforts at cloaking the results of a power struggle between the prosecution and the defense in considerations of truth and justice demonstrate that legal systems cannot afford to openly declare the will of parties to be the supreme value.'

[12] Dennis (n 9) 57.

[13] ibid 56.

[14] Dennis is aware of this possible criticism, and after noting that '[a]ll of this is not to say that the theory of legitimacy is simply a description of whatever decisions about rules of evidence are arrived at in particular contexts' (ibid 59), he describes the critical potential that the theory does retain, namely, that exclusion of relevant evidence always requires either truth-based justification or justification that refers to a significant risk of undermining the moral authority or expressive value of the verdict. But this again begs the question how the concepts of resolution and legitimacy give rise to value claims regarding the truth, as well as the broader question to what extent the reference to moral authority or expressive value can justify any concrete value claims at all.

not explain how justice is connected with epistemically warranted assertions of the truth.[15]

Communicative theories of criminal justice open the door for direct engagement with assertions of the truth and their role in conflict resolution; yet this door has not been walked through just yet. In his discussion of truth finding, Antony Duff has merely proposed that there is no tension between 'resolution' and rigid commitment to the truth, as 'resolution' is an objective concept whose specific content is not derived from the perspectives of the parties.[16] At most, the perspectives of the parties are significant only for the quality of the restorative resolution.[17] Truth finding is thus the cornerstone of resolution. Clearly, such a position invites rigid commitment to the truth rather than to epistemically warranted assertions.

Yet it can be noted that Duff's general communicative stance could have produced a more refined position that assigns a central role for epistemic properties. Duff sees the criminal justice system as a system of communication: in convicting a defendant, the court communicates to the defendant, to the victim and to the public censure of a wrong that has been committed; the aim of such communication is to facilitate repentance, reform and reconciliation.[18] Within such a theory, it is the assertion of the truth (rather than the truth itself) that matters. Assertions are communications; as such they can censure wrongdoing and, allegedly, thereby facilitate resolution. Clearly, such a claim requires further development; and it might not be fully defensible in all its parts. But it is noteworthy that communicative theories of criminal law do seem to have the potential to reflect the insight of conflict-resolution theory, namely, that assertion of the truth is an element of conflict resolution.

Be that as it may, while there are sufficient grounds for the claim that conflicts over truths require for their resolution an assertion of the truth by a third party, it has not yet been clarified why resolution might require that assertions be epistemically warranted. Perhaps for the purposes of resolution, the third party can determine the truth based on evidence about the probability of the truth that does not meet error eliminability. The question is particularly pressing given that the truth can hardly ever be reached with certainty, and hence it must be acknowledged

[15] Furthermore, some features of the criminal justice system can hardly be conceptualised with reference to any of the end-values that Dennis identifies. The reluctance to convict on statistical evidence is one example.

[16] See especially A Duff, 'Restoration and Retribution' in A von Hirsch et al (eds), *Restorative Justice and Criminal Justice: Competing or Reconcilable Paradigms* (Oxford, Hart Publishing, 2006) 43, 56 and 57. See also DHJ Hermann, 'Restorative Justice and Retributive Justice: An Opportunity for Cooperation or an Occasion for Conflict in the Search for Justice?' (2017) 16 *Seattle Journal for Social Justice* 71.

[17] See L Walgrave, 'Imposing Restoration instead of Inflicting Pain: Reflections on the Judicial Reaction to Crime' in von Hirsch et al (eds) (n 16) 61.

[18] A full statement of the theory can be found in A Duff, *Punishment, Communication and Community*, rev edn (Oxford, Oxford University Press, 2001).

by the parties and the public that any assertion of the truth by a third party might be wrong. In such conditions, why should we not accept that a conflict over truths cannot receive its ideal resolution, and opt for less than resolution through approximation instead? To state things differently, given the uncertainties associated with it, how can an outright assertion of the truth by a third party maintain any of its resolutive nature?

The next section demonstrates that the resolutive power of assertion of the truth by third parties is rooted in the condition for justified belief that underlies assertions: if this condition is error eliminability, as it is in the legal context, then assertion of the truth has resolutive properties notwithstanding the fact that the truth can hardly ever be reached with certainty. This is because assertions based on error eliminability protect the parties from the danger of fresh conflict that might emerge when the resolution is erroneous. Subsequently, the resolution indeed resolves the conflict and allows the parties to move on from it. This makes the resolution acceptable to the parties and the public, and indeed likely to be accepted by them even when they contest its content.

II. Error Eliminability and Legal Resolution

For a determination of the truth by a third party to resolve conflicts, it needs to be the product of a search that protects the parties from escalation of the conflict. The search based on error eliminability is such.

The argument will run as follows: Error eliminability has an 'open edge'. Rather than delineating the scope of information that is being evaluated, error eliminability invites identification of ever more alternatives to the proposition that is being considered, and subsequently engagement in elimination processes that logically allow reaching truth and justice. This open edge of error eliminability guarantees that the parties' rational objections to any proposed resolution will have been considered. When accompanied by appropriate procedures, error eliminability further invites the actual parties to a conflict to actively draw attention to as many alternatives or objections as they deem necessary. In such conditions, the emerging resolution (in the form of a determination of the truth) does not open the door for fresh conflict over the agency of participants, which might otherwise have emerged. Subsequently, the goal of conflict resolution is served.

A. The Open Edge of Error Eliminability

Let us observe the 'open edge' of evidential error eliminability. Error eliminability conditions the justification for belief that a proposition P is true on an increase in the probability that P is true and on the logical possibility of eliminating error. The two elements are connected: the probability of P given evidence E is increased as we engage in reducing the risk of error (and error eliminability requires that it would be logically possible to carry on with this process until the risk of error is eliminated entirely). Since error eliminability focuses on a combination of that which the evidence has revealed and that which it can logically reveal, it has an open edge: error eliminability does not impose a 'stopping point' for the process of evaluating the risk of error. While belief might be justified at the point where the posterior probability of P is high enough (typically, above 0.5), justification would be removed where it is then demonstrated that further investigation of the evidence changes this probability; and so forth. To state things differently, the 'stopping point' of the observation of the evidence is not determined. The question is then asked how the 'stopping point' is to be determined. The answer is that if we are after assertions that would resolve a conflict over truths, we need to opt for a 'stopping procedure' that would allow for such resolutive assertions.

B. The 'Stopping Procedure': Preventing Fresh Conflict Over Agency

If conflicts are to be resolved, the 'stopping procedure' must not create further independent conflict. Let us consider how such fresh conflict might emerge, and how error eliminability prevents it from emerging. It can be suggested that in the legal context, some errors in truth finding might undermine participants' agency; that the resulting conflict over agency is hardly resolvable; and that its emergence therefore undercuts the overarching goal of conflict resolution. The risk of errors that undermine agency thus needs to be neutralised where possible. This is the case even if neutralising this risk increases the overall risk of errors in truth finding that do not undermine agency; if it is to resolve conflicts, the legal system should opt for a higher acceptable risk rather than for a lower unacceptable one. Error eliminability and the procedures that accompany it allow exactly that: they neutralise the risk of fresh conflict over agency.

i. On Agency and Engagement in Error Elimination

Exercising human agency is good in itself; but in the legal context, it is also good because it is an essential part of the resolution of the legal conflict. For current purposes, agency refers to having one's intentions contribute to the shaping of one's life.[19] Legal assertions are an aspect of one's life in the relevant sense: they are resolutions of one's fundamental conflicts, and they thus form an

[19] See, eg, J McDowell, *Mind and World* (Cambridge, MA, Harvard University Press, 1994); P Hieronymi, 'Two Kinds of Agency' in L O'Brien and M Soteriou (eds), *Mental Actions* (Oxford, Oxford University Press, 2009); T Burge, 'Reason and the First Person' in B Smith and C Wright (eds), *Knowing One's Own Mind* (Oxford, Oxford University Press, 1995) 243.

aspect of one's life. These legal assertions further form an immediate basis for legal action that clearly forms an aspect of one's life. One cannot always exercise agency by opting out of the legal resolution; and when such is the case, one can only exercise agency by having one's intentions contribute to the shaping of this resolution.[20]

There is deep disagreement over the question whether the notion of agency is epistemically relevant,[21] but I will use 'agency' here in a way that should not be problematic: rather than agency in the formation of belief, I will refer to agency in the examination of evidence that provides a basis for legal assertions. Arguably, this task involves, among other intentional actions, some cognitive tasks like the intentional generation of new hypotheses in processes of eliminating the risk of error.

ii. Engaging in Error Elimination and Preventing Conflict

Legal fact-finding errors might undermine a legal party's agency when this party has no intentional part in the process that brought them about. To see this, let us first consider the formation of true (rather than erroneous) legal determinations. Where no errors are made in the formation of the legal determination, one's intentional actions or inactions contribute directly to the shaping of these legal determinations. Things are different in cases of error. In case of error, the defendant has not made a similar agential contribution to the shaping of the legal determination: by definition, the point of error 'misses' the defendant's true agential action or inaction. To the extent that the defendant's action is misinterpreted by the decision maker, although the action may remain agential, the defendant's contribution

[20] Compare with the discussion of participation in DJ Galligan, *Due Process and Fair Procedures: A Study of Administrative Procedures* (Oxford, Clarendon Press, 1996). Galligan reaches the conclusion that participation can only be justified as a means for establishing the truth (ibid 131–32) or as exemplifying respect through self-protection from accusation (ibid 140–43). Arguably, the connection between respect for the right to protect oneself by oneself can be questioned, especially noting the limitations on this right set by the criminal law. It can be suggested here that unlike participation, agency is one of the 'basic needs' that are valuable in themselves and are threatened by a truth-based resolution.

[21] Outside the boundaries of foundationalism, intentionality and agency are taken as central to the generation of belief. Some accounts have referred to intentional reflection on the reasons that underlie belief. C Peacocke, *Being Known* (Oxford, Oxford University Press, 1999) proposes an account of belief that has been taken to imply agency (see ibid ch 2 and ch 3, esp at 238). As Brandom noted, such accounts all hold on to the claim that 'discursive activity, from everyday thought to the cognition of theoretical physics, is a species of practical intentionality … and indeed, one that is intelligible as having developed out of nondiscursive practical intentionality, while still maintaining that it is a wholly distinctive variety': RB Brandom, *Perspectives on Pragmatism: Classical, Recent and Contemporary* (Cambridge, MA, Harvard University Press, 2011) 10. But see also the discussion of epistemic responsibility as responsibility for belief in S Hetherington, 'Epistemic Responsibility: A Dilemma' (2002) 85 *The Monist* 398, 401–03. Compare with K Setiya, 'Epistemic Agency: Some Doubts' (2013) 23 *Philosophical Issues* 179. See also P Boghossian, 'What is Inference' (2014) 169 *Philosophical Studies* 1. And see HL Ho, *A Philosophy of Evidence Law: Justice in the Search for Truth* (Oxford, Oxford University Press, 2008) 102–04.

to the legal determination is hardly agential. In fact, the agent does not subsequently contribute to the legal judgment at all, whether agentially or otherwise. It is taken out of the agent's hands by an error by the factfinder. An erroneous legal determination would then reflect only the misguided mental processes of the legal decision maker; it would reflect nothing but a failure in the exclusive relation between the legal decision maker and the world, in which one could have no part. The legal party would then remain a passive object of an imposed legal determination that would do away with her original conflict. Accordingly, her agency in the shaping of her life would be undermined.

This undermining of agency is the basis for a fresh conflict. This conflict over agency would be irresolvable. Establishing the truth and providing compensation will not do, as it can only be resolutive on the background of a fact-finding norm that upholds agency; a system that leaves room for violations of agency hardly adheres to such a norm. No other potential resolution seems practical and relevant here.

This has clear implications for the ability of the legal system to meet its goal. Beyond that, this also has implications for the acceptability and acceptance of erroneous resolutions, and for the acceptability and acceptance of any resolution (correct or erroneous) offered by the legal system. When erroneous resolutions lead to conflicts of agency, the legal system is not only unsuccessful; it is an active generator of avoidable conflicts that it can hardly resolve. In such conditions, any party who disagrees with the content of a resolution offered by the system would have reasonable grounds for rejecting it. The grounds would be that the reasoning process was not suitable for the purpose of conflict resolution. Such a party would be likely to reject the resolution, thus undermining the legal system's ability to achieve its resolutive goals. Accordingly, errors that undermine agency should be prevented where possible. This requires guaranteeing the agency of participants in the generation of the legal judgments, regardless of the judgments' correctness or incorrectness.

This conclusion is reinforced by the experience of other systems and organisations dealing with the risk of error. The topic has been widely considered in the literature on organisation management. Clearly, the objectives, roles, values and contexts of such organisations are remarkably different from those of the criminal justice system,[22] and accordingly we shall proceed with caution. The literature on organisation management has long recognised that strategies for minimising the risk of error are insufficient for the overall success of organisations. In fact, in the long run, low prevalence of errors is a relatively poor predictor of future success

[22] For one, unlike in other organisations, the criminal justice system does not seek only proximity to the truth in the long run. In addition, in the criminal justice system, the ultimate conflict that requires truth-based resolution precedes the error, which only works to further exacerbate it.

and survivability.[23] Error-management strategies are better predictors of success and survivability, and thus they should complement strategies for the minimisation of the risk of error.[24] Error-management strategies accept errors and work to reduce their negative consequences and to increase their positive consequences. The negative consequences of errors include 'error cascades' (where errors build on top of each other, with one leading to the next), the emotional toll that errors impose on all parties, the subsequent reduction in productivity and the reduction of trust within the organisation.[25] The positive consequences of errors include reduction of excessive confidence and an increase of attention to all errors within the organisation; the ability to learn from error so that it does not repeat; and the ability to develop, innovate and grow through confident reflection on past errors and out of trust in the organisation's ability to contain future errors.[26]

Thus, to the extent that lessons can be drawn, it is noteworthy that when error is such that it enables organisations to establish what went wrong and how to improve, it can be left behind. Thus, any irresolvable conflict and friction that might otherwise have emerged with the error (manifested in 'the negative consequences of error') are prevented. Furthermore, the relevant actors can meaningfully reflect on error and learn from it only where they have been given the opportunity to contribute to the reasoning process that produces it. Thus, guaranteeing contribution or active agency of all relevant participants throughout the decision-making process makes decisions acceptable even when erroneous.

We can now return to the legal system. Clearly, decreasing errors in the long run is important in the legal system as it is in other organisations.[27] But in addition to that, like other organisations, the legal system needs to prevent wherever possible any fundamental conflicts over agency that might arise with error. This is especially true given that the overarching goal of the legal system is conflict resolution.

[23] C van Dyck et al, 'Organizational Error Management Culture and Its Impact on Performance: A Two-Study Replication' (2005) 90 *Journal of Applied Psychology* 1228, 1230–31 (introducing data from PG Audia, EA Locke and KG Smith, 'The Paradox of Success: An Archival and Laboratory Study of Strategic Persistence Following Radical Environmental Change' (2000) 43 *Academy of Management Journal* 837; and JD Bragger et al, 'When Success Breeds Failure: History, Hysteresis, and Delayed Exit Decisions' (2003) 88 *Journal of Applied Psychology* 6).

[24] Van Dyck et al (n 23) have confirmed this finding. Similar findings in the medical context had been reported in AC Edmondson, 'Learning from Mistakes is Easier Said than Done: Group and Organizational Influences on the Detection and Correction of Human Error' (1996) 32 *Journal of Applied Behavioral Science* 5.

[25] See B Zhao and F Olivera, 'Error Reporting in Organizations' (2006) 31 *Academy of Management Review* 1012; V Rybowiak et al, 'Error Orientation Questionnaire (EOQ): Reliability, Validity, and Different Language Equivalence' (1999) 20 *Journal of Organizational Behavior* 527; PS Goodman et al, 'Organizational Errors: Directions for Future Research' (2011) 31 *Research in Organizational Behavior* 151.

[26] See SB Sitkin, 'Learning through Failure: The Strategy of Small Losses' in M Cohen and U Sproull (eds), *Organizational Learning* (Thousand Oaks, CA, Sage, 1996) 541; M Frese and N Keith, 'Action Errors, Error Management, and Learning in Organizations' (2015) 66 *Annual Review of Psychology* 661, 671–78.

[27] B Sangero, 'Safe Convictions' (2019) 30 *Criminal Law Forum* 375.

For this purpose, the legal system needs to guarantee the agency of all relevant actors in the generation of the legal resolution. When all the participants in the legal process (parties and decision makers) exercise agency in the process of fact finding, errors are no longer merely external impositions that shape the lives of one of them. They are no longer associated with a failure in the exclusive relation between one of the participants and the external world in which others could have no agential part. Rather, errors are the unfortunate outcomes of a joint agential effort that failed. Because all participants take active part in this effort, the failure is possessed by all.

This does not necessarily mean that each participant is individually responsible for the failure; but a notion of collective responsibility – something similar to the collective responsibility of all participants in a game for good or bad outcomes – becomes relevant. Errors can then be learned from: just like sports teams can reflect on the ways each member could have contributed more to the prevention of a failure, all participants who exercise agency in the legal process can reflect on the ways in which they could have done better to prevent error. And even in the unlikely event that one or several participants performed perfectly, they could still draw on the lessons of others.

Error eliminability allows space for the exercise of agency by all participants in the legal process; and the procedural rules that accompany error eliminability ensure that agency is indeed exercised by all participants. Together, they call on participants to agentially participate in the process of eliminating the risk of error; they call on them to generate hypotheses with the prospect of narrowing down relevant reference classes further and further so that the process constantly progresses towards the elimination of the risk of error. This process of generating hypotheses and examining their truth on the evidence involves the exercise of agency. Accordingly, subsequent errors would not produce irresolvable conflict over agency.

In such conditions, the resolution offered by the legal system no longer risks the creation of fresh irresolvable conflict over agency. Such resolution indeed resolves the conflict and allows the parties and the public to leave it behind; it is likely to be accepted by the parties and the public; and it is normatively acceptable and legitimate despite the risk of error. In such conditions, the legal system can carry on fulfilling its goal of resolving conflicts over truth and justice.

III. Some Procedural Implications

We have seen that the generation of resolutive legal assertions involves intentionality and agency in the process of reducing a logically eliminable risk of error, and that this makes the truth-based resolutions offered by the criminal justice system resolutive. Various procedural rules that cannot be explained with reference to a narrow search for the truth can be explained as presentations of this agency-ridden method for the generation of resolutions. This section provides a brief demonstrative survey that is focused on criminal law.

A. The Right to Silence

The right to silence has proved to be one of the more controversial procedural protections in the criminal justice system.[28] With the exception of arguments about the symbolic role of the right in signalling (lack of) faith in the police,[29] the debate has been framed mainly in terms of the right's utility or disutility in ensuring the rectitude of legal judgments. Proponents have suggested that the right to silence is a vital guarantee against false convictions.[30] Opponents have argued to the contrary. Bentham famously suggested that the right to silence was in clear tension with a narrowly defined search for the truth, since 'innocence claims the right of speaking, as guilt invokes the privilege of silence'.[31] Furthermore, as the defendant has direct access to all the information required in order to establish the truth, and exclusive direct access to some of this information (like her mental state), an effective search for the truth requires her cooperation.[32] Later opponents have suggested that these considerations are valid when defendants are provided with appropriate protections like the right to legal representation and recordings of interviews.[33] These arguments fed into legal reforms that have weakened the right to silence.[34]

The truth-related arguments in support of the right to silence can become less speculative and more principled if we take the overarching aim of the criminal justice system to be achieving truth-based resolutions, rather than plainly establishing the truth to the highest degree of accuracy. The right to silence can then be interpreted as a mechanism that prevents fresh conflicts over agency, thus allowing resolution. Under this interpretation, the right to silence grants defendants a wide range of alternative ways to exercise agency in the process of resolution. Far from reflecting passivity and lack of agency, the defendant's choice to remain silent shapes the generation of a legal resolution much like the choice to testify.

[28] For comprehensive accounts, see H Quirk, *The Rise and Fall of the Right of Silence* (London, Routledge, Taylor and Francis, 2016); S Easton, *The Case for the Right to Silence*, 2nd edn (Farnham, Ashgate Publishing Limited, 1998).

[29] For a summary of this argument, see S Greer, 'The Right to Silence: A Review of the Current Debate' (1990) 53 *MLR* 709.

[30] ibid 725–29; Easton (n 28) ch 10.

[31] J Bentham, *The Works of Jeremy Bentham* (Edinburgh, Bowring Edition, 1843) 451.

[32] ibid. For critical analysis, see S Easton, *Silence and Confessions: The Suspect as a Source of Evidence* (London, Palgrave Macmillan, 2014) esp 8–9 and 13–16.

[33] See, eg, AAS Zuckerman, 'Trial by Unfair Means – The Report of the Working Group on the Right of Silence' [1989] *Crim LR* 855. For rebuttal, see Quirk (n 28) esp ch 3.

[34] Criminal Justice and Public Order Act 1994, ss 34–37.

Remaining silent means that the prosecution's proposition [P] is to be tested only against the simple proposition [no-P]. Accordingly, the evidence only needs to be probative of [P] and incompatible with [no-P]. To take one example, the prosecution's proposition that the defendant acted with intent is to be tested against the simple proposition that she acted without intent; it is not to be tested against the more nuanced proposition that the defendant acted without intent but with hope that harm would be avoided.

This choice to have the prosecution's proposition [P] tested only against one simple [no-P] proposition is significant. It can be understood as a choice to ask the legal decision maker to conclude that not enough hypotheses have been generated and negated in the circumstances, and hence [P] cannot be established. This choice involves agency in the shaping of the legal determination, or at least in the choice of its method, and hence the legal determination cannot be reasonably rejected. In such circumstances the legal determination can function as a resolution for the legal conflict.

Accordingly, while allowing the defendant to remain silent might well have a cost in accuracy, it is still compatible with the overarching goal of truth-based resolution. In preventing conflicts over agency in cases of error, the right of silence helps in maintaining a system of truth-based resolutions.

B. Confrontation Rights

The right to confront one's accuser was never a well-established right under English law, but both American and European law recognise and value it.[35] Despite its weak status in English law, this right was invoked in the debate over the legitimacy of special measures for examination of vulnerable witnesses.[36] The aim of the following paragraphs is not to suggest that confrontation rights should be acknowledged in English law and prevent protection of vulnerable witnesses. The aim is only to show that the debate could be richer than it has been, and that confrontation rights might have more to them than previously acknowledged.

Ian Dennis and Mike Redmayne have separately offered important critical contributions to the debate over confrontation rights.[37] The emerging analysis has been roughly as follows: one value underlying confrontation rights is accuracy in fact finding. Yet sometimes, as the case is with vulnerable witnesses, promoting accuracy would require compromising confrontation rights rather

[35] See M Redmayne, 'Confronting Confrontation' *LSE Law, Society and Economy Working Paper* 10/2010 at www.lse.ac.uk/collections/law/wps/wps.htm.

[36] Youth Justice and Criminal Evidence Act 1999, ss 16–18.

[37] I Dennis, 'The Right to Confront Witnesses: Meanings, Myths and Human Rights' [2010] *Crim LR* 255; Redmayne (n 35).

than upholding them: vulnerable witnesses would tend to provide more useful information when protected rather than when confronted. Another value that might be underlying confrontation rights is a process value. Various attempts have been made to characterise this value, and Dennis helpfully draws a distinction between two types of relevant values. The first is encapsulated in an accuser's duty to face the person whom he accuses, but as Redmayne shows in great detail, it remains unclear exactly what value this might be.[38] Alternatively, the relevant process value might be the value of respect for defendants, who should be allowed to play an active role in the legal process that is equal to the role played by the prosecution. Yet as Dennis notes,[39] such a general notion of respect does not stop with the defendant; witnesses must also be respected, and when witnesses are vulnerable, this might require special measures. Hence, confrontation rights can hardly be defended.

The account proposed here can shed different light on confrontation rights. Confrontation rights provide one way for guaranteeing defendants' agency in determining the 'stopping point' for the examination of evidence, as well as for guaranteeing agency in the generation of legal determinations. Thus, they prevent fresh conflict over agency in cases of error, and accordingly they can serve as resolutions for the criminal conflict. An exchange between the defendant and her accuser might allow the defendant to generate additional (true or false) hypotheses. Furthermore, the ability of other participants to determine the 'stopping point', as well as the agency of other participants, is not similarly threatened by confrontation. Even if confrontation might increase the likelihood of erroneous resolution, it does not prevent any of the other participants from deciding that the 'stopping point' for the examination of evidence has not yet been reached or from exercising agency in the generation of the legal determination. Thus, at least a priori, confrontation rights that are not being abused serve to guarantee resolution. Clearly, the possibility of abuse should be considered; and further, as Dennis notes, a different question is what other duties of respect to vulnerable witnesses might entail for the process of generating a resolution.

[38] See especially Redmayne (n 35) 13–14 (critically examining suggestions in RD Friedman, 'Grappling with the Meaning of "Testimonial"' (2005) 71 *Brooklyn Law Review* 241 and WE O'Brian, 'The Right of Confrontation: US and European Perspectives' (2005) 121 *LQR* 481, 494); at 14–16 (showing the limits of a confrontation right based on an ignobility rationale offered in SJ Clark, 'An Accuser-Obligation Approach to the Confrontation Clause' (2003) 81 *Nebraska Law Review* 1258, if such a rationale is at all convincing); and at 18–20 (critically examining Massaro's suggestions about the connection between confrontation and fair play or decent treatment in TM Massaro, 'The Dignity Value of Face-to-Face Confrontations' (1988) 40 *University of Florida Law Review* 863, and Scallen's suggestions about the social catharsis associated with confrontation in EA Scallen, 'Constitutional Dimensions of Hearsay Reform: Toward a Three-Dimensional Confrontation Clause' (1992) 76 *Minnesota Law Review* 623).

[39] Dennis (n 37) 260.

C. Adversary

The analysis of confrontation rights can be abstracted to account for the adversarial nature of our criminal justice system. The adversarial system probably does not fare significantly better than the inquisitorial system in terms of accuracy.[40] In fact, it is arguable that adversary undermines accurate fact finding; the arguments are familiar, and there is no need to repeat them here.[41] Like in the context of confrontation rights, it might be possible to try to explain adversary with reference to human rights;[42] but in any case, it would be hard to argue that human rights are only consistent with an adversarial system. On this background, some have suggested that it is pointless to over-rationalise the adversarial characteristics of the system; they might just be attributable to legal tradition.[43]

The adversarial nature of the criminal justice system is surely attributable mostly to tradition, but it is also possible to justify it on resolutive grounds. Far from Weigend's account of a system that is accepted by the parties because it is not committed to the truth and accepted by the public because it pretends to be committed to the truth,[44] the adversarial system can be accounted for as a system that genuinely seeks the truth as a component of resolution. Such a system must neutralise the risk to agency that might undermine any resolution. This is what adversary does: each of the parties generates as many relevant hypotheses of guilt and of innocence as it wishes, introduces evidence and examines the compatibility of the evidence with the different competing hypotheses. These exercises of agency ensure that even if an error occurs, it is not an objectionable external imposition; relatedly, it does not give rise to fresh conflicts over agency that would have undercut resolution and threaten its acceptability and acceptance.

D. The Presumption of Innocence

Many attempts have been made to explain what the presumption of innocence comes to and on what grounds it can be justified.[45] It is impossible to survey these

[40] See, eg, the findings in MK Block et al, 'An Experimental Comparison of Adversarial versus Inquisitorial Procedural Regimes' (2000) 2 *American Law and Economics Review* 170 (suggesting that the systems fare differently depending on the ex-ante structure of the information available for the parties).

[41] See, eg, J Frank, *Courts on Trial: Myth and Reality in American Justice* (Princeton, NJ, Princeton University Press, 1950). A useful summary can be found in KA Findley, 'Adversarial Inquisitions: Rethinking the Search for Truth' (2012) 56 *NYLS Law Review* 911. Analyses usually also address a range of procedural and evidential rules associated with adversary. The current short analysis considers adversary in a narrow sense.

[42] And see also S Landsman, *The Adversary System: A Description and Defence* (Washington, DC, American Enterprise Institute for Public Policy Research, 1984) (defending adversary with reference to the individuation of the litigation and to its contribution to the maintenance of human rights).

[43] See Redmayne (n 35) and the references there.

[44] Weigend (n 9).

[45] A Ashworth, 'Four Threats to the Presumption of Innocence' (2006) 10 *International Journal of Evidence and Proof* 241; A Duff, 'Presuming Innocence' in L Zedner and JV Roberts (eds), *Principles and Values in Criminal Law and Criminal Justice* (Oxford, Oxford University Press, 2012) 51; L Campbell,

attempts here, but one thread is notable: most interpretations of the presumption refrain from endowing it with doxastic content; they take the presumption as calling for the development of some practical attitudes about the defendant and the course of trial, rather than as calling for plain belief in the defendant's innocence.[46] Under the assumption that belief is unintentional, this seems easy to explain: the requirement to adopt a belief in the defendant's innocence would be hard to fulfil; and to the extent that the available evidence demonstrates that the defendant is guilty, this requirement would be epistemologically unjustified.

The proposed account nevertheless allows for a plain doxastic interpretation of the presumption of innocence.[47] According to this interpretation, the presumption of innocence clarifies that mere passive belief in guilt based on the fact that some evidence is available, and that the defendant is being prosecuted, would undermine the resolutive nature of legal fact finding. The initial formation of such a belief is irrational and unfair: it is based on evidence that does not meet error eliminability (namely, the statistical fact that the defendant is being prosecuted and that most defendants are guilty). Where the factfinder holds such an irrational and unfair belief, and the defendant is asked to refute it and would be determined guilty if she did not, the entire reasoning process is irrational and unfair. This itself is enough to undermine the legal determination on grounds of irrationality and unfairness. In addition, such a determination will not be suitable as a resolution: it will give rise to fresh conflict, which might not be over agency but over the fairness of the procedures, yet it would nevertheless undermine the goal of conflict resolution. The presumption of innocence thus directs legal actors to a rational reasoning. Such a direction is not impossible to meet, and it is justified in a system whose overarching aim is truth-based resolution.

'Criminal Labels, the European Convention on Human Rights and the Presumption of Innocence' (2013) 76 *MLR* 681; D Hamer, 'A Dynamic Reconstruction of the Presumption of Innocence' (2011) 31 *OJLS* 417; RL Lippke, *Taming the Presumption of Innocence* (Oxford, Oxford University Press, 2016); L Laudan, *Truth, Error, and Criminal Law: An Essay in Legal Epistemology* (Cambridge, Cambridge University Press, 2006) esp 93–96.

[46] Lippke (n 45) might be coming close to an epistemic interpretation, but it seems that his proposal should be read as calling for practical attitudes rather than beliefs.

[47] Compare with Laudan (n 45), who refers to belief in the defendant's 'probatory' innocence; this comes to a call for juries to ignore the status of the defendant as a defendant.

7

From Respect to Cost Analysis in Criminal Judgments*

This chapter focuses on the negative value of errors based on evidence that does not meet error eliminability. It is demonstrated that in the special context of criminal law, false convictions based on such evidence have higher negative value than other false convictions. Given this added negative value, an argument in support of error eliminability can rely on a cost-based analysis that is guided by decision-theoretic principles and compares error eliminability with accuracy-focused rules of decision making.

The argument about the higher negative value of false convictions based on evidence that does not meet error eliminability will run as follows: such entirely possible false convictions are profoundly tragic in the Aristotelian sense. The tragedy is of the falsely convicted defendant as well as of the falsely convicting state. This aesthetic characteristic of the false conviction has moral significance: tragedies undermine the value of choice; they capture situations where a seemingly insignificant original choice leads to a completely disproportionate disaster despite all effort to avoid it. Thus, false impositions of liability based on evidence that does not meet error eliminability have particularly high negative value.

The argument that, given this high negative value, rationality requires that we insist on error eliminability will make use of decision-theoretic principles. It will be shown that in the evidential conditions of the criminal justice system, the likelihood of tragic errors is unknown and probably unknowable. Maximin will then be applied, leading to the conclusion that evidence that is not based on error eliminability should be excluded.

The analysis will address in turn various types of legal evidence that do not meet error eliminability, including 'bad character evidence;' other statistical evidence that indicates propensity; and statistical evidence that does not indicate propensity.

* Parts of this chapter were published previously in L Levanon, '"Bad Character", Tragic Errors and Deep Ignorance' (2019) 39 *Legal Studies* 676.

I. Evidence of Past Misconduct

Loosely defined, 'bad character evidence' is evidence of the defendant's similar past misconduct. As we shall see, the law has been ambivalent about admitting such evidence to support an inference that the defendant is more likely to have committed the offence at issue. The inference would work as follows: the defendant has committed similar misconduct before; people who have committed misconduct are more likely to commit similar offences than random members of the population; hence the defendant is more likely to have committed the offence at issue than a random member of the population. Such inference is different from inferences based, say, on an identified motive to commit a certain type of misconduct. The motive can be examined to reveal how strong it is, how much force it has given the specific personality of the defendant and so on. It can, in other words, be individualised. The same is not the case when it comes to past misconduct: while past misconduct signifies the existence of a motive or reason to commit offences of a certain type, it does not identify this motive or reason. Hence, individuation is impossible, and the inference is based on a correlation that can be observed across the relevant population between past and future commission. Available data demonstrate that this inference is valid where the previous offence is recent; and the inference would be stronger for some types of offences than it would be for others.[1]

The inference from past misconduct thus fails to meet error eliminability. It is based on the generalisation that many offenders are recidivist (because they have a persisting reason to commit offences, and/or because past commission creates reasons for further commission or erodes reasons against further commission). This generalisation is not true for all offenders: some offenders are not recidivists. They commit one or more offences and then they stop. Nevertheless, the inference would be from the class of all offenders to the defendant, without room for a further narrowing down of the reference class until it captures only recidivist offenders. Where the evidence takes the form of such a generalisation, the possibility of error cannot be eliminated. Furthermore, since the generalisation essentially captures some non-recidivist offenders, if the inference from past misconduct is applied to all offenders, some errors are logically inevitable. In such conditions, it is irrational to believe that any specific offender is recidivist. There is no reason to believe that the defendant at issue (rather than any other defendant who committed crime before) does not belong with the non-recidivist offenders; accordingly, the assertion that the defendant is recidivist cannot reflect justified legal belief and hence also legal knowledge.

[1] M Redmayne, *Character in the Criminal Trial* (Oxford, Oxford University Press, 2015) esp 22–24.

The case of inferences from past misconduct helps reveal some additional implications of error eliminability in the legal context. Let us begin by examining the law in some more detail, and then move on to unfolding these additional implications of error eliminability.

A. The Law

Since the early nineteenth century, the common law had been ambivalent about evidence of 'bad character'. A rule of exclusion emerged,[2] which was initially associated with the probative value of the evidence and then with the possibility of prejudice.[3] Yet the common law never resorted to blanket exclusion. Rather, the rule of exclusion 'was subject to exceptions from the moment of its birth'.[4] At first these took the form of categories of admissibility based on the purpose for which the evidence was introduced. Relying on a list devised by Cross, Redmayne notes that 'bad character evidence' was admissible for the purposes of

> rebutting a defence of accident or involuntary conduct, rebutting the accused's plea of ignorance or mistake of fact; rebutting an innocent explanation of a particular act or of the possession of incriminating material; proving identity; and rebutting a defence of innocent association.[5]

Most of the categories had something in common. Redmayne suggests that apart from proving identity, all the categories allowed admission of 'bad character evidence' for the purpose of rebutting 'confession and avoidance' defences.[6] In 'confession and avoidance' the defendant admits facts that the prosecution seek to prove, but she argues for the existence of additional facts that preclude liability. Significantly, in such cases the defendant bluntly and transparently fails herself. The defendant: (i) puts herself in a difficult position that allows the prosecution to easily connect her to the offence at issue; and (ii) subsequently decides to make a partial confession, endorsing some of the circumstances of the offence and thereby completing a significant part of the task for the prosecution. Through her miscalculated moves the defendant thus puts herself on the defensive: she now needs to provide independent evidence to rebut the charges. In most of the common law categories, this transparent self-failing opened the door to the introduction of further prosecution evidence of the defendant's 'bad character'. The significance of transparent self-failing for decisions about admissibility of 'bad character evidence' will be discussed further in section I.F.

[2] Redmayne (ibid 93) mentions the unreported decision in Cole from 1810 as the point of emergence of the rule of exclusion.

[3] Redmayne (n 1) 97.

[4] ibid.

[5] ibid.

[6] ibid 128, relying on R Cross, *Evidence*, 5th edn (London, Butterworths, 1979) 378–93.

Notably, such failing of oneself could also be traced in one subcategory of proof of identity, namely, in modus operandi cases. The clearest example was *Straffen*,[7] which concerned a 'singularly bizarre crime which Straffen had himself committed twice the year before', to use John Spencer's lucid description.[8] The defendant in this case thus devised a 'criminal fingerprint'. This is a transparent act of self-failing; it involves taking a clear risk that one would be directly connected to specific past or future offences. In the similar 'brides in the bath' case of *Smith*,[9] three of the defendant's wives died of drowning in bathtubs shortly after making financial arrangements that would benefit the defendant if they died. Here, transparent self-failing consisted of one of the following: either devising a 'criminal fingerprint', or failing to correct a clear impression that such a 'fingerprint' has been devised. In these modus operandi cases the error is so remarkably obvious that self-failing can be identified even without partial confession.[10]

The only subcategory that did not require the defendant to have bluntly and transparently failed herself was proving identity in cases where a witness's testimony was available against the defendant. Here, the defendant did not self-failingly connect herself to the offence at issue; rather, the alleged connection between the defendant and the offence was mediated by an external indicator (the testimony). This subcategory can be understood as a first sign of future legal developments: it signalled that the defendant's conduct in the run up to trial was to be set aside, and instead the focus should be on probative value. Specifically, this subcategory focused on the probative value of one type of incriminating evidence that existed in addition to bare past misconduct, namely, the testimony.

This shift of focus continued to unfold in *Boardman*,[11] where the common law categories were replaced by a test of 'striking similarity' between past misconduct and the conduct at issue. The 'striking similarity' test focused on probative value of incriminating data that could not be introduced without revealing bare 'bad character evidence', namely, data regarding a similar pattern of commission that the defendant endorsed. *Boardman* established that only where such data were highly probative could the defendant's past misconduct be revealed to the jury. Yet the decision did not complete the shift of focus to considerations of probative value by considering the independent value of bare past misconduct and by generalising to all incriminating data that might exist in addition to bare past misconduct, and it has been criticised on this ground.[12]

It was the Criminal Justice Act (CJA) 2003 that concluded the shift of focus from the defendant's blunt and transparent self-failing to considerations of

[7] *R v Straffen* [1952] 2 QB 911.

[8] JR Spencer, *Evidence of Bad Character*, 2nd edn (Oxford, Hart Publishing, 2009) para 1.72.

[9] *R v Smith* (1916) 11 Cr App R 229.

[10] This can be distinguished from having one's physical fingerprint found in the scene of crime, which is not necessarily associated with any transparently erroneous behaviour that was sure to turn the defendant into a suspect of crime.

[11] *DPP v Boardman* [1975] AC 421.

[12] Redmayne (n 1) 130.

probative value. The 2003 Act defines evidence of 'bad character' in section 98, as 'evidence of, or of a disposition towards, misconduct'; and 'misconduct' is defined in section 112(1) as 'the commission of an offence or other reprehensible behaviour'. Section 101(1) sets seven gateways for admission of 'bad character evidence'. For current purposes, the relevant gateway is gateway (d), which makes the evidence admissible if 'it is relevant to an important matter in issue between the defendant and the prosecution'. This gateway has relaxed the common law's striking similarity (or enhanced relevance) requirement, and in this way it has signified completion of the transition to a strict regime of probative value. According to section 103(1)(a), matters in issue between the defendant and the prosecution include, amongst other things, 'the question whether the defendant has a propensity to commit offences of the kind with which he is charged, except where his having such a propensity makes it no more likely that he is guilty of the offence'. Section 103(2) further mentions one way of proving propensity, namely, by introducing evidence of previous convictions of an offence of the same description or category as the offence of which he is accused. Admission is subject to section 101(3), which requires exclusion where the evidence would have an adverse effect on the fairness of the proceedings. Other gateways allow the introduction of 'bad character evidence' where all parties agree to it;[13] where it is the defendant who introduces it,[14] or who raises the issue of his character or of another person's 'bad character';[15] where it is important explanatory evidence;[16] and where it has substantial probative value for an important matter in issue between the defendant and a co-defendant.[17]

These provisions changed the exclusion regime in more ways than one. The definition of 'bad character evidence' that they adopt is exceptionally broad, at least in some respects. Significantly, Federico Picinali has noted that in addition to evidence of previous commission of comparable crimes, propensity evidence might include evidence of other indicators of propensity, such as affiliations and group memberships.[18] The discussion in this section focuses on evidence of previous commission of comparable crimes; extending the argument to other indicators of propensity, and indeed to naked statistical evidence that does not indicate propensity,[19] will follow.

[13] CJA 2003, s 101(1)(a).

[14] CJA 2003, s 101(1)(b).

[15] CJA 2003, s 101(1)(g).

[16] CJA 2003, s 101(1)(c).

[17] CJA 2003, s 101(1)(e).

[18] F Picinali, 'Generalisations, Causal Relationships and Moral Responsibility' (2016) 20 *The International Journal of Evidence & Proof* 121, 129.

[19] For example, in the bus companies example that is a variation on the American case of *Smith v Rapid Transit, Inc* 58 NE 2d 754 (Mass 1945). See the discussion in GL Wells, 'Naked statistical evidence of liability: is subjective probability enough?' (1992) 62 *Journal of Personality and Social Psychology* 739; or the rodeo stadium example in LJ Cohen, *The Probable and the Provable* (Oxford, Clarendon Press, 1977) 74–75.

As for the scope of admissibility, *Hanson*[20] was one of the first decisions to interpret the CJA 2003 provisions, and it remains relevant. The decision focuses on probative value. Analysing the probative value of bare evidence of past misconduct for proof of propensity, the Court of Appeal noted the significance of the number of instances of past misconduct. Analysing the possible impact of admission on the fairness of proceedings, the Court addressed mainly the probative value of other available incriminating data. Here, the Court referred to the level of similarity of past commissions to the offence at issue and, more generally, to the strength of the prosecution case. The Court also mentioned the importance of the respective gravity of past and present offences. Last, *Hanson* outlined a warning that the trial judge should make when admitting propensity evidence.[21]

It is fairly consensual that by completing the shift of focus to probative value, the 2003 Act extended the scope of admissible evidence of previous misconduct.[22] Yet examination of the case law that followed *Hanson* has led Redmayne to conclude that it is impossible to describe it with much precision, especially given that the Court of Appeal has granted trial judges a broad discretion in applying the law.[23] Redmayne notes that where probative value in the circumstances of the case is the main consideration, this is not necessarily a bad thing;[24] after all, these circumstances change from one case to another in a way that may require particularistic judgement.

B. Tragic Errors

When a belief cannot be justified based on error eliminability, a subsequent erroneous conviction would be profoundly tragic in nature. To see this, we can compare errors based on evidence of past misconduct that fails to meet error eliminability to errors based on evidence that meets error eliminability. Assume first that we have CCTV evidence of the highest quality in which the defendant can be seen committing robbery, and that based on this evidence the defendant can be identified with certainty by the maximally perceptive factfinder. In fact, the factfinders in his trial are less than maximally perceptive, and hence they come to conclude that they can only identify the defendant to a likelihood of 98 per cent. The defendant is convicted, alas wrongfully – unfortunately, his conviction falls within the 2 per cent likelihood of error. The error is of course sad and frustrating; some might say that it is 'tragic' in the plain sense of the term; but this is what it comes to, and nothing more than this. The meaning of this error comes only to the

[20] *R v Hanson* [2005] EWCA Crim 824, [2005] 2 Cr App R 21.

[21] ibid.

[22] Redmayne (n 1) 167; AL-T Choo *Evidence*, 4th edn (Oxford, Oxford University Press, 2015) 263–64.

[23] Redmayne (n 1) 169.

[24] ibid 169–72.

fact that CCTV evidence has been wrongly assumed to provide that which it did not provide. In such circumstances the error is a highly unfortunate chance event.

Now assume that the same defendant is convicted based on evidence of a similar and unusual way of him committing robbery on past occasions – evidence that again creates a mere 2 per cent likelihood of error, this time because 98 per cent of offenders who commit such robberies are recidivist. Here, too, the conviction falls within these 2 per cent. But here, the meaning of the false conviction is different and more profoundly tragic: it is a false conviction based on past conduct whose statistical implications the defendant has, in fact, almost heroically beaten. This is a tragedy at a scale that is better left for the theatre. It is hard enough for the legal system to live with the disaster of any false conviction; living with the overwhelming tragedy of falsely convicting those who have beaten all odds based on the very same odds they have beaten is more than what some legal systems have been willing to do.

C. The Elements of Tragedies

To clarify this argument, the materials of which tragedies are made should be observed. Nowadays the word 'tragedy' is used loosely to refer to bad events that cause suffering and regret. Any false conviction would therefore easily qualify as a tragedy in this sense. However, the theoretical-theatrical concept, and particularly the original Greek theoretical-theatrical concept, has a narrower meaning. To comprehend this narrower meaning, we can observe Aristotle's account of tragedy in his *Poetics*.[25] While probably non-exhaustive,[26] this account is illuminating.

In terms of content, Aristotle's account captures what we can call the profound tragedy, where a disproportionate disaster or total destruction befalls the hero not by some entirely arbitrary fate but by his own misjudgement or by his human weaknesses (known as *hamartia* in Greek tragedy).[27] The Aristotelian tragedy is

[25] According to Aristotle's definition of a tragedy, it 'is an imitation of an action that is serious, complete and of a certain magnitude; … in the form of action, not of narrative; through pity and fear effecting the proper purgation of those passions': Aristotle, *The Poetics of Aristotle*, 3rd edn, ed with critical notes and tr SH Butcher (1902) pt VI, available at www.gutenberg.org/files/1974/1974-h/1974-h.htm.

[26] The Aristotelian account has been criticised as overly narrow, in the sense that it does not even capture all types of Greek tragedies. See GR Noyes, 'Aristotle and Modern Tragedy' (1891) 13 *Modern Language Notes* 6, 11–12. See further P Woodruff, 'Aristotle on Character in Tragedy, or Who is Creon? What is He?' (2009) 67 *The Journal of Aesthetics and Art Criticism* 301; M Pabst Battin, 'Aristotle's Definition of Tragedy in the Poetics' (1975) 33 *The Journal of Aesthetics and Art Criticism* 293. Yet Aristotle's account was probably not meant as an exhaustive definition of a tragedy. See Noyes, 'Aristotle and Modern Tragedy', this footnote, at 7.

[27] See Aristotle (n 25) pt IX; D Frede, 'Necessity, Chance, and "What Happens for the Most Part"' in A Rorty (ed), *Essays on Aristotle's Poetics* (Princeton, NJ, Princeton University Press, 1992) 197, 205 and 212. The extent to which *hamartia* involves (limited) guilt is controversial. See TCW Stinton, 'Hamartia in Aristotle and Greek tragedy' (1975) 25 *The Classical Quarterly* 221.

thus made of an imperfect protagonist making what initially looks like a limited error, but which ends up having extremely destructive consequences. The structural components of the Aristotelian tragic plot are the following:[28] a sequence of events that are connected as causes and effects;[29] an element of surprise;[30] reversal of the situation/intention, where an event ends up having the opposite effect to that which was intended or expected;[31] a moment of recognition, where the protagonist comes to realise his error;[32] and a scene of suffering (or a tragic incident), where the painful impact of the disaster manifests itself.[33]

In terms of its effects, the tragic course of events stimulates pity and fear.[34] Aristotle further elaborates the means by which this effect is produced, or the circumstances that in his mind strike us as most terrible or pitiful. According to Aristotle, pity and fear are stimulated when the tragedy happens between persons who are near or dear to one another;[35] and where the protagonist is above the common level and is characterised by goodness and propriety[36] but is nonetheless true to life and fairly consistent.[37] The tragic hero should remind us of ourselves,[38] 'a man who is not eminently good and just, yet whose misfortune is brought about not by vice or depravity, but by some error or frailty'.[39] In this way tragedies demonstrate that we are our biggest enemies; and this insight is terrible and frightening.

D. The Defendant's Tragedy

The story of a false conviction based on evidence of previous misconduct is such a profound tragedy. It is a story of a disaster whose origins trace back to the defendant's limited but apparently fatal error. The erroneous choice is the past choice to commit some crimes. Indeed, this means that the story is not one of a merely understandable human misjudgement that leads to the disproportionate destruction. After all, we do not consider past misconduct as understandable misjudgement but as a condemnable moral wrong. But the story is, nevertheless, a story of a blameworthy but presumably narrow and bounded choice that somehow leads to catastrophe.

[28] Aristotle (n 25) pts IX et seq.
[29] ibid pt IX.
[30] ibid
[31] ibid pt XI.
[32] ibid.
[33] ibid pt XII.
[34] Aristotle (n 25).
[35] ibid pt XIV.
[36] ibid pt XV.
[37] ibid.
[38] ibid pt XIII: 'for pity is aroused by unmerited misfortune, fear by the misfortune of a man like ourselves'.
[39] ibid.

Let us observe how the catastrophe unfolds. The past choice to commit some crimes puts the actor in the claws of the gloomy recidivism statistics. And the statistics are gloomy. They are gloomy not because they show that an actor who previously committed crime is almost certain to commit further similar crimes (they do not show this[40]); the statistics are gloomy because they show that an actor who previously committed crime is much more likely to commit further similar crimes than an actor who did not previously commit crime.[41]

These statistics have two meanings. First, they have purely evidential meaning: they simply indicate that the actor is statistically more likely than a random person to have committed the misconduct at issue.[42] Second, the statistics have a substantive meaning: they indicate that the choice to refrain from crime is more challenging and difficult for this actor than for others who did not commit crime.[43] Compared with others, the actor who committed crime is apparently subject to particularly strong forces that push him towards further crime commission. There may be many such forces: the actor may have developed the self-perception of a criminal; may have crossed the internal Rubicon that usually stops people from crime commission; may have befriended other criminals who encourage further crime commission, etc. Even if such forces do not prove to be operative for a particular actor, reality still presents them to the actor as traps to be avoided, and this in itself is challenging. This second, substantive meaning of the statistics is morally significant: it implies that the actor faces a difficult moral challenge.

The actor who previously committed crime is therefore faced with a challenging test. But he then almost heroically stands up to the challenge. He fights the forces that push towards crime commission and wins; he beats the odds. And while many in his position manage to do the same, his achievement is still impressive (and so is that of similar others). They should all be compared with others who do not face similar challenges at all. When such actors manage to evade the traps of past misconduct, they win over the statistics that indicate they are more likely than others to commit crimes. The achievement of every such actor is almost heroic.

Alas, against all expectations, the statistics then nevertheless chase the actor all the way to his false conviction for other crimes. Just as it seems that the actor has so impressively situated himself next to law-abiding citizens and escaped the

[40] See Redmayne (n 1) 16–21.

[41] ibid 22–24 (Table 2.7).

[42] For an elaborate critical discussion of the ways to analyse the probative value of evidence of previous misconduct, see ibid 35–41.

[43] If this were not the case, the statistics would have been nothing more than 'spurious' generalisations that cannot be used in a criminal trial. See F Picinali, 'Generalisations, Causal Relationships and Moral Responsibility' (2016) 20 *The International Journal of Evidence and Proof* 121, 122–23. For critical discussion, see A Pundik, 'Against Racial Profiling' (2017) 67 *The University of Toronto Law Journal* 175, 188–89.

fate of a criminal, the fate of a criminal knocks on his door. It suddenly becomes apparent that while he managed to beat the morally significant metaphysical implications of the error, its morally insignificant evidential implications cannot be evaded. The evidence created by his original misconduct brings about a false conviction, or at least contributes to this outcome.[44]

The story is thus, in the end, a story of an actor who finds himself unable to escape the punitive implications of the statistics he had erroneously put himself into, and whose human journey ends in a disproportionate disaster. Like an Aristotelian profound tragedy, it is a story that stimulates extreme pity and fear, and for the same reasons.

The profoundly tragic aspect exists even if the defendant has not gone through the unlikely process of full reform but rather did not commit the crime on the occasion at issue for other reasons, for example because she was too tired or busy doing something else. To see this, we should think of the probability of commission per opportunity to commit crime (usually expressed in Bayesian terms[45]). For a defendant who has already committed crimes, the probability of commission per opportunity is very high. With every such opportunity that the defendant encounters, she also encounters the gloomy statistics she has put herself in. Whenever such an offender chooses not to take an opportunity to commit a crime – be the reason for that choice as it may be – she beats the odds. Every decision to engage in non-harmful activity rather than to take an opportunity to commit crime involves a small but nevertheless almost heroic victory over the statistics. Alas, the statistics still chase her all the way to her false conviction.

Arguably, there is a difficulty with the defendant who has not fully reformed when her case is observed through the prism of probability per time unit (rather than per opportunity).[46] According to this argument, while such a defendant did not commit the crime during the relevant opportunity, she did not thereby confront and beat the high odds of crime commission over the same week or month. As the relevant time period has not been exhausted, the same odds are still there, waiting to be confronted. Thus, when probabilities are observed per time unit, the defendant has not yet beaten the odds. In such circumstances her false conviction based on these statistics is, arguably, not profoundly tragic.

This argument relies on several inaccuracies. First, such a defendant is actually expected to commit fewer crimes per (sufficiently long) time unit than a

[44] Where the evidence does not contribute to the false conviction, it is not clear that the false conviction is profoundly tragic. Yet it is hard, if not impossible, to say whether the evidence contributed to the false conviction; and, as explained in section I.D, the fact that there are some cases in which the evidence did contribute to the false conviction is the significant one when making general decisions regarding the admissibility of evidence of previous misconduct.

[45] See L Levanon, 'The Law of Police Entrapment: Critical Evaluation and Policy Analysis' (2016) 27 *Criminal Law Forum* 35.

[46] ibid.

similar fellow defendant who decided to commit crime early in the relevant time period, and this already indicates an initial process of distancing herself from crime, or of reform. Accordingly, false conviction based on the low likelihood of reform is still profoundly tragic. In addition, with every day that goes by without her committing crime, this defendant's likelihood of repetition drops (as recidivism rates drop with time[47]). Thus, when the defendant postpones her criminal activity, she reduces the likelihood that she will ever return to it, thereby starting to reform. For this reason too, her false conviction based on the low probability of reform is still profoundly tragic. This is true even if in the end this defendant does not reform: falsely convicting for something that took place exactly within the time period when the defendant opened the door for reform, and doing so based on the low likelihood of reform, is profoundly tragic no matter how things turned out in the end. Last, observing probabilities per time unit only provides part of the picture; understanding the full meaning of the choice to engage in non-harmful activity in the relevant time period must also have regard to the above-mentioned probabilities per opportunity.

The only cases where false conviction of a defendant who has not fully reformed based on evidence of previous misconduct is not profoundly tragic are the following: (i) the case of a defendant who did not commit the relevant crime because she was busy committing another similar crime; and (ii) the case of a defendant who did not commit the relevant crime but had already committed a similar recidivist crime, say on the day before. It is hard to say whether in such cases we would still feel uncomfortable using evidence of previous misconduct and taking the risk of a mistake. In any case, there are still grounds for a general rule of exclusion whose aim is to avoid rare but profoundly tragic false convictions of reformed defendants. After all, a rule that excludes probative evidence of past misconduct would essentially presume that it is justified to exclude some perfectly good evidence to avoid certain errors.

E. Comparing the Defendant's Story with that of the Greek Tragic Hero

We can now examine how the characteristics of the Greek tragedy present themselves in Sophocles' *Oedipus Rex*, which Aristotle considered the purest example of a tragedy;[48] and, by way of comparison, how they present themselves in the story of the defendant who is falsely convicted based on previous misconduct. The examination will start with content and then move to the structure of the plot and the means by which the tragic effect is achieved.

[47] Redmayne (n 1) 26–27.
[48] See M Barstow, 'Oedipus Rex as the Ideal Tragic Hero of Aristotle' (1912) 6 *The Classic Weekly* 2.

The content of *Oedipus Rex* is familiar enough: Oedipus has been given a prophecy according to which he will kill his father and sleep with his mother. Trying to escape this prophecy, he leaves his home in Corinth and the people he believes are his biological mother and father. Alas, his fate (or the prophecy) cannot be escaped, and Oedipus ends up discovering that after leaving his home, he committed these horrors against his true biological parents without realising who they were. Notably, the origins of the disaster trace back to the crime of killing a stranger on a crossroad.[49] The implications of this crime seemed to have been limited but eventually revealed themselves as disastrous (the stranger was later revealed as Oedipus' biological father).

This story bears strong similarity to the story of the defendant that has already been outlined. Like Oedipus, this defendant lives in the shadow of a prediction: the statistics predict that she will end up being destroyed by repeated convictions of further crimes. In what initially looks like a successful attempt to escape this prediction, she refrains from further crime commission. But, like Oedipus, this defendant's fate cannot be escaped, and she ends up being falsely convicted based on the statistics and thereby being destroyed. Here too, the origins of the disaster trace back to crime commission whose implications seemed to have been limited but eventually revealed themselves as disastrous.[50]

The plots of both *Oedipus Rex* and the defendant's story have the above-mentioned structural characteristics of the Aristotelian tragedy. As already demonstrated, in both stories the chain of events flows as a causal chain. Furthermore, in both stories the destruction of the protagonist is surprising: Oedipus seems to have evaded the prophecy when leaving Corinth for the city of Thebes, and his discovery that the prophecy has been realised is astonishing. Similarly, the defendant seems to have escaped the claws of statistics when she refrains from further crime commission, and her false conviction based on these statistics is no less astonishing. Moreover, in both cases there is Reversal of Situation. In *Oedipus Rex* the messenger brings information that is supposed to free Oedipus from his worries (namely, that Merope was not his real mother), but this message produces the opposite effect, leading to the discovery that Jocasta is his mother. In the defendant's case, the trial is supposed to reveal the truth and free the defendant from false suspicion, but it ends up producing the opposite effect when the defendant is falsely convicted. In addition, in both stories there is a moment of recognition. Aristotle notes that 'The best form of recognition is coincident with a Reversal

[49] There is disagreement in the literature on the *hamartia* in *Oedipus Rex*, but many trace it to this killing that is later revealed as parricide, which also opens the door for his marrying his biological mother. See I Hyde, 'The Tragic Flaw: Is It a Tragic Error?' (1963) 58 *The Modern Language Review* 321; L Golden, 'Hamartia, Atë, and Oedipus' (1978) 72 *Classical World* 3.

[50] At least under the assumption that Oedipus' *hamartia* was indeed the ignorant killing of the person at the crossroad.

of the Situation, as in the Oedipus.'[51] The same applies for the defendant who comes to realise her disaster as the evidence is presented against her and seals her false conviction. Last, in both stories there is a Scene of Suffering where the protagonist is mortified: Oedipus plunges Jocasta's pins into his eyes, and the defendant's suffering is, presumably, apparent as the court finds her guilty.

As for the tragic effect, while both stories stimulate extreme pity and fear, the means that achieve the tragic effect are admittedly more strictly Aristotelian in *Oedipus Rex* than they are in the defendant's story. Unlike in *Oedipus Rex*, the defendant's tragedy does not involve family or friends. Furthermore, unlike Oedipus, who comes from the ruling classes and who accordingly is considered above the common level, the defendant is not above the common level and is not necessarily characterised by goodness and propriety. But at least to the extent that this defendant is fully or partly reformed, her intentions are good and we can identify with her. Moreover, like Oedipus, the defendant is true to life and fairly consistent, and this too allows identification.

To conclude, the defendant's story has the content and structure of an Aristotelian tragedy. The absence of some characteristics that Aristotle considered as best producing the tragic effect does not necessarily prevent the development of this effect. The defendant who is falsely convicted based on her past is therefore very similar to Aristotle's tragic hero.

F. Back to the Law

We can now go back to observing the law. The analysis proposed so far can shed light on the common law exceptions to the rule of exclusion of 'bad character evidence'. It was noted that almost all of these exceptions involved cases where the defendant failed herself one more time, above and beyond her bare past misconduct, and this time bluntly and transparently so. But this additional moment of blunt and transparent self-failing affects our evaluation of the defendant's entire erroneous course of conduct and its outcomes in several ways.

First, it deprives the defendant's original error (the bare past misconduct) of its limited scope, turning it into one in a sequence of risky behaviours. Second, a subsequent false conviction based partly on the original error no longer comes as a complete surprise: the defendant who has transparently turned herself into a suspect has also openly taken all the risks associated with a criminal justice process, including that of a false conviction. That this might actually lead to her being falsely convicted is hardly astonishing. Third, the theatrical disproportionality of a false conviction is no longer measured only against the single original error but against the combination of this error with the following act of

[51] Aristotle (n 25) pt XI.

blunt self-failing. Accordingly, the disaster seems less disproportionate. Fourth, her blunt and transparent self-failing makes the defendant significantly harder to identify with. The defendant therefore loses many of the characteristics of a tragic protagonist, and the false conviction loses many of the characteristics of a tragic outcome.

It can thus be suggested that the common law categories captured cases where the admission of 'bad character evidence' no longer had the potential to lead to profoundly tragic false convictions. Only in these cases was admission exceptionally allowed. Clearly, this is not to suggest that the common law categories exhausted the cases where admission of 'bad character evidence' would not lead to tragedies; neither is it to suggest that all the categories were accurate and fully explicable along the suggested lines. Still, the proposed analysis does demonstrate that the common law's approach may have had its grounds. In addition, this analysis can explain why the categories only partly overlap with the pool of cases in which other strong evidence is available against the defendant. Last, the analysis sheds different light on the transition completed by CJA 2003 into a regime of probative value: this transition has removed the distinction between profoundly tragic errors and other errors.

II. Statistical Evidence that Indicates Propensity

We are now in a better position to move on to the next type of evidence, namely, naked statistical evidence indicating propensity (such as evidence of low socio-economic background, etc). Like evidence of past misconduct, this evidence does not meet error eliminability. The inference based on such evidence is as follows: the defendant belongs in class X; members of class X are more likely to commit (such) offences than random members of the population; hence the defendant is more likely to have committed the offence at issue. Since the evidence guarantees that not all members of class X commit (such) offences, if the inference is applied with respect to all members of class X, errors are certain to occur. Furthermore, the risk of error cannot logically be eliminated when relying on such evidence; the evidence imposes a 'stopping point' for the narrowing down of the reference class; it does not allow for carrying on the narrowing-down process until all possible error cases have been removed from the reference class.

The arguments about tragedies can further apply to such evidence. To see this, assume that the defendant is wrongly convicted based on naked statistical evidence that indicates propensity, such as evidence of unchosen group affiliation – evidence that again creates a mere 2 per cent likelihood of error. According to the proposed argument, this false conviction is also profoundly tragic; possibly, it is even more profoundly tragic than a false conviction based on previous misconduct.

To clarify this argument, the statistical significance of affiliations needs to be analysed. The statistical significance of affiliations is connected to two aspects of such affiliations. The first is the unchosen one (eg, being born with a certain group affiliation). This aspect is statistically 'escapable', as the person can exclude himself from the relevant reference class by making the right choices (the statistics for the economically deprived defendant are not the same as the ones for the economically deprived defendant who invested in her studies, spent most of her free time playing the recorder, volunteered in the community, etc).[52] If the defendant made the right choices, the naked statistical evidence concerning unchosen affiliations would have not probative value and would therefore be irrelevant evidence. False conviction based on this evidence would be out of the picture.

Second, the statistical significance of affiliations is connected to exactly these endless daily choices that the defendant makes and whose background conditions are introduced to her by the unchosen aspect of affiliations (such as choice of friends, choice of time to invest in education, decisions on how to spend one's free time, etc). Erroneous daily choices put the defendant deeper and deeper in the claws of crime statistics, as they affect her motivations to commit crime. Yet, much like the tragic *hamartia*, such erroneous choices are perfectly understandable in the circumstances and overall fairly blameless. Where the defendant has made such erroneous daily choices that indeed put her in the claws of statistics, her winning over the statistics becomes even more admirable and heroic than in the case of previous misconduct – where the erroneous choice that put her in the claws of statistics was also blameworthy and risky. Consequently, the inability to escape the punitive implications of the statistics becomes even more profoundly tragic. The defendant in this case is in fact identical to the Aristotelian tragic hero. The feeling stimulated by this inability is one of great pity and dread of our own affiliations with the seemingly innocent choices they impose on us and with their potential disasters.

III. Statistical Evidence that Does Not Indicate Propensity

We have yet to observe naked statistical evidence that does not indicate propensity. Such evidence includes, for example, DNA evidence introduced for purposes of identification, and evidence that the defendant belongs in a group of a specified number of persons with information available about the majority of them. Examples include the evidence explored in the famous blue and red bus

[52] For a discussion of the reference class problem, see L Levanon, 'Sexual History Evidence in Sexual Assault Cases: A Critical Reevaluation' (2012) 62 *University of Toronto Law Journal* 609.

companies example,[53] or in the equally famous rodeo stadium example.[54] Before examining the relevance of the concept of tragedy to an analysis of erroneous judgments based on such evidence, it should be noted that using such evidence does not provoke the same type of moral outrage that using propensity evidence provokes.

The argument about profoundly tragic errors is relevant for such evidence too. To see this, we can focus on a criminal law variation of Cohen's rodeo stadium example. In this version, a rodeo is attended by 1,000 spectators, 100 of whom have paid for admission and 900 of whom have not paid. The probability for each random spectator that he did not pay is thus 0.9. The question is whether a conviction of a random spectator would be profoundly tragic.

It appears at first sight that the answer is in the negative. In this example, the prior odds of commission are not known to be particularly high. Those spectators who paid are not known to have belonged in any reference class members of which are less likely to pay than the general population. Therefore, their choice to pay does not involve beating any gloomy prior odds of commission, and erroneously obliging them to compensate based on the 0.9 posterior probability of commission is indeed sad but not profoundly tragic.

However, this account does not yet consider the impact of admission on incentives and its implications for the negative value of false findings.[55] As we shall see further in section VI.B.ii, a rule of admission reduces the incentive for spectators to pay for entry: they know that provided that enough spectators do not pay, they would be found liable whether they have paid or not, so they might as well not pay. Thus, under admission regime, the prior odds of their paying are decreased – they are decreased, as we eventually learn, to 0.100. If they nevertheless do the right thing and pay, they thereby succeed in beating these somewhat gloomy odds; and deciding against them based on the very odds they have beaten is profoundly tragic.

Perhaps in such circumstances an erroneous decision against whoever paid entry based on the odds that she did not pay entry is even more profoundly tragic given that it is *only* the legal system that imposed the higher odds of commission on whoever chooses to make such an understandable choice (let us assume) as attending rodeo: prior to setting a rule of admission, none of the spectators had any special motivation not to pay, and therefore it is possible that for many of the other spectators who did not pay (thereby establishing the statistics on which the legal system ultimately claims to rely) the legal rule actually *tipped the balance* in favour of not paying.

[53] This is a variation on the American case of *Smith v Rapid Transit, Inc* 58 NE 2d 754 (Mass 1945). See discussion in Wells (n 19).

[54] Cohen (n 19) 74–75.

[55] The impact of incentives will be further discussed in section VI.D.

The same is true for convictions on DNA crime-scene samples that do not contain a full DNA profile. To state things briefly: if citizens know that they can be convicted on DNA evidence that carries an ineliminable risk of error (no matter how many scientists will check the sample and with what means, it might still erroneously point to them), their incentive to refrain from crime commission is reduced. If they nevertheless refrain from crime and are then convicted based on such DNA samples, their conviction is profoundly tragic.

IV. A Mutual Tragedy: The Error of the Legal System

But this is not where the account of Aristotelian tragedy ends. Hegel's interpretation of the Greek tragedy can take the analysis another step forward.[56] It has the potential to shift the focus for a moment to the legal system's adoption of an inappropriate evidential regime, adding dimensions to the tragedy and exposing its full scale.

In his famous analysis of Sophocles' *Antigone*,[57] Hegel provides a more nuanced picture of the tragedy. He does so by bringing the law maker to the front. For Hegel, both Antigone, who disregards the law of the city, and Creon, who seeks to enforce the law of the city, are representatives of laws: Antigone represents the more particular law of the family, and Creon represents the more general law of the city. And each of them acts as a human law maker who brings the law to life, and accordingly could have chosen a different and more inclusive representation of the law. Consider Creon first. Creon is not merely a representative or an applicator of the law of the city that prohibits burial, equivalent to the legal factfinder; rather, he has a creative role equivalent to that of a legislature or a court that sets precedent in choosing how to shape and represent this law. The opportunity to choose how to shape and represent the law has two implications: first, in using these opportunities and making these choices Creon becomes responsible for their outcomes; and, second, in making his choices Creon is subject to his own character and fate. Creon is therefore a tragic hero. But Creon is a tragic hero in a story that unfolds as a mutual tragedy of two protagonists. Like Creon, Antigone also makes choices that make her responsible for their content and consequences. She chooses how to shape and represent the more particularistic law of the family that demands burial, and hence she is responsible for the content and consequences of the law of the family, and she is also subject to her own character and fate in choosing this content and hence its consequences.

The choices of both protagonists are erroneous. Creon's insistence on too rigid a representation of the law of the city becomes an instance of technocratic

[56] GWF Hegel, *The Phenomenology of Spirit* (1807), tr AV Miller; analysis and Foreword by JN Findlay, rev edn (New York, Oxford University Press, 1976) esp paras 470–73.

[57] In Sophocles, *The Three Theban Plays: Antigone, Oedipus the King; Oedipus at Colonus*, tr R Fagles; Introduction and Notes by B Knox (New York, Penguin Books, 1984).

stubbornness that is just as erroneous and short-sighted as Antigone's original disregard of the law of the city (and her rigid insistence on the law of the family).[58] Creon's error has all the characteristics of a tragic error that leads to an unexpected and disproportionate disaster, while the dangers of Antigone's error are evident from the start. Nevertheless, the two errors complement one another and integrate in a course of development that ends in an extended and mutual tragedy. Just as it seems that the errors of both have been retrieved – Creon changes his mind and Antigone should live notwithstanding her crime – Antigone's characteristic 'impatience of heart'[59] brings about an excessive and disproportionate materialisation of the risks of the two original errors. Antigone, Haimon and Eurydike are all dead.

Hegel emphasises the mutual contribution of Creon and Antigone (acting in their law-making capacity) to this mutual disaster:

> The movement of the ethical powers against each other and of the individuals calling them into life and action have attained their true end only in so far as both sides suffer the same destruction … and since each itself calls forth this opposition … each is responsible for the guilt which destroys it.[60]

Hegel thus suggests that the disaster is possessed by both, because neither of the two makes a plainly unacceptable fallacy – one that has no grain of truth in it and that can therefore justifiably be regarded as having determined the course of events.[61] Rather, when they bring laws into life, each of them represents a different aspect of the truth, and their error is in failing to mutually acknowledge this. Their responsibilities and their fates are thus intertwined; each of them could have taken the opportunity to change the course of events and rescue not only himself but also the other, but failed to do so.

Viewed in the light of this analysis, the tragedy of a false conviction based on evidence that does not meet error eliminability is not only the tragedy of a defendant who faces a court; it is also the tragedy of a legal system in its legislative capacity. The defendant's error has the characteristics of a tragic error, as demonstrated above. Thus, while particularistic like Antigone's error, it has the tragic structure of Creon's error. The error of the legal system in its law-making capacity is not a purely tragic error; it intertwines with the defendant's tragic error too, in a course of events that leads to an extended and mutual tragedy. When the legal system insists rigidly and technocratically on accuracy, it makes an error that has the structure of Antigone's evident error: it is an error whose dangers are

[58] See M Thibodeau, *Hegel and Greek Tragedy*, tr HJ Wilhelm (Lanham, MD, Lexington Books, 2013), noting (ibid 128) that 'Both Antigone, the representative of the law of the family, and Creon, the defender of the law of the city, are annihilated because they acted one-sidedly and partially. Both believed their actions to be nothing but the realization of justice, but both were forgetful or oblivious of the hidden law, the subterranean law that was lying in wait.'

[59] This expression is taken from Stefan Zweig's psychological tragedy *Ungeduld des Herzens* (1939).

[60] Hegel (n 56) para 472.

[61] Compare with the factfinder who simply misinterprets the evidence.

clear from the outset. It is evident from the moment of adopting such a rule that it would lead to the legal system's contributing to tragic false convictions, thus, as we shall further see in the next section, exacerbating injustice.

The tragedy is thus, in the end, a mutual tragedy for the defendant and the state: the defendant is falsely convicted based on statistics into whose claws she put herself; and the state contributes to a tragic false conviction based on the statistics that it unwittingly relied on with excessive rigidity.

V. Practical Implications: Aesthetics, Ethics and the Value of Choice

The most obvious question left to be considered is whether there might be a connection between aesthetics and ethics, or between aesthetic value and ethical value or disvalue. Amongst the various theories about such a possible connection, Kant's is one of the most modest and unambitious ones; and perhaps this is where its convincing force lies.[62]

With the utmost brevity and necessary simplification, Kant's account suggests that the aesthetic captures the natural world's purposiveness or orientation towards human cognition. It thus symbolises the status of persons as ends, and it allows cognising persons as ends in the only realm where they can be so cognised, namely, the realm of the natural world. For Kant, morality is indeed based on reason and independent from aesthetics; but there is a relation of symbolism or analogy between the aesthetic and the moral. Notably, the analogy between the aesthetic and the moral further provides a basis for an account of an internally generated moral feeling; and the moral feeling, in turn, makes morality possible for human beings in the natural world.

Even under these relatively weak assumptions, tragedy emerges as a morally and legally relevant category: the aesthetic impact of tragedy is powerful and timeless because tragedy symbolises morally relevant categories. The aesthetic awe stimulated by tragedy is analogous to the moral feeling stimulated by the discovery of a moral truth; and this awe is so strong because tragedy, like all good art in Kant's account, in fact captures a moral truth and gives it a sensual representation.

As may be clear by now, this moral truth does not concern any particularly great amount of suffering or loss that tragedies allegedly involve. The amount of suffering or loss that any event involves is contingent and depends on its particular circumstances. A tragic course of events may well involve less suffering than

[62] I Kant, *Critique of the Power of Judgment*, ed P Guyer; trs P Guyer and E Matthews (Cambridge, Cambridge University Press, 2000). See also P Guyer, *Kant and the Experience of Freedom* (New York, Cambridge University Press, 1996); P Guyer, 'Feeling and Freedom: Kant on Aesthetics and Morality' (1990) 48 *The Journal of Aesthetics and Art Criticism* 137.

other extremely unfortunate courses of events. Consider, for example, the false conviction of a parent of the murder of her child. The amount of suffering that such a parent is made to bear is almost beyond imagination, and it is most probably greater than the amount of suffering brought about by a defendant's false conviction of burglary based on previous similar burglaries she committed. Still, the parent's false conviction lacks the characteristics of a tragedy in the theoretical-theatrical sense (the parent does not make an error that despite every impressive effort chases her all the way to the totally disproportionate disaster of a false conviction). The same is true, for example, about a false conviction of a genius violinist whose career, and indeed her contribution to society, is thereby brought to an end. Here too, the contingent loss and suffering are enormous, but the course of events is not profoundly tragic. The appropriate response to such instances would involve mainly great sorrow, but it would not involve the extreme fear characteristic of tragedies. Thus, something other than loss and suffering makes tragedies distinctly negative.

It can be suggested that the moral truth that tragedy captures concerns the erosion of the value of choice; tragedies capture choices that end up eroding the value of choice.[63] Choice is of course valuable for reasons of respect for persons; but it is also valuable for other reasons. Choice is valuable, amongst other things, as a limited yet effective defence against the arbitrariness of any external forces, human or inhuman, that might detract from one's welfare.[64] Choice is free; it is not caused by arbitrary forces external to agents, and thus it can protect from them. But tragedies demonstrate that the power to make free choice has an almost paradoxical cost: it entails the power to make choices that unleash wholly surprising, strong and now uncontrollable external forces to whose arbitrariness we thereby become vulnerable. Let us focus on the convicted defendant. If it were not for the defendant's power to make (bad) original choices, the unpredictable arbitrary forces that eventually push her to prison despite every impressive effort to beat them would not have been unleashed. The value of this defendant's choices is thus eroded by her own unfortunate choice. The same goes for the law maker's choice to insist rigidly on accuracy, which ends up bringing its own disaster in the form of causing exacerbated injustice. Arguably, this is the tragic element that provokes fear in all of us who value our power of choice; and this is also what makes tragedies distinctly negative, especially in the legal context, where the value of choice is foundational and fundamental.

A tragic false conviction is thus a false conviction that involves erosion of the value of the defendant's choice. Such a tragic false conviction is accordingly

[63] I do not lose sight of the fact that the Greeks were interested in personality and fate rather than in the human power of choice

[64] Full development of this suggestion goes beyond the scope of this book. For several different suggestions about the value of choice, see TM Scanlon, *What We Owe to Each Other*, rev edn (Cambridge, MA, Harvard University Press, 2000) 251–55.

morally worse than equivalent non-tragic false convictions; in fact, it is the worst possible outcome of the criminal justice process. This has two implications. First, as far as defendants are concerned, tragic errors could end up as impositions of the worst possible outcomes on the worst off. Since this is the case, they should be prevented where possible on grounds of unfairness, as we have seen in the previous chapter. Preventing them would involve adopting error eliminability, thus refraining from convictions that rely on the various types of evidence that have been discussed in this chapter. Second, if tragic errors are indeed worse for defendants than other equivalent non-tragic errors, a simple cost analysis might demonstrate that they should be prevented, as we shall see in the next section. This point is exacerbated by the added negative value of tragic false convictions for the legal system.

VI. Error Eliminability and Cost Analysis

The analysis so far has demonstrated that rejecting error eliminability leads to profoundly tragic false convictions; and that tragic false convictions are morally worse than equivalent non-tragic false convictions. Accordingly, the argument from respect and justice for the adoption of error eliminability receives another dimension in the context of criminal convictions. Yet in the evidential conditions of the criminal justice system, there is also a costs-based argument to make for the adoption of error eliminability: since the more tragic the error the more negative value it has, and since the likelihoods of each type of error are unknown and probably unknowable, maximin requires ruling out the most tragic error by way of adopting error eliminability. Here again, the argument is made with reference to 'bad character evidence', but we shall see later that it is applicable to other evidence that fails to meet error eliminability.

A. The Problem

Let us consider 'bad character evidence'; the argument will then generalise to all types of evidence that were discussed earlier. The decision whether to admit or exclude 'bad character evidence' can be made based on the expected negative values of errors associated with a rule of admission and with a rule of exclusion: the rule that is associated with lower negative values should be preferred. For purposes of convenience, I will refer to such negative values hereinafter as 'costs'. Estimating the cost of errors involves identifying the different costs associated with different types of errors and the likelihood of different types of errors under the two types of rules (admission and exclusion). The likelihood of errors, in turn, is not determined directly by the evidence or its absence, but rather by the factfinders' interpretations of the evidence or its absence. Yet the evidential conditions that prevail in the criminal justice system are such that we are deeply ignorant about factfinders' interpretations of the evidence or its absence. Derivatively, we are also deeply ignorant about the overall negative values associated with a rule of admission and with a rule of exclusion. Then, decision theory and the maximin rule are used to advance the argument that considering the difference in the costs of possible errors under a rule of admission and under a rule of exclusion, a rule of exclusion should be preferred; this rule is error eliminability.

It is often argued that juries over-estimate the probative value of evidence of previous misconduct, or alternatively convict in order to punish for previous misconduct.[65] One of Redmayne's notable contributions to the research of evidence of previous misconduct was his careful and thorough analysis of the existing empirical research on bias. While indecisive, the conclusions of this analysis are far from being insignificant. Redmayne concludes that we cannot know whether evidence of previous misconduct is likely to be biasing, and that there are reasons to think either way.[66] Furthermore, Redmayne notes that in some cases, evidence of previous misconduct might even have the unexpected outcome of reducing the likelihood of conviction.[67] This might be the case where introduction of evidence of previous misconduct seems to the jury to be unfair;[68] or, alternatively, where absent the evidence, the jury would have made unfounded and more condemning speculations.[69]

The picture we end up with regarding the expected outcomes of admission or exclusion thus becomes remarkably obscure: both a rule of admission and a rule of exclusion might or might not hamper juries' judgment in either of two ways (for or against the accused) and to an unknown extent.[70] Accordingly, we cannot know how many errors and of which type (profoundly tragic or not) would be brought about by each of the rules. It is therefore impossible to know which rule might minimise the negative value of errors.

The difficulty is a general one in the law of evidence. It occurs where there are reasons to think the evidence overall valuable and other reasons to think it overall

[65] For presentation and analysis of the relevant mock jury studies and real trial studies, see Redmayne (n 1) 53–59.

[66] ibid 60.

[67] ibid 55, citing such findings with respect to the impact of dissimilar convictions in S Lloyd-Bostock, 'The Effects on Juries of Hearing about the Defendant's Previous Criminal Record: A Simulation Study' [2000] *Crim LR* 734.

[68] Redmayne (n 1) 55.

[69] See J McEwan, *The Verdict of the Court: Passing Judgement in Law and Psychology* (Oxford, Hart Publishing, 2003) 169–70; Spencer (n 8); Lord Justice Auld, *A Review of the Criminal Courts in England and Wales* (Lord Chancellor's Department, 2001) ch 11, paras 118–20. See also L Laudan and RJ Allen, 'The Devastating Impact of Prior Crime Evidence and Other Myths of the Criminal Justice Process' (2013) 101 *Journal of Criminal Law and Criminology* 493, 515 and 522.

[70] Redmayne's proposed solution seems to reflect the assumption that the lack of knowledge with respect to prejudicial inferences is such a non-starter, that it must be set aside. See Redmayne (n 1) chs 2 and 12.

damaging, and we cannot evaluate the probability of its being valuable or damaging. The evidence (might) pull in different directions.

Indeed, this difficulty goes beyond the law of evidence; it is a difficulty long known to decision theorists and referred to as 'deep ignorance'.[71] Deep ignorance is a condition where the likelihood of different outcomes of different courses of action are unknown and unknowable, since a sufficiently broad range of evaluations can be supported by good reasons.[72] Thus, unlike in conditions of mere uncertainty, cost expectancies cannot be calculated, and a decision about the appropriate course of action cannot be made based a principle of cost minimisation. As the principle of cost minimisation is inapplicable, different principles of decision are needed for conditions of deep ignorance.

B. Decision Theory: Applying Maximin

As we have already seen when considering Rawls's justification for his principles of justice, decision theory proposes several decision rules for conditions of deep ignorance.[73] These include the maximin rule and the lexical maximin rule (leximin). The following discussion applies these rules to the problem of bias in the context of evidence of previous misconduct. It examines the possible outcomes of a rule of admission and a rule of exclusion. It does so with reference to the types of possible errors under each regime, given the ways juries might interpret the evidence or its absence. It demonstrates that the range of possible outcomes under a rule of admission and under a rule of exclusion is, in fact, qualitatively equal: considering the possibility that juries might 'fill in the gap' where the evidence is excluded and presume propensity, profoundly tragic errors are possible not only under a rule of admission, but also under a rule of exclusion. Next, it is demonstrated that the possible outcomes of a rule of admission and of a rule of exclusion are nevertheless quantitatively different: profoundly tragic errors made under a rule of admission are more tragic than those made under a rule of exclusion. Accordingly, principles offered by decision theory lead to the conclusion that exclusion is preferable to admission; or that error eliminability should be adopted as an evidential principle.

[71] R Aboodi, A Borer and D Enoch, 'Deontology, Individualism and Uncertainty: A Reply to Jackson and Smith' (2008) 105 *The Journal of Philosophy* 259, 270.

[72] For a comprehensive analysis of uncertainty and theories of resolving uncertainties, see VR Walker, 'Theories of Uncertainty: Explaining the Possible Sources of Error in Inference' (2001) 22 *Cardozo Law Review* 22.

[73] For a clear introduction, see M Peterson, *An Introduction to Decision Theory* (Cambridge, Cambridge University Press, 2009) ch 3. To go further, see, eg, PH Giang, 'Decision Making under Uncertainty Comprising Complete Ignorance and Probability' (2015) 62 *International Journal of Approximate Reasoning* 27 and the references there.

i. Initial Application: Errors and Profoundly Tragic Errors

To apply maximin to admission of evidence of previous misconduct clearly, two unrealistic assumptions are made: first, it is assumed that evidence of the defendant's previous misconduct is the only available evidence; and, second, it is assumed that juries' possible estimations of the likelihood of recidivism are radical, so that over-estimation means estimation of 100 per cent likelihood and under-estimation means estimation of 0 per cent likelihood.

The two relevant acts are admission and exclusion of the evidence. The three relevant states are: (i) juries over-estimate the likelihood of recidivism given the defendant's past; (ii) juries estimate correctly the likelihood of recidivism given the defendant's past; and (iii) juries under-estimate the likelihood of recidivism given the defendant's past. Where the evidence is excluded, these three states are further differentiated: under all of them, juries might assume no past, the correct past, or an excessive past. The five relevant possible outcomes are the following: true acquittal, false acquittal, true conviction, false conviction and tragic false conviction.

Tragic false conviction is a false conviction based on the defendant's previous misconduct, whether or not it involves over-estimation of the likelihood of recidivism. It has been demonstrated in section I that such a conviction is tragic where juries estimate the likelihood of recidivism correctly. Over-estimation of this likelihood by the juries does not negate the tragic nature of the conviction: it is the reliance on the defendant's poor odds, rather than the accuracy of the estimation of these poor odds, that makes the false conviction tragic.

Tragic false conviction can occur either where evidence of previous misconduct has been introduced, or where it has not been introduced but juries assume rightly or wrongly that the defendant has a past involving misconduct. We have already seen why tragic errors are possible where the evidence is introduced. Where the evidence is not introduced but juries fill the gap by rightly assuming that the defendant has a past involving previous misconduct, the outcome is similar to that of admission, and there is a similar risk of tragic errors. Where the evidence is not introduced, and juries wrongly assume that the defendant has a past involving misconduct, erroneous convictions would still be tragic: Unfortunate as this may be, the statistics indicate that, at the very least, defendants are indeed more likely to have previous convictions than random citizens (and to the extent that they have such previous convictions, they are more likely to have committed the offence at issue).[74] Accordingly, the fact that a person has been accused of crime indicates that there are strong forces pushing him to commit crime; indeed the forces pushing such a person to commit crime are stronger than the forces pushing random

[74] These assumptions are not in conflict with the presumption of innocence. For a discussion, see Levanon (n 52).

citizens to commit crime. Given these statistical realities, where the defendant has beaten the odds by not having committed past crimes, and accordingly by not having such a past (and hence he is no longer more likely to have committed the offence at issue), his false conviction based on the odds that he has beaten is still profoundly tragic.

As for the costs of each outcome, it is assumed that true results have no relevant costs; that false convictions are worse or more costly than false acquittals; and that tragic false convictions are worse or more costly than other non-tragic false convictions. The first and second assumptions do not require explanation. The third assumption (that tragic false convictions are worse than other non-tragic false convictions) attributes additional costs to profound tragedy. It relies on our natural strong response to tragedies – a response that implies such additional costs. In addition, this assumption can rely on the additional negative value, beyond that of any false conviction, that tragic false convictions involve;[75] as well as on the disrespect towards the defendant that the legal system arguably demonstrates when it allows tragic false convictions to happen.

Now, let us observe the respective acts, states and outcomes as summarised in Tables A–D in the appendix to this chapter. The observation leads to the following conclusions: if juries do give some weight to evidence of previous misconduct, but where the evidence is excluded they assume that the defendant has no past of previous misconduct, then maximin would recommend excluding the evidence. The reason is that under this assumption, the worst possible outcome of exclusion is false acquittal, and this outcome is better than the worst possible outcome of admission, namely, tragic false conviction.

However, assuming again that juries give some weight to the evidence, but that following exclusion juries might actually assume that the defendant does have some past of previous misconduct, maximin becomes less helpful. The reason is that under this assumption, the worst possible outcomes of exclusion and of admission are equally bad (tragic false convictions). In such circumstances, we should apply leximin and examine the second worst possible outcomes. Yet this too does not take us far, as the second worst possible outcomes of admission and of exclusion are also equal (false acquittal); and other outcomes are true outcomes and therefore good outcomes.

The same is true assuming that juries do not attribute any weight to the evidence: the worst outcomes under a rule of admission and of exclusion are equally bad (false acquittals); and other possible outcomes are true outcomes and therefore good outcomes.

Thus, under such assumptions, maximin and leximin do not take us far in deciding the question of admission.

[75] As we have seen, the Aristotelian tragedy does not necessarily involve moral judgements. But if a moral judgement is applied to tragic conditions, it is often the case that in such conditions failing to prevent the tragedy when one has the power to do so (eg by excluding evidence of previous misconduct) would be unjustified.

ii. Taking the Analysis Forward: The Role of Incentives

Reconstruction of the incentive argument originally proposed by Sanchirico[76] and further developed and extended by Enoch, Spectre and Fisher[77] can get the analysis going. According to this argument, admission of evidence of previous misconduct creates a disincentive for potential defendants with a past of misconduct to refrain from the proscribed act.

Where evidence of previous misconduct is admissible, potential defendants with a past of misconduct *know* that their past will be considered during trial; they *know* that it might be over-estimated by the juries; and they *know* that they might be falsely convicted on the basis of their past. Thus, the possibility of a tragic false conviction becomes visible to them. It is this visibility that reduces potential defendants' motivation to refrain from further crime, with the implication that they are more likely to commit such crime. Arguably, this visibility does more than that: it actually increases the motivation to commit further crime; it creates a positive incentive for further crime commission. If potential defendants know that their prospects of a good life are diminished because of the possibility of tragic false convictions, they have a positive incentive to balance this out by taking what they consider as 'more' of life (for example by way of stealing property or taking criminal revenge, etc) in the time that is left before the expected false conviction. Thus, the visibility of possible tragic errors puts potential defendants deeper into the claws of the recidivism statistics. But the deeper potential defendants are trapped in these claws, the more heroic is their eventual decision to refrain from further crime, and the more profoundly tragic is their eventual false conviction. If this is true, a rule of admission involves a risk of errors whose tragic nature is particularly profound; it involves a risk of errors that are more profoundly tragic than other tragic errors. A decision to opt for a legal rule of admission therefore has particularly low minimal value obtainable with it.

The same does not apply to the minimal value obtainable with a decision to opt for a rule of exclusion. Where the rule is one of exclusion, the possibility of tragic false convictions is far less visible to potential defendants. Unless highly sophisticated or unusually pessimistic, they are not expected to think that juries would assume they have a past of misconduct absent evidence of such misconduct (and indeed, this is the assumption that lies in the heart of any incentive-based analysis of evidence of previous misconduct). Thus a decision to opt for a rule of exclusion does not reduce potential defendants' motivations to refrain from the

[76] CW Sanchirico, 'Character Evidence and the Object of Trial' (2001) 101 *Columbia Law Review* 1227.

[77] D Enoch and T Fisher, 'Sense and "Sensitivity": Epistemic and Instrumental Approaches to Statistical Evidence' (2015) 67 *Stanford Law Review* 557; and D Enoch, L Spectre and T Fisher, 'Statistical Evidence, Sensitivity, and the Legal Value of Knowledge' (2012) 40 *Philosophy and Public Affairs* 197.

proscribed act in a way similar to a decision to opt for a rule of admission. A rule of exclusion therefore does not increase the odds of commission and put potential defendants deeper in the recidivism statistics, and accordingly it does not make their eventual decision to refrain from crime more heroic. Accordingly, a false conviction reached in exclusion regime may well be profoundly tragic, but it is not as profoundly tragic as a false conviction reached in admission regime. A decision to opt for a legal rule of exclusion therefore does not have particularly low minimal value obtainable with it.

If this is the case, maximising the minimal value obtainable with the admissibility decision, as required by the maximin rule, entails opting for exclusion. The worst outcome of exclusion (profoundly tragic false conviction) is still better than the worst outcome of admission (more profoundly tragic false conviction).

Note that in this analysis contingent incentives play a role, but it is not a justifying role: the way it is applied here, maximin does not recommend exclusion based on the added value of discouraging crime (which is a contingency). Rather, the justification for exclusion is the profoundly tragic and unfair nature of possible errors.

C. Can the Analysis Generalise?

The next question is whether this analysis applies only to evidence of previous misconduct, or whether it generalises to support a sweeping principle of error eliminability. The answer is that it generalises at least to an extent. The costs analysis would apply with the same force to all evidence that imposes an ineliminable risk of error; whose presence might bias juries; and whose presence the juries might assume. It would thus apply to much statistical evidence that indicates propensity based on affiliation.

It is, however, harder to say to what extent the analysis would apply to statistical evidence that does not indicate propensity, like partial cold-hit DNA evidence. The existence of such evidence is unlikely to be presumed by the juries. It is possible that this makes for a simple case for exclusion without having to refer to incentives. Under a rule of exclusion, tragic false convictions would be avoided. Under a rule of admission, it is at least arguable that juries might or might not give such evidence more weight than they should; that it is unknown if and at what level of likelihood they would do so; and, therefore, the worst possible outcome is a false conviction that would be tragic due to the statistical nature of the evidence, as we have seen. Maximin would then recommend exclusion.

If all this is correct then, in addition to the case from respect and justice, there is also a case based on cost analysis for adopting error eliminability as a general evidential principle in criminal law.

Appendix: The Range of Possible Outcomes under a Rule of Admission of 'Bad Character Evidence' and under a Rule of Exclusion of 'Bad Character Evidence'

Table A Possible Outcomes under a Rule of Admission

	Juries over-estimate to 100%		**Juries estimate correctly**				**Juries under-estimate to 0%**	
Admission	True conviction	Tragic false conviction	True acquittal	False acquittal	True conviction	Tragic false conviction	True acquittal	False acquittal

Table B Possible Outcomes under a Rule of Exclusion, Assuming Juries' Over-estimation

	Juries over-estimate to 100%					
Exclusion	**Juries assume no past**		**Juries assume correct past**		**Juries assume excessive past**	
	True acquittal	False acquittal	Tragic false conviction	True conviction	Tragic false conviction	True conviction

Table C Possible Outcomes under a Rule of Exclusion, Assuming Juries' Correct Estimation

	Juries estimate correctly					
Exclusion	**Juries assume no past**		**Juries assume correct past**		**Juries assume excessive past**	
	True acquittal	False acquittal	True conviction	Tragic false conviction	True conviction	Tragic false conviction

Table D Possible Outcomes under a Rule of Exclusion, Assuming Juries' Under-estimation

	Juries underestimate to 0%					
Exclusion	**Juries assume no past**		**Juries assume correct past**		**Juries assume excessive past**	
	True acquittal	False acquittal	True acquittal	False acquittal	True acquittal	False acquittal

PART III

Responsibility

8

Epistemic and Moral Responsibility*

Error eliminability is a condition for justified belief and subsequently for assertion; it is a condition for just action that responds appropriately for reasons of respect; and it is a condition for effective resolution of conflicts over truth and justice. The convergence of the epistemic and the practical is accounted for by reference to the conceptual priority of respect for persons, which overarches the practical and epistemological projects.

Adherence to error eliminability is thus a matter of epistemic and moral responsibility. It is associated with our duties to ourselves and to others. And in the legal context, responsibility is crucial: without responsibility of legal decision makers for the content of their epistemic and practical judgements, legal institutions might lose public trust and legitimacy. This chapter unfolds this responsibility with an emphasis on the value that it has in the legal context.

I. Legal Assertions and Epistemic Responsibility

Accounts of assertions usually emphasise that asserting involves epistemic responsibility. The relevant responsibility might or might not be for believing the content of the assertion;[1] but be that as it may, an assertor is responsible at least for other epistemic characteristics of the assertion.

The exact nature of this responsibility will thus depend on the specific account of assertions and the norm that regulates them. Williamson, for example, suggests that the knowledge norm of assertion reflects relations of responsibility for the truth of the asserted proposition:

> To make an assertion is to confer a responsibility (on oneself) for the truth of its content; to satisfy the rule of assertion, by having the requisite knowledge, is to discharge that responsibility, by epistemically ensuring the truth of the content. Our possession of such speech acts is no more surprising than the fact that we have a use for relations of responsibility.[2]

* Parts of this chapter were published previously in L Levanon, 'Statistical Evidence, Assertions and Responsibility' (2019) 82 *MLR* 269.

[1] Compare with S Hetherington, 'Epistemic Responsibility: A Dilemma' (2002) 85 *The Monist* 398.

[2] T Williamson, 'Knowing and Asserting' (1996) 105 *Philosophical Review* 489, 522. See also T Williamson, *Knowledge and Its Limits* (Oxford, Oxford University Press, 2002) 268.

Brandom similarly regards assertions as regulated by a knowledge norm, but he suggests that an assertor confers on herself responsibility for providing a justification (demonstrating a warrant) for the assertion:

> This use [of the notion of assertion] suggests taking the commitment involved in asserting to be the undertaking of justificatory responsibility for what is claimed. In asserting a sentence, one not only licenses further assertions on the part of others, but commits oneself to justifying the original claim. The responsibility in question is of the sort Baier calls 'task-responsibility', requiring the performance of a task of some kind for its fulfilment. Specifically, one undertakes the conditional task responsibility to justify the claim if challenged.[3]

Thus, for Brandom, responsibility is not discharged simply by adhering to the norm of assertion; it is discharged by demonstrating, if challenged to do so, that one has adhered to the norm of assertion. Possibly, if one cannot demonstrate this, one can legitimately be subject to epistemic criticism. This account of epistemic responsibility can also fit a conception of assertions as regulated by a norm of warranted belief, as suggested here. And as we shall see in section II, it reflects a demanding concept of responsibility.

A. Why Epistemic Responsibility?

The question is why assertions should confer epistemic responsibility at all, or what value might there be in a concept of assertions that confers epistemic responsibility. At least in the legal context, the answer is twofold: first, the value of epistemic responsibility is derived from the value of practical and moral responsibility of legal institutions, and accordingly the value of epistemic responsibility is practical and moral; and, second, epistemic responsibility is also of independent epistemic value.

To see this, we should begin by observing the epistemic function of assertions. Assertions are not only regulated by a norm of warranted belief; they also grant warrant to others to believe and to assert. As Brandom notes, when one asserts, hearers are entitled to repeat the content of the assertion while taking the fact that one asserted it as a warrant for their own assertion, and they are further entitled to use the content of the assertion as a premise.[4] Assertions thus turn epistemic warrant from a private matter to a social collaborative exercise. Social cooperation has epistemic advantages: considering the limitations of our mental capacities, the epistemic project of accessing new information that can be rationally believed and asserted would have been severely limited without such cooperation. When we

[3] R Brandom, 'Asserting' (1983) 17 *Noûs* 637, 641–42.
[4] ibid.

can rely on the assertions of others as warrant, we can explore the implications of these assertions without fully grasping their original epistemic basis. If the implications turn out to be untenable, we can return the original assertor and ask her to provide her justification.

Epistemic social cooperation is thus based at least on the entitlement to ask for justification; and the other side of such entitlement is epistemic responsibility of assertors of the kind described by Brandom. If assertors are not normatively committed either to demonstrate why their assertion is epistemically warranted when asked to do so, or at least to include in their assertions an 'exclusion clause' that clarifies that the rationality of any specific assertion will not be demonstrated, there will be no ground for epistemic cooperation.

But exactly what value does epistemic cooperation have in the legal context? As might be clear by now, the value of epistemic cooperation is, firstly, practical and moral. Legal institutions generate practical and moral values by making epistemically warranted assertions that confer responsibility on themselves towards the parties and the public; accordingly, their epistemic responsibility as assertors is of practical and moral value.

The next section examines practical and moral values in detail; here, we can focus on one kind of moral value that is specifically associated with epistemic cooperation. As we have seen, legal assertions about wrongdoing comply with reasons to respect wronged persons by countering the challenges that wrongdoing poses. Epistemic social cooperation then allows members of the public to use these assertions directly as bases for their own assertions about wrongdoing; and when members of the public make such assertions, they too counter the challenges posed by wrongdoing (as they have a moral reason to do). This, in turn, is an independent moral good.

In addition, as they generate practical and moral values by making epistemically warranted assertions, legal institutions also generate non-legal epistemic value, in the sense that their assertions can be used as premises in other assertions that are of social epistemic interest. Examples would include historical analyses of crimes, contemporary documentaries about persons of wide social interest, etc. Thus the epistemic responsibility of legal institutions, first, is practically and morally valuable; and, second, also has incidental value that is purely epistemic.

It is therefore not surprising that epistemic cooperation is institutionalised in the legal system. In part, this institutionalisation formalises responsibility, and in this way it ensures that responsibility is discharged. Institutions fulfil various functions, but in part they are mechanisms of responsibility; they are entities defined by a social function and formalised to ensure that this function is fulfilled. Institutions are constantly evaluated on their success in fulfilling this function, and as part of this evaluation, they are expected to justify their moves. The social function of institutions thus comes with epistemic responsibility; and in the legal context, this responsibility is morally and practically valuable.

II. Legal Assertions and Practical Responsibility

We can now look more closely at the practical and moral responsibility associated with assertions. Sanford Goldberg's analysis of the responsibilities of assertors has already indicated that assertions might give rise not only to epistemic responsibility, but also to moral responsibility. Goldberg first considers epistemic responsibility. He notes that others are entitled to expect an assertor to know the content of his assertion, and that the assertor is responsible to satisfy these expectations about his epistemic position.[5] He explains that some of the entitlements of others are connected to specific professional or other roles of the person making the statement, and others are more general entitlements shared by all members of the epistemic community as such.[6] According to Goldberg, what makes others entitled to hold these expectations is the social-institutional context and its underlying rationale: we would not have exchanged information and practised as we do (generally or in specific contexts) if it were not for these mutual expectations. Thus, the source and conditions of responsibility are in social practice and in its constitutive rationale.[7]

Despite references to epistemic expectations, Goldberg's analysis seems to go beyond epistemic responsibility. Goldberg treats assertions as social institutions similar, for example, to promises. He notes that our epistemic presuppositions inform not only our epistemic practices, but also our practical engagements with one another.[8] Accordingly, his account implies that assertors might have moral or practical (rather than merely epistemic) responsibilities. If this is indeed the case, further clarification is due about the source of such responsibilities. As noted, Goldberg identifies the source of responsibility in social practices and in their

[5] See S Goldberg, *To the Best of Our Knowledge: Social Expectations and Epistemic Normativity* (Oxford and New York, Oxford University Press, 2018); S Goldberg, 'Should Have Known' (2017) 194 *Synthese* 2863; S Goldberg, *Assertion: On the Philosophical Significance of Assertoric Speech* (Oxford, Oxford University Press, 2015) section 1.1 (and see his discussion of ethics, ibid section 7). A concise statement of this position can be found in *To the Best of Our Knowledge* at 127 ('My claim is that epistemic responsibility in the broader sense … is simply a matter of satisfying all of the legitimate epistemic expectations on one.')

[6] For elaboration, see Goldberg, *To the Best of Our Knowledge* (n 5) ch 5.

[7] In *To the Best of our Knowledge* (ibid 106–07), Goldberg writes 'But we might ask: what *entitles* us to have such epistemic expectations of one another? My answer is that these epistemic expectations reflect a number of presuppositions that inform our engagements with one another. These engagements are of two main types: information-exchanging engagements (where the aim is to share information), and practical engagements (where the aim is to act together or in coordination with one another).'

[8] In *To the Best of Our Knowledge* (ibid 110), Goldberg writes 'our practices of information-exchange and practical engagement with one another have a rationale supporting them – that is, participation in these practices avoids practical irrationality – only if we are entitled to expect certain things of other epistemic subjects; but these engagements *do* have a rationale supporting them (one can deny this only at the cost of a profound distortion of our lives as fundamentally social creatures); so we are entitled to have the expectations.'

rationales; but it is at least arguable that social practices and their rationales can hardly work to legitimise our expectations from one another. After all, existing practices may not have a rational or legitimate rationale, or they may reflect an irrational or illegitimate way to meet a legitimate rationale.

A. Responsibility for Externalised Burdens

We can begin with the moral and practical responsibility of legal decision makers for the burdens that error imposes on the legal parties and on the public. To motivate the argument on the essence and value of responsibility for burdens on the parties and on the public, it is worthwhile outlining some general characteristics of responsibility. The literature has made impressive progress in highlighting the types and nuances of responsibility.[9]

Analyses of responsibility usually capture instances in which an attitude or action is attributable to an agent; the agent is answerable for this attitude or action; and the agent is further accountable for this attitude or action. Attributability concerns the relation between an agent and an action or attitude: the action or attitude reflects a relevant property of the agent. In Scanlonian accounts, this property is the agent's reason as reflected in her rational judgement;[10] in other accounts this property goes beyond the agent's reason to include, for example, emotional commitments that (allegedly) cannot be rationally grounded.[11] Answerability refers to a legitimate demand by others that the agent rationally justify her judgement with reasons. Accountability refers to others' normative ability to appraise the agent's judgement, or to blame her when a moral judgement does not respond well to valid reasons; and on some views also to respond with certain moral emotions like resentment or indignation.[12] The exact relation between these concepts is contentious: on Scanlonian accounts, the concepts converge – attributability gives rise to answerability and accountability; on other accounts, like the one advanced by Shoemaker, attributability does not necessarily give rise to answerability, and

[9] See esp PF Strawson, 'Freedom and Resentment' (1962) 48 *Proceedings of the British Academy* 1; G Watson, *Agency and Answerability: Selected Essays* (Oxford, Oxford University Press, 2004); M McKeena, *Conversation and Responsibility* (Oxford, Oxford University Press, 2012); D Shoemaker, *Responsibility from the Margins* (Oxford and New York, Oxford University Press, 2015).

[10] See TM Scanlon, *What We Owe to Each Other* (Cambridge, MA, The Belknap Press of Harvard University Press, 1998) 272; A Smith, 'On Being Responsible and Holding Responsible' (2007) 11 *Journal of Ethics* 465, 469.

[11] See D Shoemaker, 'Attributability, Answerability and Accountability: Toward a Wider Theory of Moral Responsibility' (2011) 121 *Ethics* 602, 608–09.

[12] This is a familiar interpretation of PF Strawson, 'Freedom and Resentment' in G Watson (ed), *Free Will*, 2nd edn (Oxford, Oxford University Press, 2003) 72.

answerability does not necessarily converge with accountability.[13] There is no need for us to examine these differences of view in detail. Legal judgments are properly attributable to legal decision makers who are answerable and accountable for them.

That legal decision makers carry moral responsibility for legal judgments and for any errors in these should be clear by now. As we have seen in chapters 4 and 5, legal judgments include assertions that have moral value or disvalue. First, as demonstrated in chapter 4, epistemically warranted assertions work to prevent probabilistic imposition of liability and to counter the moral challenge posed by wrongdoing, thus meeting the demands of the obligation to respect persons. Second, as demonstrated in chapter 5, epistemically warranted assertions are required by the notion of retributive fairness whenever retributive judgements are made. Since epistemically warranted assertions have moral value, agents who make such assertions are morally responsible for any moral value or disvalue associated with their assertions. They are further morally responsible for any additional burdens that are imposed based on these assertions.

The moral responsibility of legal decision makers for their judgments is stringent; it consists of attributability, answerability and accountability. Assertions made in legal judgments and their moral consequences are attributable to legal decision makers; they reflect their rational judgement not only about factual truths, but also about moral truths. In addition, legal decision makers are answerable for these assertions and for their moral implications: legal decision makers are, in Shoemaker's terms, connected to their judgments in a way that renders them able in principle to cite the reasons they took to justify them[14] Last, legal decision makers are accountable even in a strict sense of accountability as openness to moral indignation and resentment. Because of the moral significance of their assertions, failure would have moral implications, and moral failures deserve moral condemnation.[15] Furthermore such condemnation is specifically important in institutional contexts such as the legal context, as we shall see in the next subsection. Accordingly, moral resentment is appropriate.

It can be suggested that a similar account applies to the decision makers' responsibility for aspects of their judgments that have prudential value for specific citizens. As we have seen in chapters 6 and 7, assertions concerning truths are practical tools that facilitate resolution; and in addition, in certain conditions they reflect rational decision making about costs. Such practical consequences

[13] See Shoemaker (n 9); Shoemaker (n 11); AM Smith, 'Attributability, Answerability, and Accountability: In Defence of a Unified Account' (2012) 122 *Ethics* 122.

[14] Shoemaker (n 11) 616.

[15] This is not the place to consider why this is so, but see ibid, suggesting at 619–24 that moral failures undermine relationships.

have prudential value for the parties to the legal conflict, and to an extent also for members of the public who enjoy the existence of institutions that would support them in times of conflict. Accordingly, legal decision makers are responsible for decisions that impact such prudential values in the three above-mentioned senses. The decisions that should bring about these consequences are properly attributable to legal decision makers; legal decision makers are capable of citing their reasons for taking those decisions; and since conflict resolution and rational decision making are constitutive of legal institutions, legal decision makers are accountable in the strictest sense for decisions that fail to rationally resolve conflicts over truth and justice.[16]

Before moving on, it can be noted that we are now in a position to better understand the way we describe our judgements based on statistical evidence that does not meet error eliminability. Consider the toss of a coin whose centre of gravity is diverted in a way that creates a 0.9 likelihood of it falling on side X rather than on side Y. When asked what was the outcome of yesterday's toss, which I did not witness, I might say something like 'I can only guess that it was X.' But when I say 'I can only guess' I make more than an epistemological statement; I also make a statement of practical normativity – that I will not be responsible for any negative implications of error in any domains where justification requires error eliminability (so, not only the epistemological domain, but also the moral domain where reasons of respect are relevant, and the practical domain where resolution is valuable).

B. Why Responsibility for Externalised Burdens?

There is no need to consider here the question why practical and moral action should sometimes give rise to responsibility. That such is the case is a sufficiently well-established starting point of discussions of responsibility. The question that still merits attention concerns any special value the moral and practical responsibility of the legal decision maker might have.

The moral and practical responsibility of legal decision makers is valuable as one aspect of political responsibility, which is in turn a condition for the legitimacy of political institutions. Legal decision makers judge on behalf of legal institutions; and legal institutions require political legitimacy. Any normative

[16] For Scanlon, where the relevant action or attitude is implicated in our relations with one another, the relevant responsibility for this action or attitude is moral. Remember here also Raz's suggestion that failing to treat something valuable in a way that is consistent with its value is morally wrong. An institution whose function is to bring about valuable consequences (or to realise their value) treats such consequences as valuable when it ensures they are brought about; when it fails to ensure they are brought about without good reason, it treats these consequences in a way that is inconsistent with their value.

conception of political legitimacy requires the availability of reasons that justify the right to rule. These reasons might be found in an 'overlapping consensus' over principles of justice,[17] or they might be found in the fact that citizens are more likely to comply with the reasons that apply to them anyway if they are under the political authority's rule.[18]

Responding to reasons that can justify the right to rule, and being able and willing to point to these reasons and to be held accountable for exercises of the right to rule, thus form the foundations of political legitimacy. In other words, responsibility for exercises of authority is a foundation of political legitimacy. Indeed, in his study of political legitimacy, Jean-Marc Coicaud notes that one of the presuppositions of political legitimacy is political responsibility. Responsibility is 'the manifestation of a power that accepts the constraints imposed by the right to govern'.[19] If they are to maintain the right to govern, political institutions need to allow attribution to them of the consequences of their actions; they need to justify their actions with reference to the common interest rather than to any private interests; and they need to accept 'sanctions' or criticism where they err.[20] Coicaud explains that the value of such responsibility is that it prevents rulers from acting against the common good, and it further preserves a peaceful and cooperative society.[21] And this value is the value of political legitimacy.

This analysis, which primarily has the political system in mind, is also applicable to legal institutions. To maintain their legitimacy, legal institutions need to be responsible for their judgments. They need to allow attribution of the judgments to them. They further need to be able to point to reasons of justice that guided them; such reasons of justice would be legitimising reasons (either because they are hypothetically consensual, or because in meeting them the state assists citizens in identifying the reasons that apply to them, or for any other reason). Last, legal decision makers need to accept criticism when they err. The value of the moral and practical responsibility of legal decision makers for externalised burdens is thus in ensuring the legitimacy of legal institutions.

C. Substantive Responsibility: The Decision Maker's Burden

We can now move on to analysing responsibility for the burden of error carried by the decision maker. Legal errors can be practically burdensome not only for the legal parties and for the public, but also for the decision maker. A legal error

[17] As suggested by 'public reason' political philosophers, who follow Rawls's stance on legitimacy.

[18] Compare with J Raz, 'Authority and Justification' (1985) 14 *Philosophy and Public Affairs* 3.

[19] JM Coicaud, *Legitimacy and Politics: A Contribution to the Study of Political Right and Political Responsibility* tr and ed DA Curtis (Cambridge, Cambridge University Press, 2002) 33.

[20] ibid 33–36.

[21] ibid 37–38.

is always burdensome for legal decision makers, because it reflects a failure in fulfilling their practical and moral role; and failure is burdensome. In addition, a legal error becomes even more burdensome for the legal decision maker where the decision maker imposes or reallocates burdens without having trust in the truth of her judgment, or when she imposes or reallocates burdens without being able to rule out the possibility that this would fail to reflect the value of a defendant's actions. The decision maker would not necessarily be responsible for these burdens that she has to carry. Rather, the decision maker would only be responsible for any burden she ends up carrying if the law allowed her to decide the case otherwise and while maintaining trust in the truth of her decision. For the law to allow such trust, error eliminability should be adopted. Let us see why this is so.

Scanlon's account of responsibility is particularly helpful here, as it addresses not only one's responsibility for burdens imposed on others, but also one's responsibility for burdens imposed on oneself. Scanlon identifies what he terms 'substantive responsibility'. Substantive responsibility concerns one's obligations and one's claims against others.[22] Where it comes to a burden that the actor herself carries, the actor is substantively responsible for that burden where and only where the social arrangement that allocates this burden has provided the actor with sufficient opportunities to make a valuable choice that would avoid the burden.[23] Substantive responsibility, in turn, diminishes the actor's grounds for rejecting the social arrangement that allocates the burden.[24]

Now, one reason an error might burden the legal decision maker is that she decided without rationally trusting the truth of her decision. Where the decision maker judges without rationally trusting the truth of her judgment, and the judgment is erroneous, the decision maker's frustratingly regrettable judgment and the burdens associated with it weigh on her too. The legal decision maker who falsely convicts a defendant and sentences him to imprisonment while ignoring the lack of reason to trust the truth of this decision will carry not only the burden of the failure but also a long-lasting burden of self-criticism and guilt. This might explain the intuition that legal decision makers (and indeed other decision makers who impose or reallocate burdens) should be entitled to 'listen to themselves'.[25] Because an error might become particularly burdensome to her if she does not 'listen to herself', the legal decision maker owes it to herself to decide only when she has reason to trust the truth of her decision, if

[22] ibid.

[23] Scanlon (n 10) 251. The value of choice, in turn, depends on the reasons that make us prefer choice-sensitive arrangements – including, for example, instrumental reasons, reasons having to do with the representative value of choice, or reasons having to do with the symbolic value of choice. See Scanlon's discussion, ibid 251–53.

[24] Scanlon draws here a distinction between responsibility as attributability and substantive responsibility (for an initial account, see ibid 248).

[25] This will be discussed further in section II.D, when considering the role that the decision maker's substantive responsibility plays in the legal system.

at all possible; and if she does not trace reason to trust the truth of any relevant proposition, she owes it to herself to refrain from imposing new burdens or reallocating any existing burdens.

The decision maker would not be able to rationally trust the truth of her decision when error is logically ineliminable. As we have seen, error eliminability justifies outright belief; and outright belief involves nothing but trust in the truth of one's judgement. If the evidence does not provide the decision maker with the substrate for eliminating the risk of error, if it prohibits narrowing down the reference class until it only captures true propositions, then the decision maker will need to decide despite being logically incapable of eliminating the risk of error notwithstanding any skill and effort. In such a situation, the decision maker would have no rational grounds for thinking that if an error occurs, it does not occur in the case at hand, and she would not be able to rationally trust the truth of her judgment.

It is thus the burden of an erroneous practical decision whose truth she could never have rationally trusted for which the legal decision maker may or may not be substantively responsible, depending on the opportunities to avoid the burden that the decision-making arrangement allows her. The legal decision maker can avoid this burden if she rationally gains trust in the truth of her decisions by ensuring that they meet error eliminability. Minimising the risk of error would not be enough, as the decision maker may well have no trust in the truth of her decisions even in cases where the risk of error is negligible. But epistemic credentials in the form of error eliminability can allow her to avoid the burden. They would ensure that it is logically possible to eliminate the risk of error. If error eliminability is met, it is possible that when the investigation of the evidence stops, the point has been reached where the evidence captures only cases in which the proposition in question is true. It is then left for the decision maker to judge if she estimates that this point has been reached; and it is here that her skill and expertise play a role. If she is confident that this point has been reached, she would trust the truth of her judgment.

Accordingly, when denied the opportunity to develop trust in the truth of her practical decisions by epistemically ensuring them, the decision maker is not substantively responsible for the burden of any erroneous decisions she makes despite having no trust in their truth. She would then have valid grounds to reject the decision-making arrangement that did not allow her opportunity to avoid this burden. She may justifiably ask 'Why did you make me decide based on such evidence? Why did you not let me listen to myself and avoid this outcome?' But once allowed the opportunity to develop trust in the truth of her practical decisions by epistemically ensuring them, the decision maker becomes substantively responsible for the burden of any erroneous practical decisions she makes despite having no trust in their truth. Once allowed the opportunity to ensure that there is proper epistemic justification for believing in the truth of her practical decisions, the decision maker who fails to take this opportunity and errs no longer has valid grounds to reject the decision-making arrangement.

Another reason why practical errors might burden the decision maker is that she decided without being able to rule out the possibility that this would end up disrespecting the defendant. When the possibility of disrespect remains without negation, the judgment only 'probably respects' the defendant, and accordingly the judgment is disrespectful and objectionable. The decision maker then carries the burden of a double failure: the failure to act on reasons of respect that she competently identifies, and the failure to make the right decision. Her responsibility for this double burden will depend on the question whether she was given an opportunity to avoid it. When the decision maker is required by law to act against reasons of respect that apply to her, and when this further ends up in a failure to decide as the truth in fact requires, she would not be substantively responsible for this burden. She would then have a valid claim against the legal system that did not allow her to avoid this burden.

If this is correct then substantive responsibility is tied to the assertoric foundation of decisions, which is also their moral foundation. A legal decision maker who is not required to assert facts but rather to infer liability based on probabilities is not substantively responsible for burdensome practical errors, and she has valid grounds to object to the legal decision-making arrangement in case of such errors. By contrast, a legal decision maker who is required to make assertions that reflect epistemically warranted belief and hence also comply with reasons of respect is substantively responsible for burdensome practical errors, and she has no valid grounds to complain if she nevertheless decides without having faith in her decision and against her moral reasons, and ends up erring. Accordingly, if the legal decision-maker's substantive responsibility for errors is important, legal decision-making should involve assertions.

D. Why Substantive Responsibility?

There are good reasons to maintain the legal decision maker's substantive responsibility for burdening practical errors. First, we saw that lack of substantive responsibility means that the legal decision maker has a valid claim against the system; the claim would be that the system is unfair to her: it does not grant her the freedom she deserves to exercise her rational capacities. Thus, if we are to avoid unfairness to the legal decision maker, we should have in place a legal system that is based on assertions and subject to the norm of warranted belief. Second, if a decision maker is not substantively responsible for her decisions, the legitimacy of the system might be undermined. As we have seen, the foundation for legitimacy is responsibility. When it comes to legal institutions, the relevant responsibility is not only the responsibility of the factfinder towards the parties and the public; it is also the responsibility of the factfinder towards herself. If the legal factfinder cannot be responsible towards herself for the burden she carries, a split would emerge between her civil capacity and her institutional capacity; the institution would then lose its legitimacy for her as a citizen.

Notably, legal decisions can be (and usually are) based on evidence that allows respect and provides epistemic warrant. Thus, demanding that the decision maker takes decisions in whose truth she has no trust and whose outcomes involve disrespect would burden her unnecessarily; there is no strong reason to place the decision maker in a position where she has no sufficient opportunity to avoid this burden. In such circumstances, forcing her to choose between carrying the burden and changing profession would be unreasonable. Thus, the legal decision maker's lack of responsibility does strengthen her ground for rejecting the decision-making arrangement.

It may be interesting to note here that when it comes to legal decisions on causation, the legal system is rightly more lax about the demand for epistemic warrant. Consider, for example, cases where a defendant points a gun towards an old and frail victim who then dies of cardiac arrest. It is reasonable to suppose that if the cardiac arrest was not caused by the defendant's act, this fact would not find expression on any evidence. Thus, the evidence of the proximity in time between the defendant's act and the victim's cardiac arrest does not meet error eliminability. Is a finding of causation possible?

It is arguable that if properly explored, the evidence would nevertheless allow for elimination of the risk of error: in addition to time proximity, one can observe physiological signs of fear, and then also traces of neurological responses that would allow eliminating the risk of error. I confess that I doubt if such is the case; I suspect that causation is a non-empirical concept. This is not the place to explore this heavy question in full, but the following can be noted: evidence can show that X follows Y; any conclusion that Y causes X adds to the information provided by the evidence. There is hardly ever case-specific evidence available that would indicate that it was the defendant's act that caused the outcome. This is all the more so in cases of causation by omission, where it needs to be shown that had the defendant acted, the outcome would not have been brought about.[26] In all these cases, causation can only be sought to be established with reference to probability calculations (eg in cases of multiple factors that might have caused the outcome) or to statistics on causation in the relevant reference class (eg in cases of causation by omission). These are then complemented by non-empirical content.

Yet if error eliminability cannot be met in the context of causation, it is possible to defend a finding of causation based on this very impossibility. Because it is,

[26] For a discussion of the problems in proving causation by omission, see S Tofaris and S Steel, 'Negligence Liability for Omissions and the Police' (2016) 75 *CLJ* 128.

presumably, impossible to meet error eliminability when deciding causation, the legal decision maker's errors are less burdensome to her; and in any case, her lack of responsibility for her epistemically unwarranted finding does not mean that she has valid grounds to reject the decision-making arrangement.

This seems to have had rather far-reaching implications for proof of causation in civil cases: it has not only allowed reliance on statistical evidence that fails to logically allow the elimination of error, but has also opened the door for lowering the standard of proof for causation below preponderance of evidence where considerations of justice for the parties justify such a move.[27] In most of the relevant cases several liabilities are being decided, even though it is known that only some of them are true.[28] Had such decisions been required where case-specific evidence might exist, the decision maker would have had a valid claim against the arrangement: she could have argued that she was denied the opportunity to make respectful decisions whose content she trusted in conditions where it is possible to allow her this opportunity. But since the decisions are legitimately based on statistical evidence that does not meet error eliminability, the decision maker's claim against the decision-making arrangement is weak. Requiring her to decide several liabilities despite knowing that some of the decisions are wrong adds little to what is legitimately required from her anyway in a causation regime that is based as it must be on statistical evidence (namely to decide despite not trusting the truth of her decisions). It does not give rise to any new and valid claims against the decision-making arrangement.[29]

[27] See S Steel, 'Justifying Exceptions to Proof of Causation in Tort Law' (2015) 78 *MLR* 729; S Steel, *Proof of Causation in Tort Law* (Cambridge, Cambridge University Press, 2015).

[28] Steel, 'Justifying Exceptions' (n 27); and Steel, *Proof of Causation* (n 27).

[29] In 'Justifying Exceptions' (n 27), Sandy Steel has defended three exceptions to the civil standard of preponderance of evidence in proof of causation. Steel's proposed defence relies on considerations of justice for the parties. Naturally, all of Steel's examples are examples of judgments based on naked statistical evidence. But let us assume for a moment that 'case-specific' evidence is freely available for proof of causation. Consider, for example, the application of Steel's Defendant Indeterminacy Rule that concerns cases where it is impossible to prove on balance of probabilities which defendant amongst a group of defendants was the cause of C's injury. Steel gives the following example: two hunters shot different bullets in the direction of C, but a hospital employee X maliciously disposes of the injuring bullet in a way that makes it impossible to identify the injurer based on the injuring bullet. Here, Steel convincingly defends the position that both D1 and D2 should be liable to C in full or in proportion to the likelihood that each of them was a cause of the injury. But consider the following variation on Steel's example, where the evidence is 'case-specific': two of X's assistants testify that they saw X disposing of the bullet. The two assistants are equally reliable witnesses, but one of them testifies that it was D1's bullet and the other testifies that it was D2's bullet. Here, it seems hard to defend the proposition that a court may find the two defendants liable. Such a finding would lead to justified claims by D1 and D2 that the court just failed to do its job. If the court really cannot decide which of the testimonies is more reliable, an acquittal for lack of sufficient evidence seems like the reasonable and expected outcome (though really we would expect the court to be able to narrow reference classes further and decide accordingly). Here, requiring the court to make a finding against the two defendants would provide grounds for a claim by the decision maker that she is required to make a disrespectful finding in whose truth she has no trust, where it is possible to refrain from such a requirement.

III. Conclusions

Legal judgments include assertions of fact. Accordingly, they are regulated by a norm of rational belief. This norm is also a norm of respect and justice, of resolution of conflicts over truths, and of rational cost-based decision making in the evidential conditions of the criminal justice system. Since they include such assertions, legal judgments confer responsibility on the legal decision maker. This responsibility is at the same time epistemic, moral and otherwise practical. It works to allow epistemic cooperation, to maintain justice for the parties, to allow fairness to decision makers and to legitimise legal institutions.

PART IV

Beyond Legal Fact Finding

9

Applications

The focus of this book has been on legal practice, even though some of the conclusions that have been reached are of more general applicability. This chapter broadens the perspective. It explores some concrete applications of these general conclusions that go beyond the context of legal determination of liability. It begins with an analysis of decision making by artificial intelligence (AI); this analysis shows that AI decides based on evidence that does not meet error eliminability. Next, several specific contexts are examined in which the use of AI (or of evidence that does not meet error eliminability) might be relevant. The focus is on social and political contexts; the context of natural experimental sciences is only briefly commented on. Throughout the discussion, I set aside the questions whether and in which contexts there might be reasons that override reasons of respect.

The general question that should guide the choice of evidential practices in these specific social and political contexts is whether reasons of respect are relevant (whether the evidential practice might be inconsistent with the general value of persons as ends in themselves, or whether it might be inconsistent with the special value of a specific person). Where reasons of respect are relevant, evidential practices have the potential to cause or risk disrespect, because they do not allow us to accurately identify these reasons or to accurately identify instances in which they are not met. Respect is then replaced by 'probable respect'; and 'probable respect' cannot respect. Thus, where reasons of respect are relevant, such evidential practices would need to be rejected in favour of an epistemically solid ones that further rule out instances of disrespect.

So how can we identify contexts in which evidential rules cause or risk disrespect? To answer this question, the content of the judgement or action made in each specific context needs to be distilled: the judgement or action might directly concern the value of persons, and hence evidential practices that do not support belief in the value of persons would be inconsistent with respect for persons. Alternatively, the judgement or action might indirectly concern the value of persons because, if erroneous, it would either cause disrespect (for example, would place a person below a welfare threshold or would involve the worst outcomes for the worst off) or would reflect disrespectful presuppositions.

A subsequent related question concerns resolution: if the context of the judgement or action is a context where resolution is required, evidential norms that allow for effective resolution are required; and as we have seen, these would also be the norms that allow just and epistemologically solid judgements.

I. Artificial Intelligence

No one is (yet) seriously speaking of replacing the judicial system with AI. But questions about AI are lively in some areas of the criminal justice system and in many other areas. These include a range of private and public distributional decisions, such as decisions about insurance pricing for individuals, eligibility for loans and mortgages, eligibility for state benefits, etc. There are many ethical questions surrounding the use of AI in a wide range of contexts.[1] This section demonstrates that some of the questions (though by no means all of them) originate in the fact that the evidence AI essentially uses is evidence that does not meet error eliminability.

Artificial intelligence systems are initially fed with premises and conclusions in the form of 'if X then Y' or 'if X then not-Y'. The premises and the conclusions can of course include different parameters and combinations of parameters. The systems then start providing output for ever more complicated input. Some AI systems have machine-learning capabilities. These systems are further exposed to a very wide range of data about previously decided cases, and they can then trace parameters that, despite not having been signalled as relevant for the desired conclusions, in fact correlate with Y or not-Y conclusions. They can then add these parameters to the process of drawing conclusions in new cases, and to further analyse these new cases to identify even more such parameters.

Yet some inferences from premises to conclusions are not computable,[2] and others can only be computed probabilistically. The problem goes deep, but there is no need to explore it here in full. For current purposes, it is enough to note that many of the limits on algorithmic decision making stem from the fact that AI cannot generate entirely new hypotheses that will only later be confirmed on evidence, the way humans do. People can use whatever little evidence already exists to generate a well-confined selection of entirely new good hypotheses that can then be confirmed by further exploration of the evidence. Even with machine-learning capabilities, AI cannot do this as effectively as humans: AI can hardly imagine entirely new hypotheses that are consistent with the evidence but given preexisting conceptual limitations are not yet identifiable on the evidence.

[1] See SM Liao (ed), *Ethics of Artificial Intelligence* (Oxford, Oxford University Press, 2020); see also at www.statewatch.org/media/documents/news/2019/mar/ep-study-Understanding-algorithmic-decision-making.pdf

[2] This has been shown in H Putnam, '"Degree of Confirmation" and Inductive Logic' in PA Schilpp (ed), *The Philosophy of Rudolf Carnap* (La Salle, IL, Open Court, 1963) 761, 781–82. The argument is that predictive inferences based on past observations necessarily fail to take into account the possibility that the hypothesis based on which they are interpreted might be false.

Accordingly, the way in which humans use evidence means that error is logically eliminable on it (with the help of the capacity to generate entirely new hypotheses that are consistent with the evidence). The way in which AI uses evidence means that error is logically ineliminable on it: any new hypothesis must not only be consistent with existing evidence, but also be confirmed by this evidence within the preexisting conceptual framework; AI cannot generate a new hypothesis and then seek information to which the existing evidence might lead but which is not already identifiable on this evidence. For AI, all evidence is thus reduced to its 'naked' statistical form.

Let us consider in some detail that which AI cannot do, and which results in failing to meet error eliminability. First, while AI can identify new parameters that fall under the concepts with which it is familiar, it cannot (use a hunch to) generate new concepts that will, in turn, extend its range of parameters. Accordingly, even if AI can generate some hypotheses, it cannot generate any entirely novel hypotheses.[3] It could not, for example, have predicted the existence of black matter, and it could not have generated the concept of spacetime. Or, to move down to Earth, a sentencing AI could not have generated the concept of psychopathy before it was hypothesised, and subsequently it could not have started taking it into account in sentencing. This logically bars the full elimination of error on the evidence.

Second, AI does not (have the hunch that might direct it to) focus on certain parameters rather than others. The work of AI is based on its capacity to 'scan' huge numbers of parameters and to identify significant correlations, rather than on well-focused new hypotheses. It could be thought that this is an advantage; but given the risk of spurious generalisations, it is also a disadvantage. There might be correlations between exposure to a specific poem about flowers in childhood and anti-social behaviour in adulthood, but any generalisation based on these correlations would falsely imply a causal link. Artificial intelligence that identifies such a correlation might nevertheless rely on it inappropriately. Alternatively, it would need to engage in semi-scientific research of this correlation to identify whether it might imply causation; this would involve tracing alternative possible causes for the anti-social behaviour of adults who have been exposed to this poem. This would be costly and might end up badly: it is not clear that all such hypotheses can be scientifically refuted, and it is even less clear that AI can scientifically refute all such hypotheses based on the information it has.

This is intuitive, but it can also be understood if we think of conventional ways of establishing causation. Hill's criteria are often taken as the standard.[4] These criteria include, amongst other things, the strength of the statistical correlation; its consistency; its specificity (ruling out alternative explanations); the

[3] This was Putnam's point, originally made on the method of logical induction.

[4] AB Hill, 'The Environment and Disease: Association or Causation?' (1965) 58 *Proceedings of the Royal Society of Medicine* 295.

plausibility of a causal relation; the existence of similar known causal relations; and the coherence of a causal relation with other related and known causal relations. Clearly, fully satisfying all these criteria is an infinite task; it is impossible to complete, given virtually endless possible alternative explanations and virtually endless known causal relations. Accordingly, not all the criteria are met in all cases; and it is also logically possible that all the criteria are met in a certain series of experiments even where there is no causal relation. Still, talented scientists would be able to establish causality. If causation is a non-empirical concept as I noted in chapter 8.II.D that I suspect it is, it is clear how this is possible. Since no algorithmic or imitable thinking is involved, AI would not be able to do this even with machine-learning capabilities. Its evidential and conceptual basis would be limited to that with which it has been supplied; and where such is the evidential and conceptual basis, error is logically ineliminable.

It could be objected that all this does not mean that AI would be worse than a person at predicting the right results, especially considering the practical inability to eliminate human error. It is probably true that once technology advances enough, this could be the case. Still, as we have seen, in some contexts reasons of respect still override accuracy. Furthermore, when it comes to science, if the focus shifts merely to providing the most accurate predictions about specific cases based on the available evidence, science will lose its explanatory properties and its aspiration to find ever more general laws that apply to ever wider phenomena. Relatedly, the experimental sciences provide another context in which error eliminability needs to be met, and in this evidential respect the context of experimental sciences is similar to the context of the legal trial. This is a similarity that was famously highlighted by Cohen.[5]

The problems associated with the failure to meet error eliminability can be alleviated but they cannot be resolved. A sufficiently strong and sophisticated AI might one day be able to arrive infinitely close to meeting error eliminability. If it scans through huge amounts of data and generates huge numbers of hypotheses about relations between variables, and if it has learnt by trial and error what kinds of variations on preexisting concepts might be plausible, and what kinds of hypotheses are more likely to be true, AI might be using evidence that would allow it to reduce the risk of error close to zero. Yet error would still remain logically ineliminable on the evidence, because the endless process of learning which hypotheses should be generated would be based solely on analysis of errors rather than on human imagination; in fact, errors would become an essential feature of the system. Accordingly, in contexts where there is reason to meet error eliminability, the use of AI as a 'final judge' would be hard to defend.

Before we proceed, another comment about transparency and responsibility might be appropriate. Artificial intelligence that is based on machine learning

[5] LJ Cohen, *The Probable and the Provable* (Oxford, Clarendon Press, 1977); see the discussion of Cohen's work in ch 1.

deploys processes that often lack transparency for users: when the system provides a decision, it does not provide the list of parameters that have been used, neither does it provide details about the way in which they have been used. Users do not have access to the algorithm that was used (and in some machine-learning methods, the algorithm is unexplainable), to the data that were used to train the machine or to the process of selecting training data.

This raises difficulties in contexts that require responsibility for decision making that go beyond those that have already been discussed. As we have seen, responsibility in the sense of answerability requires that the decision maker would be able to defend her decision with appropriate reasons if challenged: AI cannot provide such a defence.

Vincent Chiao rightly comments that such lack of transparency characterises human decision making as much as it characterises AI decision making. He notes:

> [O]ur understanding of why a human decision-maker decided a close case this way rather than that way is itself far from perfect, particularly once we discount that person's own subjective reports – even reports that take the form of ex post legal rationalisations.[6]

The issue is, however, not with the transparency and intelligibility of the decisions as such, but with their relevance for responsibility as answerability. Various factors might have affected a human judgement, but what matters for purposes of answerability is whether the person who made this judgement gave appropriately heavy weight to the relevant reasons and can thus defend it with reference to these reasons.

It could be suggested that the judgement only needs to be defensible with reference to appropriate reasons *in principle*, and thus not necessarily by the person who made it; it needs to be defensible by the system rather than by any specific individual. Such defensibility is to be tested by appeal processes. And appeal processes on judgements by persons and by AI can always be led by humans.[7] The difficulty with this view is that it places appropriate and inappropriate reasons on a par, as long as they lead to an acceptable outcome that can also be defended with reference only to legitimate reasons. Answerability serves to signal that there are appropriate and inappropriate reasons, and that we expect the decision maker to rely only on appropriate reasons. This is important in institutional contexts where legitimacy needs to be maintained. At least if legitimacy depends on institutions' increasing the likelihood that people would act on the (appropriate) reasons,[8] institutions should themselves be guided only by these reasons. If 'answerability' does not rule out of consideration inappropriate reasons, the

[6] V Chiao, 'Fairness, Accountability and Transparency: Notes on Algorithmic Decision-Making in Criminal Justice' (2019) 15 *International Journal of Law in Context* 126, 136.

[7] ibid 134–35.

[8] Compare with J Raz, 'Authority and Justification' (1985) 14 *Philosophy and Public Affairs* 3 (and see the discussion in ch 8 of this book).

likelihood that people and indeed institutions abide by appropriate reasons is reduced in the long run (and indeed in any specific case). Thus, the legitimacy of institutions is at least eroded.

Given these limitations of AI decision making, the question of where AI can legitimately be used to generate binding decisions would depend on context. The following sections consider some specific contexts.

II. Algorithmic Sentencing: Predicting how a Human Would Make Retributive Judgements

In 'Predicting Proportionality: The Case for Algorithmic Sentencing',[9] Vincent Chiao suggests that statistical evidence that fails to meet error eliminability can be used to predict the decisions of judges in specific cases about proportionate sentences. These predictions would be provided to the sitting judge, thus helping to ensure that sentencing is aligned across the system. Under this suggestion, the relevant data that AI would be using include data about the case at issue (this might include, for example, information about the defendant's past misconduct, familial status, employability, etc) and data about judgments in similar cases. From this, the probability that a judge would assign a sanction X would be inferred. Chiao suggests that at least initially, this AI output would serve as a non-binding recommendation for the sitting judge.

Chiao notes that such an algorithm would perform a reasoning process that is very close to the reasoning process required by current sentencing guidelines:

> Looking beyond computerized sentencing aids, one might think of a proportionality prediction as a case-specific application of the first two steps of sentencing as established by the definitive guidelines set out by the Sentencing Council for England and Wales. Under that framework, a sentencing court is asked to first establish the category in which a given crime falls by ranking the crime according to the degree of harm inflicted as well as the offender's culpability. In the second step, the sentencing court is referred to a range of sentences for that category of offence as well as a 'starting point' within that range. The court is then required to take into account a non-exhaustive list of case-specific aggravating and mitigating factors, adjusting the starting point accordingly. The remaining steps modify the sentence for systemic factors, such as early guilty pleas, time spent in pre-trial detention, and so forth.[10]

Such a non-binding algorithm would have many advantages that Chiao mentions. Mainly, it would increase fairness and predictability across the system. Given these advantages, it is possible that there might be reason to generalise: such an algorithm can be relevant not only for decisions about proportionality in

[9] V Chiao, 'Predicting Proportionality: The Case for Algorithmic Sentencing' (2018) 37 *Criminal Justice Ethics* 238.

[10] ibid 250.

sentencing, but also for a significantly wider range of judicial decisions and other judgements – potentially also for legal fact finding. It might not be as needed in such other contexts as it is in the context of sentencing, because decision making in other contexts is allegedly already less unpredictable than in the context of sentencing, but it would at least not be objectionable. Or would it?

Chiao's proposal seeks to dismantle some of the objections to AI by redefining its task: rather than asking that AI would make the appropriate decisions, AI is asked to predict what human judges would decide; and it is assumed that human judges would usually make appropriate decisions. Yet this rephrasing of the task for AI does not in fact change its task: AI is always fed with human judgements on the basis of which it predicts what human decision makers would do if they could push those capacities that they share with AI to their limit. There is nothing special in the context of sentencing. There might be some deeper and more controversial assumptions at play in the context of sentencing, like the assumption that the 'rightness' of sentences depends only or mostly on uniformity across the system; or alternatively the assumption that getting it uniform has nothing to do with getting it right, but it is still valuable. Yet such assumptions do not change the basic fact that in the context of sentencing like in any other context, the task for AI is to predict what persons would do, ideally when they decide both rightly and uniformly.

But if this is the case, the problems associated with algorithmic decision making would feature in the context of sentencing as in any other context. To see this, return to judgements of proportionality in sentencing. Assume for a moment that the algorithm's recommendations are binding on judges, as Chiao implies that they might be at some point. Would judicial decision making then be objectionable? I suspect it would. First, as noted, decision making by AI would open the door for reliance on factors that should not be relied on even if they accidentally lead to the correct result, and this would undermine the legitimacy of legal institutions regardless of the correctness of the outcome. Second, such decision making would be based on evidence that does not meet error eliminability. It does not meet error eliminability because it does not allow narrowing down the relevant reference class based on factors that had not featured in sentencing or elsewhere before, as well as based on factors that had rightly featured in sentencing before but without finding any well-articulated expression on the evidence or in judgments.

Consider first how AI would respond to factors that should impact sentencing but have not featured in previous decisions. The decision-making algorithm would ignore such factors. Even if it has learning capabilities, identification of new relevant factors would still depend on the concepts with which the AI is already familiar (entirely novel ones would not be identified). In such conditions, if the algorithmic output is, say, that there is 80 per cent likelihood that the system would impose a sentence of seven years' imprisonment in the case at issue, the case at issue would fall within the 20 per cent likelihood that the system would impose a different (higher or lower) sanction. The defendant would thus be subject to an erroneous, disproportionate sanction that would further be objectionable on grounds of disrespect, as explained in chapter 5.

Perhaps more fundamentally, any assumption that all the factors that rightly impacted sentencing before can be captured by a sufficiently sophisticated AI is over-optimistic (or perhaps over-pessimistic). Some such factors exist and rightly impact the decisions of human judges without being articulated by the judges or indeed by the parties who introduce evidence, and thus without being accessible to AI.[11] Factors whose existence is at least implied in the presentation of the evidence might be captured by AI, but completely 'silent' ones would essentially fail to be captured. A raw judicial intuition that a specific defendant had better not be sent to prison, which is based on an unarticulated evaluation that prison would be very damaging for her, is such a 'silent' factor. As we have seen, Chiao acknowledges this elsewhere when he notes that human decision making is not fully transparent, even though the factors he has in mind are ones that might well inappropriately impact decision making. But like with medical doctors, an intuitive grasp of relevant factors is part of the skills that human judges use. This intuitive grasp is an aspect of the human ability to generate good new hypotheses on little evidence. AI can hardly generate such hypotheses, especially where the evidence is mediated to it by persons who do not give expression to the full data that the evidence contains.

The existence of new or unarticulated factors that should impact sentencing is also why legislative schemes never provide an exhaustive list of factors that would determine sentencing. Indeed, an ideal algorithm would capture more relevant factors than any legislative regime ever could, but it would still be logically incapable of capturing all the relevant factors (while it is logically possible for a human judge to capture them). As we have seen, AI would in fact build error into the system as a logically essential feature that is a condition of machine learning.

If this is correct, then no matter how strong and sophisticated the algorithm is, where the algorithm is binding, erroneous judgments based on statistical evidence that does not meet error eliminability would be made; disproportionate sanctions would be imposed based on a statistical prediction. This would lead to most of the difficulties that have been identified in previous chapters.[12] We can mention the main ones briefly. If a human judge needs to 'sign off' the judgment then problems of substantive responsibility emerge, as we have seen in chapter 8. But even if no one needs to 'sign off' the judgment, the evidential regime would still be problematic for reasons of respect and of public resolution. Consider respect first. As we have seen, where retributive justice is at stake, reasons of respect for persons require adopting an evidential regime that logically allows ruling out the possibility of error; it requires adopting error eliminability. Relatedly, an error based

[11] At least, such factors are not articulated until a judge is challenged to further defend her decision (and sometimes even when challenged).

[12] Obviously, difficulties associated with reasons to assert that wrongdoing has been committed are irrelevant at the sentencing stage.

on evidence that fails to meet error eliminability might well lead to the imposition of the worst consequences on the worst off, or bring people below a minimal threshold of welfare. Whether or not such an outcome is brought about would depend on the circumstance or on the factors that have been 'missed' by the algorithm: if, for example, some personal characteristics of the defendant have been missed, which means that the sanction would weigh particularly heavily on her, then the disproportionate sanction might well come to be the worst consequence for the worst off. The point is a general one: if the evidential regime blocks out some relevant information, it cannot rule out consequences that relevant reasons of respect require ruling out. A binding algorithmic regime would thus be an unjust one. And consider resolution: sentencing is part of the resolution of the criminal conflict. We have seen that an evidential regime that fails to meet error eliminability undermines resolution: in cases of error the agency of the losing party would be undermined in a way that creates irresolvable conflict. For this reason too, binding algorithmic sentencing that fails to meet error eliminability would be inappropriate.

III. Algorithmic Prediction of Students' Grades

Algorithmic prediction of students' grades based on statistical evidence that fails to meet error eliminability merits independent discussion, if only because of the strong public response to its utilisation during the COVID 19 pandemic.[13] As a reminder, during the academic year 2020–21, A-level exams could not take place in the United Kingdom because social-distancing measures were in place. Instead, Ofqual (The Office of Qualifications and Examinations Regulation) decided to determine the final grades for year 13 students with the help of an algorithm. The algorithm calculated the grades based on three parameters:

(a) the historical grade distribution of schools from the three previous years (2017–19);
(b) the rank of each student within her own school for a particular subject, based on a teacher's evaluation of the student's likely grade had the A-levels gone forward as planned;
(c) the previous exam results for a student per subject.

The publication of the grades led to wide protests that led the Government to retract them and endorse teachers' evaluations instead.

That there is a problem with determining grades algorithmically is clear. Part of the problem was that the specific algorithm was a bad algorithm: it was inaccurate, it was biased, it gave an advantage to private schools that teach students

[13] See at www.bbc.co.uk/news/explainers-53807730.

in small classes and so on.[14] But let us imagine a good algorithm that would provide accurate predictions for 90 per cent of the students. Would the use of such an algorithm be appropriate? If all that has been said so far is correct, the answer is no.

To see this, we need to consider the nature of the judgement about students' grades and the nature of the evidence the algorithm uses. Judgements about students' grades are what has been referred to in this book as 'retributive in a loose sense'; the basis for allocating them is desert. The relevant sense of desert here is not moral desert for moral action; it is non-moral desert that relates to an intellectual accomplishment. Accordingly, reasons of respect are at play, but they are not reasons of respect for persons as valuable in themselves; they are reasons for respect for all that is valuable in any way. Furthermore, the relevant judgements have a public dimension, and while they do not resolve a conflict or disagreement, they do resolve a pending question about students' levels of knowledge and skills. In addition, these judgements have another aspect: they are predictors of future academic success, and accordingly they are used in the allocation of university places.

Now for the evidence. It is easy to see that while the abovementioned parameter (b) meets error eliminability, parameters (a) and (c) do not. A teacher's prediction is based on her close familiarity with the individual student; reasons are thus available to support the proposition that the assessment is not erroneous in any specific case. The teacher can refer to her overall impression of the student's understanding of the subject; to her estimation of the level of effort that the student will put into preparation for final exams; to the level of support that the student will be provided prior to final exams; to her evaluation of the student's ability to handle the stress of final exams; and so on. By contrast, past performance of a student and past performance of students at the same school do not provide reasons in support of the proposition that if an error occurs, an error does not occur for each individual prediction. These two parameters were in many instances decisive: they led to rejection of teachers' evaluations and to the adoption of grades that were instead modelled on these parameters.

With such an evidential procedure, the loosely retributive judgement about students' grades cannot be a fair judgement of what they deserve. It is based on an evidential rule that does not allow ruling out the possibility of error; and reasons of respect require that such an evidential rule would itself be ruled out or rejected. When students complete educational tasks, they exercise intellectual skills. These exercises should not be treated in a way that is inconsistent with their value; respect requires that such treatment should be ruled out. Accordingly, an evidential regime that does not allow ruling out the possibility of error in the form of

[14] See at www.theguardian.com/education/2020/aug/21/ofqual-exams-algorithm-why-did-it-fail-make-grade-a-levels; https://blogs.lse.ac.uk/impactofsocialsciences/2020/08/26/fk-the-algorithm-what-the-world-can-learn-from-the-uks-a-level-grading-fiasco/.

misevaluation should itself be ruled out. Furthermore, the algorithmic judgement about students' grades would not facilitate real resolution of pending questions about their skills and abilities; it would generate further conflict over the agential contribution of students to this resolution (as it in fact did). This is at least undesirable; and it undermines the legitimacy of the deciding institutions.

What about the allocation of university places? There is a sense in which a university place is deserved; if my daughter works hard and does well, I will think that she deserves the benefit of a place at a good university. In some countries it is thought that everyone deserves a place at a good university; offering places to everyone is part of the social roles of universities. But as far as universities in the United Kingdom are concerned, desert depends on academic merit. Yet in another sense, universities allocate places based on utilitarian grounds associated with the benefits for them in having students who will perform well. In this respect, universities operate like private providers who prioritise their own interest. Now, in a normal year, most universities decide based on performance of the individual student in tasks that have a dual role: they are individual demonstrations of merit, and they are also statistical predictors of academic success. But while alternative statistical predictors were available, the individual demonstration of merit was unavailable in 2020–21. Could universities then rely solely on sufficiently accurate and unbiased statistical data that do not meet error eliminability in making their decisions?

The answer is in the negative, because fairness and respect remain relevant when universities decide to whom to provide. Respect here is responsiveness to the value of students' academic merit; since academic merit is valuable, it should be treated consistently with its value. Accordingly, universities' response to students' academic merit should not be decided on probabilistic grounds. It should be decided on evidence that meets error eliminability, namely on individual demonstrations of merit.

The next section considers decisions by private providers in the free market. Yet it can already be said here that while such decisions are indeed hardly constrained by considerations of fairness and respect, this is only because the conditions of the free market ensure fairness and respect to the extent that they need to be ensured. The conditions of the free market ensure that multiple providers will be available, so that if one of them errs and subsequently denies provision, another will get it right. But the higher-education market is not a free market in the relevant respects. For some of its 'products' there are only very few 'providers'. Such is the case when it comes to tutorial groups of two to three students;[15] to proximity to one's home; to particular strength in a student's area of interest; or to particularly high student satisfaction rates. And in such conditions, universities cannot fairly decide to whom to allocate places based on evidence that does not allow eliminating the possibility of error for each individual candidate. Respect for students'

[15] For better or for worse (and there is a lot that is 'for worse', but it does not concern us here), this might explain the individualised admission criteria of universities that offer such a tutorial system.

demonstrations of academic merit requires that the risk of error in the allocation of such exclusive resources be logically eliminable, and that there would be reasons available in support of the proposition that it has been eliminated. Note, however, that the status and stringency of such reasons of respect would be different from that of reasons to respect persons as valuable in themselves. There is no need for us to develop this point further here.

It can further be added that for those students who would have performed well in exams notwithstanding gloomy statistics, the decision to rely on statistics led to profoundly tragic errors and hence, as we have seen, to great injustice. Since the probability of such tragic errors was unknown, maximin would have advised rejecting altogether the method that allowed for them.

IV. Allocation of Resources in the Private and Public Domains

Resources are often allocated based on closed lists of factors that track substantive entitlements. Banks and mortgage providers decide eligibility to loans based on statistical predictions of candidates' future income; insurers decide rates based on statistical evaluations of future risk; and so forth. In all these cases, the evidence on which decisions are based does not meet error eliminability. There could be cases in which current income turns out not to be a good predictor of future income, past financial achievements turn out not to be a good predictor of future achievements and medical history turns out not to be a good predictor of future health. Yet the possibility that such is the case at issue cannot be tracked on the evidence; error is ineliminable. Where, if at all, might reliance on such evidence be inconsistent with relevant reasons of respect?

To answer this question, an initial distinction should be drawn between financial decisions made in the free market by private actors (who do not represent a public agency) and public distributive decisions. Private financial actors do not allocate resources but exchange them; they do not do so as an exercise of authority; and the welfare interests that they serve are not always fundamental ones that should be met for reasons of respect for persons (though other reasons of respect might be at play). More significantly, the rules of the free market contribute to ensuring that the activity of the market as a whole is as fair and consistent with respect as it should be: no one is wrongly denied that which she can afford.

Let us consider how the free market can work to ensure fairness (at least in theory; the question whether the free market is successful is a different one). Consider a person who requires a loan. It could, of course, be the case that a person is, say, erroneously denied a loan by a specific provider (in fact this person would be able to pay it back, but the information that supports this proposition is not taken into account by the provider). But the rules governing the operation of the free market should allow this person to approach a range of other providers, or to apply for a different loan, etc. If the relevant information that takes the person outside the class of those who would not be able to pay back is highly individualised, the market should operate in a way that makes it possible for the person to carry the costs of individuation of the risk-evaluation process. Thus, the free market should work to guarantee that 'respect disasters' that are within its remit do not occur. It should work to ensure that the principles of financial exchange can in relevant cases be applied based on sufficiently individualised evidence that meets error eliminability. In such conditions, there is no reason to further oblige any individual provider to comply with error eliminability. It is enough that there is sufficient economic incentive to guarantee that at least some providers act based on error eliminability. If this is not the case, and the entire market miscalculates the risk, then there is a market failure that should be corrected. This would be the case where, for example, the same algorithm is shared by all or most providers.[16] But where mechanisms that correct market failures exist, a provider's error does not reflect a structural failure to respect. In the context of economic markets, reasons of respect do not require that a benefit from a specific provider be available to anyone; they only require that the benefit be available.[17]

If this is correct, then while no specific private provider should be required to base its decisions on evidence that meets error eliminability, the state should ensure that the market is free enough to incentivise some providers to decide based on such evidence.

Things are different when it comes to public distributive decisions. The (somewhat simplified yet largely valid) assumption is that there is only that much that a free market can do; some people will be denied of some products not because they are erroneously judged to be unable to afford them but because they really cannot afford them. Thus the free market cannot guarantee that some basic welfare interests are served the way reasons of respect for persons require. If these welfare interests are to be guaranteed, some of the wealth accumulated in society needs to be authoritatively redistributed by the state. Here, the relevant welfare interests are ones that should always be guaranteed if respect is not to be threatened by 'probably respecting'; there are no multiple providers who work on economic incentives of the free market, and thus no mechanisms that guarantee that error eliminability is ever met in a way that responds well to reasons of respect for persons; and the decisions are authoritative decisions that seek to resolve potential conflicts over distribution. In such conditions, alternative mechanisms that ensure that rules of distribution indeed rule out 'disrespect disasters', and that they are correctly applied, need to be adopted.

Accordingly, governmental compliance with error eliminability becomes relevant. Reasons to comply with error eliminability include reasons of fairness and

[16] The Chinese social credit system, which started off in the commercial sector when China transformed to a market economy, is probably one such example. See at www.forbes.com/sites/traceyfollows/2021/10/07/are-social-credit-systems-coming-to-the-west/.

[17] There are, of course, valid general questions about the fairness of a free-market mechanism (as compared with other economic arrangements), but such questions go beyond what is needed for the purposes of the current discussion.

respect, and reasons of public resolution (which might also have legitimising properties). We have seen that demanding that the authority act from behind a veil of ignorance (ie in evidential conditions in which error is logically eliminable) allows identifying the relevant reasons of respect. These reasons, in turn, themselves demand reasoning out distributional error; they demand ruling out arrangements that logically allow for some 'distribution disasters'. But this is not where the role of error eliminability in guaranteeing respect ends. Once the appropriate arrangement is adopted, error eliminability enters the picture once again in the context of its application. In addition to the substantive arrangement, the evidential regime also needs to be such that logically allows applying the arrangement correctly, or logically allows ruling out the possibility that an application is erroneous. Thus, where reasons of respect are relevant, they require adopting an evidential regime that allows elimination of the risk of error in the application of distributive arrangements or rules. The question in applying a fair rule of distribution is who is entitled to receive any specific financial benefit, or whose basic welfare interests are at stake if they do not receive such benefits? And this question needs to be determined based on evidence that meets error eliminability. Furthermore, where distributive decisions are made based on evidence that meets error eliminability, a real resolution of distributive questions is provided: parties would not reasonably reject the distribution on the basis that it created fresh conflict. As we have seen, this is practically desirable; possibly, it also legitimises the distributive decisions and the institutions that make them.

V. Automated Cars and Other Dangerous Machines

If they are not already safer than human drivers, the day will probably come when automated cars are able to reduce the number of car accidents. Still, automated cars are designed so that the holder of a driving licence must not only sit in the driver's seat, but also indicate every so often that she is alert to the conditions of the road. In the end, she is in charge. But should she be? And will we require that a person constantly check the conditions of the road together with the algorithms, even if it transpires that human intervention does more harm than good? Similar questions arise in the context of all means of transport, of all dangerous machinery, as well as of automated warfare (even though there would be some context-specific considerations there).

Once software improves enough and the question becomes relevant, it will be a difficult one. It is clear that reasons of respect are at play, because risks to the life and limb of persons are at play. That automated cars do not reason and cannot respect or disrespect is important, but it is not conclusive: as with all AI, the question is whether their use should be authorised to begin with. Cars are dangerous, and where it is irrational to believe that a certain move will not bring about a concrete risk to persons, the move should be avoided. The software used in automated cars can calculate which moves would avoid risk based on a list of familiar factors, but it cannot 'further investigate' the evidence to discover whether new factors are at play (at least not until an error has occurred from which it can 'learn'). Thus, the evidential basis for use of automated cars does not meet error eliminability as required by reasons of respect. In such conditions, it is arguable that the authorisation of automated cars is objectionable.

There are, however, other considerations at play. Remember that the state merely authorises the use of automated cars. Using automated cars, or using any cars in a system where automated cars are in use, is a voluntary choice; it is not an imposition. There are, of course, costs to opting out, and the level of freedom one has in deciding whether to use cars is debatable. But at least some element of choice exists. There is value in the choice to participate that, arguably, is consistent with the value of persons (as ends) in themselves. On the other hand, and significantly, where activities involve a risk to life, a person who carries the burden of error can no longer live a life of respect notwithstanding the error.[18] So how should the different considerations play out?

I hesitate whether to compare the authorisation of automated cars to the authorisation of the use of vaccination against Covid-19 that endangers the life of some people. There are significant differences, but there might still be something to learn from the comparison. To remind, at some point during the Covid-19 pandemic it emerged that the Astra-Zeneca vaccine caused deadly blood clots in some people. What EU countries did was to compare the risk of hospitalisation and death associated with the vaccine with the risk of hospitalisation and death associated with Covid-19; the comparison was made for different age groups under different infection levels.[19] The vaccination was not authorised for those groups who were more likely to be harmed from the vaccine than from Covid-19 under low levels of infection. Thus, the benefits of the vaccine were measured as accurately as possible, but an ineliminable risk of error remained. Notably, in the context of these vaccinations, unlike in the context of automated cars, there was no other choice available: countries could not have chosen to let doctors evaluate risks and benefits on an individual basis, because neither evidence nor good hypotheses were yet available. In the circumstances, authorisation was based on evidence that did not meet error eliminability, while leaving the choice whether to get vaccinated in the hands of individuals.

Clearly, not all authorisations are the same: some are expected to lead to very high rates of uptake and others are not, all depending on the essence of what is being authorised and the social circumstances. Some are communicated as mere authorisations, and others are communicated as a recommendation and sometimes a professional recommendation (as is normally the case with the use of medicines).

[18] There are difficult questions involved, but the point is merely that actualisation of capacities is itself valuable or merits respect; this does not mean that a longer life is more valuable than a shorter life: in the relevant capacity-related sense, they are equally (and some would say infinitely) valuable.

[19] European Medicines Agency, Annex to Vaxzevria Art 5.3: Visual Risk Contextualisation (EMA/234525/2021) at www.ema.europa.eu/en/documents/chmp-annex/annex-vaxzevria-art53-visual-risk-contextualisation_en.pdf.

But if there is a general lesson to be learnt, it might be that whenever mere authorisation is on the cards of the use of means that statistically reduce the risk to life and limb, this evidence should still be as 'individuated' as possible in the circumstances. For automated cars, for example, it should be considered whether they minimise risk for highway users but not for users of country roads, or (perhaps) whether they minimise risk for older drivers but not for experienced younger drivers, etc. Authorisation for those who are likely to benefit might be legitimate, as long as it leaves the ultimate choice whether to make use of it in the hands of individuals.

VI. Profiling and Individual Risk Prediction Based on Group Affiliation

Profiling is a decision to act in the face of a probabilistic risk that is associated with characteristics of a group. Profiling can be the basis for various types of actions. In the sense to be considered here first, it is the basis for 'intermediate action' taken by a public authority. Such action would take the form of a search or further investigation. It is aimed at removing the uncertainty associated with the risk (or eliminating the risk) with the help of evidence that meets error eliminability; it does not reflect a decision to take or reject that risk. It is thus comparable not to a decision by a medical doctor to remove a suspicious lump, but to conduct a scan that would determine if the lump is innocent or not. Accordingly, even though the decision is usually taken by an authority in response to the possibility of wrongful conduct, it does not involve false imposition of a retributive burden.

Since this is the case, profiling seems at first sight to be unproblematic. If there is statistical evidence that increases the probability that I have committed crime, there seems to be nothing problematic about examining further evidence that would serve to confirm or refute the proposition that I have committed crime. Such would be the case even if I am made to carry a burden in the process of examination (like being invited to a police interview, or even charged with an offence); the legitimacy of imposing such burdens is presumed by any rule-based social or political arrangement. As long as nobody takes me to have committed crime (irrationally believes that I committed crime, asserts that I did so, or imposes on me burdens as if I did so), it is hard to see valid reasons to object to the process of examination.

Still, we find profiling problematic. At least sometimes; at least when it involves risk evaluation based on group affiliation, and especially racial group affiliation. Some attempts have been made in the literature to consider why. Some concerns have been raised about the reliability of such evidence, noting difficulties in gathering and analysing the relevant data.[20] But it is not clear that even under the

[20] MR Smith and GP Alpert, 'Searching for Direction: Courts, Social Science, and the Adjudication of Racial Profiling Claims' (2002) 19 *Justice Quarterly* 673; SN Durlauf, 'Racial Profiling as a Public Policy Question: Efficiency, Equity, and Ambiguity' (2005) 95 *American Economics Review* 132.

assumption that the data are accurate, we would be at ease with profiling. It has also been suggested that profiling is stigmatising and offensive for individuals and groups.[21] Yet this requires further elucidation: if the assumption about offence and stigma is correct, why should it not be similarly offensive to be suspected based on one's belonging with the group of persons against whom first-hand testimony is available? After all, all evidence can validly be described in statistical terms. Amit Pundik has suggested that the main concern is with autonomy:[22] probabilistic evidence that predicts risk based on group affiliation presumes that people are predetermined by their contingencies; they lack free will. This presumption is problematic if made in a system that seeks to confirm whether one is blameworthy, as blameworthiness presupposes free will. Yet this account too is problematic, because free will does not mean lack of contingent pressures that might give agents reasons to take certain actions; it only means that in the end, one is free to act or refrain from action notwithstanding any pressures and associated increased likelihoods.

To see why risk evaluation based on group affiliation is problematic, we must first take note of its public and often institutionalised context. The main practices that have raised objections are ones by security agencies; they include, for example, selection for police searches or for enhanced security checks in airports. In such public and institutionalised contexts, judgements have more than one layer. They are at the same time the public judgements made by institutions and, at another level that should normally be sidelined, the private judgements of individual decision makers. Furthermore, these judgements are received by members of the public, who interpret them based on their own presuppositions. This can turn a simple picture into a more complicated one. It can turn judgements from judgements that are strictly about probabilistic risk to judgements that have a dualistic nature: they are public judgements about a probable risk (or about the profiled person as a probable source of risk), but they can also be judgements about an existing risk (or about the profiled person as an actual source of risk). If a judgement is the latter, the profiled person is taken to have interpreted her realities as giving her reasons to harm; she is not taken to be merely exposed to realities that she might interpret as giving her reasons to harm. Yet such an interpretation of reality is a moral failure. Accordingly, the judgement can and often does become condemnatory and retributive.

The retributive element of the judgement can take different forms. First, a public judgement about risk can be accompanied by a private attitude of blame and resentment. This private attitude is then perceived or interpreted as public. Second, even the public judgement can reflect resentment and thereby endow the burden

[21] DA Harris, *Profiles in Injustice: Why Racial Profiling Cannot Work*, rev edn (New York, New Press, 2003); WM Carter, Jr, 'A Thirteenth Amendment Framework for Combating Racial Profiling' (2004) 39 *Harvard Civil Rights-Civil Liberties Law Review* 17; PW Beck and PA Daly, 'State Constitutional Analysis of Pretext Stops: Racial Profiling and Public Policy Concerns' (1999) 72 *Temple Law Review* 597.

[22] A Pundik, 'Against Racial Profiling' (2017) 67 *University of Toronto Law Journal* 175.

associated with searches and security checks with condemnatory meanings. This would be the case, for example, where profiling tracks race, the institutions are racist, and the allocated burden is thereby conceived as an attempt to affirm suspicion or even as implicitly punitive. Third, even when a judgement does not reflect private or public resentment, the combination of its institutional context with pre-existing social attitudes might lead to resentment by the public. The public wrongly interprets the judgements of authorities as if they were judgements about an existing risk, and then conceives these interpretations as authoritative. This, in turn, works to reaffirm the public's misguided presuppositions and attitudes.

Where the judgement is retributive, reasons of respect become relevant, and they require basing those judgements on error eliminability rather than on statistics as in profiling. Thus, in social and political conditions that are receptive of racism or other forms of bias against groups, at least the imposition of (any) burdens based on profiling is objectionable.

This might mean that profiling based on characteristics that do not merit protection could still be legitimate. It is arguable, for example, that profiling certain gamers or alcoholics, if there is evidence to indicate that they are more likely to commit certain wrongful acts, would not be objectionable. Still, it is not clear that this is not too delicate a distinction: societies are divided, and resentment of anyone who can be constructed as 'other' is too easily provoked or just awakened. If the police start stopping and searching alcoholics, this might easily be interpreted as, and stimulate, resentment towards alcoholics. Alcoholism would then become a characteristic that merits protection.

As already implied, profiling can also provide a basis for decisions to accept or reject a risk (rather than for decisions to remove uncertainty or engage in elimination of the risk of error). Profiling can, for example, provide a basis for preventive detention or for the imposition of harsher or more lenient criminal sanctions on an individual based on risk evaluation. If all that has been said so far is correct, these decisions are no different from decisions to act to remove uncertainties. In the context of such decisions, reasons of respect are relevant; and respect requires that reasons be available to support the proposition that if error about risk occurs, it does not occur in the case at issue. The 'naked' statistics that underly profiling cannot provide such reasons.

VII. Personal Attitudes

David Enoch and Levi Spectre have noted that just as we think that belief based on 'naked statistical evidence' is unjustified, we also think that the development of attitudes like resentment based on 'naked statistical evidence' is unjustified.[23]

[23] D Enoch and L Spectre, 'Statistical Resentment, or: What's Wrong with Acting, Blaming and Believing Based on Statistics Alone' (2021) 199 *Synthese* 5687.

I am not justified in resenting any single colleague based on the evidence that most of my colleagues have been talking ill of me. Enoch and Spectre suggest that resentment lies at the intersection of the epistemic and the practical, and for this reason it is particularly interesting. Still, after a long exploration, they conclude that the search for a theory that unifies the epistemic and the practical cannot succeed.

The puzzle becomes less mysterious once it is acknowledged that epistemic conditions and practical conditions of respect are similarly uncompromising; both have the same error-eliminating structure (arguably, because respect for persons is one of the values that underlies epistemology). Both epistemic conditions and conditions of respect require the availability of reasons to think that if an error occurs, it does not occur in the case at hand. The rationality of believing is thus at the same time the rationality of thinking and acting respectfully. The case of resentment is nothing but a good demonstration of this. It shows how a practical attitude that is responsive to reasons of respect and an accompanying belief that is responsive to epistemic reasons are justifiable on the same grounds, namely, the availability of reasons to think that if an error occurs, it does not occur in the case at hand.

Let us see why this is so. Rather than being on some intersection of the epistemological and the practical, resentment is a practical attitude; and it is regulated by practical reasons of respect. If, as Raz suggests, reasons of respect for persons are reasons to think, talk and act in ways that are consistent with the value of persons, then resentment is practical in any relevant sense. When Raz talks of 'thinking' of persons as a practical matter that is regulated by reasons of respect, he refers to thinking in a very broad sense that 'applies to our fantasies, imaginings, wishes, emotions, as well as to our plain beliefs'.[24] Thus, even if resentment were a belief (or essentially included a belief), it would be practical: beliefs are governed not only by epistemological norms but also by practical norms of respect, and in this way they have a practical aspect as we have already seen. But resentment is not a belief: resentment itself is an attitude. Notably, the same goes for admiration, like and dislike, envy, and a range of other attitudes that Enoch and Spectre mention and that respond to the value of individuals' actions or thoughts. That such attitudes usually come together with beliefs that a person deserves them is not accidental, but it does not mean that these attitudes are, in some way, beliefs or partly beliefs. It is not even clear that they are conditional on belief. I can resent all my colleagues if I have reason to think that most of them are speaking ill of me; resentfulness here is perhaps an aggressive defence mechanism that protects me from disappointment in any specific colleague if and when I come to justifiably believe that she has spoken ill of me. Furthermore, that these attitudes might or might not be chosen hardly matters. Either way, they can be disrespectful of persons and, hence, as Raz notes, morally wrong.

What do norms of respect require when it comes to attitudes like resentment? And how do such requirements relate to epistemic norms? Clearly, falsely resenting

[24] J Raz, *Value, Respect, and Attachment* (Cambridge, Cambridge University Press, 2001) 161.

a person involves treating a person in a way that is inconsistent with the value of his conduct, or failing to respect his conduct. As we have seen, respect requires that before we resent, reasons be available for us to think that if error in the form of false resentment might occur, it would not occur in the case at issue; respect requires reasoning out error (and it further requires doing so successfully). If such reasons are unavailable, our resentment is only probably consistent with the value of the person's conduct, and thus in fact inconsistent with this value. Accordingly, respect requires ruling out or rejecting any evidential regime that does not allow identifying such reasons. Respect thus requires that error eliminability be adopted as an evidential condition for resentment. But we saw in chapter 1 that error eliminability is also the evidential condition of rational belief; and it was argued in chapter 5 that this is not accidental but rather a manifestation of the role of knowledge in guaranteeing respect for persons. If this is correct, it is not only irrational (because unresponsive to reasons of respect) to resent a person based on statistical evidence indicating that he spoke ill of me; it is also irrational to believe that this person spoke ill of me based on such evidence.

What about pre-resentment (or pre-pride), namely, resenting based on individualised evidence that another will give me reason to resent her or to be proud of her, etc?[25] Assume that my evidence is that my colleague has a very strong motive to speak ill of me (I recently blocked his promotion for reasons that I know he cannot understand, and he had admitted to me before that 'letting off steam' helped him deal with difficult situations). Even in the face of such strong individualised evidence, it would be irrational for me to resent him before I have any evidence that he has spoken ill of me. But why?

One reason might be priors: when no one has spoken ill of me yet, the prior probability that any of my colleagues will do so in, say, the next fortnight is presumably low (it is the probability that a person in a workplace like mine will be spoken ill of by another colleague in a certain fortnight); after someone has spoken ill of me, the prior probability for each of my colleagues is significantly higher (1/n, where n is the number of my colleagues). On the background of this higher prior probability, it makes sense that my evidence can increase the posterior probability that my colleague has spoken ill of me enough to justify resentment, notwithstanding any other practical considerations at stake.

Still, sometimes the evidence is sufficiently strong to make it highly probable that a person will act in a certain way even on the background of low priors. And we would nevertheless think that pre-resentment is inappropriate. To see why, we should return to error eliminability. Remember that resentment is governed by error eliminability, and that error eliminability requires that the evidence would logically allow elimination of the risk of error. But the evidence logically allows eliminating the risk of error only when it is open for investigation and narrowing down of the reference class. Reasons thus need to be available to think that if my

[25] Enoch and Spectre (n 23) 5693.

colleague might change his mind, he will not do it on this occasion; that if external circumstances might stop him, they will not stop him this time (if he catches Covid and resorts to resting in bed, it will not happen before he has executed his intentions; if a fierce storm diverts his attention, it will not happen before he has executed his intentions, etc). Such reasons might be readily available when predictive evidence indicates that conduct has already taken place, the way evidence of a motive does when it is introduced in trials: since all the information on the conditions that prevailed at the time of commission is then readily available on the evidence that comes before us, the evidence would supply us with 'information that there is more information', and so it would logically allow us to eliminate the risk of error. But such reasons are hardly ever readily available in the case of predictive evidence that indicates that a person will do something in the future.[26] Since all the information about all the internal and external circumstances of a person in the future is scattered over too many pieces of evidence that would not come before us, we would suffice with a semi-statistical generalisation about the likelihood that a person with such a motive would act on the motive; it is accordingly logically impossible to eliminate the risk of error on the evidence. And for this reason, evidence that predicts conduct that has not yet taken place does not meet error eliminability, much like 'naked statistical evidence'. It is therefore irrational to believe based on it, or to develop any attitudes or emotions that might not be consistent with the value of people's conduct based on it.

VIII. Beliefs about Groups and the Problem of Prejudice

The convergence of the conditions of knowledge and the conditions of respect can explain why it seems problematic to entertain (positive or negative) beliefs about groups. Such beliefs would take the general form of 'group X is good/bad at …'. We often condemn such beliefs as racist or prejudicial. Clearly, more often than not these beliefs are epistemically unjustified: there is no evidence available that supports them, only anecdotes, rumours and tales whose claims become more grandiose each time they are told. But can there be such a belief that is epistemically justified? And, if so, how can it be morally bad?

The answer is that beliefs about groups can hardly ever be epistemically justified. Propositions like 'group X is good/bad at …' often rely on statistical evidence that does not meet error eliminability and hence does not justify belief (nor any practical attitudes that might disrespect). The proposition 'group X is good/bad at …' is not a shortened or lazy formulation of the proposition 'there is high prevalence of people who are good/bad at … in group X'. Rather, the proposition 'group

[26] Such reasons might be available when the predictive evidence concerning the future relies on non-probabilistic laws of nature to indicate that a natural phenomenon will take place in the future.

X is good/bad at ...' implies causation. It implies that there is a genetic or social cause that increases the prevalence of people who are good or bad at something in the group. And while statistical evidence does not fail to meet error eliminability where all that it seeks to support is propositions about prevalence, statistical evidence does not meet error eliminability when supporting propositions about causation.

This should by now be familiar. Consider evidence like '90 per cent of the members of group X perform well in Y exams, while only 60 per cent of members of groups A and B perform well in Y exams'. The proposition 'there is comparatively high prevalence of people who do well in Y exams in group X' is a proposition about correlation that is logically deducible from this evidence (so no inductive inference is involved at all, and error is of course logically eliminable). This is why if we find out that a member of group X did not perform well in Y exam, we might justifiably be surprised.[27] But the proposition 'members of group X are good at Y exams' already implies new information; it implies that there is a causal link between membership of the group and performance in exams, even if it does so without suggesting what the causal link between membership and performance might be: it might be genetic or cultural, or whatever other causal links one might envision. Where such propositions are based on statistical evidence, it is impossible to reason out error in the determination of causation. To allow reasoning out error, the evidence needs to meet error eliminability. It needs to allow the factfinder to reason out alternative hypotheses such as coincidence, an independent cause like average age and so on. In other words, the evidential basis of a scientific or legal proof is required for a belief to be justified.

Might a dedicated researcher be able to trace such evidence? It has already been noted that causation might be a non-empirical concept, with the implication that there is no point trying to establish it conclusively with reference to evidence. But might it be possible to establish causation as we normally do in and outside the legal system, for example with reference to Hill's flexible criteria that were mentioned in section I? The answer might well be in the negative. The relevant traits are never exclusive to the group; non-members can and are often good or bad at the relevant things. Furthermore, in total numbers, there might well be more non-members than members who possess the trait. In such circumstances, it is possible that the trait is in fact caused by membership of a group that crosses the group in question. To be able to negate this possibility, the exact genetic or social factor that is causally connected with the trait needs to be identified, and then its prevalence in possible crossing groups needs to be examined. Now, any reference to group membership as a cause of a trait remains fuzzy about the exact factor or factors that are at play; and there can be a vast number of such factors and combinations thereof. Accordingly, the ability to examine whether the relevant factors are indeed more

[27] Enoch and Spectre (n 23) 5693.

likely to appear in the group in question than in any crossing group (or rather the ability to effectively identify various relevant crossing groups in which these factors might be at play) is very low if not absent. Until we have accurately identified what might be the cause, we cannot examine and negate the possibility that it is caused by a crossing group membership; hence, we cannot establish the alleged causal connection between membership of the group in question and a trait. Thus, it is doubtful if even a dedicated researcher can trace evidence that justifies belief that group membership 'causes' any comparative advantages or disadvantages. Subsequently, it is irrational to hold beliefs about such comparative advantages or disadvantages; and it is irrational (and essentially disrespectful) to develop related attitudes towards the group.

BIBLIOGRAPHY

Aboodi, R, Borer, A and Enoch, D, 'Deontology, Individualism and Uncertainty: A Reply to Jackson and Smith' (2008) 105 *The Journal of Philosophy* 259, 270.

Allen, RJ and Stein, A 'Evidence, Probability, and Burden of Proof' (2013) 55 *Arizona Law Review* 557.

Annas, J and Barnes, J (eds), *Sextus Empiricus, Outlines of Scepticism*, 2nd edn (Cambridge, Cambridge University Press, 2000).

Aristotle, *The Poetics of Aristotle*, 3rd edn, ed with critical notes and tr SH Butcher (1902) at www.gutenberg.org/files/1974/1974-h/1974-h.htm.

——, *The Works of Aristotle: Organon or Logical Treatises of Aristotle*, vol 2, tr T Taylor (Dilton Marsh, Prometheus Trust, 2001).

Arrow, K, 'Some Ordinalist-Utilitarian Notes on Rawls' Theory of Justice' (1973) 70 *Journal of Philosophy* 245.

Ashworth, A, 'Four Threats to the Presumption of Innocence' (2006) 10 *International Journal of Evidence and Proof* 241.

Aubert, V, 'Competition and Dissensus: Two Types of Conflict and of Conflict Resolution' (1963) VII *Conflict Resolution* 26.

Audia, PG, Locke, EA and Smith, KG, 'The Paradox of Success: An Archival and Laboratory Study of Strategic Persistence following Radical Environmental Change' 43 (2000) *Academy of Management Journal* 837.

Ayer, AJ, *Language Truth, and Logic* (London, Gollancz, 1936).

Bach, K, 'Applying Pragmatics to Epistemology' (2008) 18 *Philosophical Issues* 68.

Bach, K and Harnish, R, *Linguistic Communication and Speech Acts* (Cambridge, MA, MIT Press, 1979).

Barstow, M, 'Oedipus Rex as the Ideal Tragic Hero of Aristotle' (1912) 6 *The Classic Weekly* 2.

Bayes, Rev T, 'An Essay toward Solving a Problem in the Doctrine of Chances' (1763) 53 *Philosophical Transactions of the Royal Society of London* 370.

Beck PW, and Daly, PA, 'State Constitutional Analysis of Pretext Stops: Racial Profiling and Public Policy Concerns' (1999) 72 *Temple Law Review* 597.

Becker, K and Black, T (eds), *The Sensitivity Principle in Epistemology* (Cambridge, Cambridge University Press, 2012).

Becker, K, *Epistemology Modalized* (New York and London, Routledge, 2007).

Bentham, J, *The Works of Jeremy Bentham* (Bowring Edition, Edinburgh, 1843).

Bercovitch, J and Jackson, R, *Conflict Resolution in the Twenty-first Century: Principles, Methods, and Approaches* (Ann Arbor, MI, University of Michigan Press, 2009) 153.

Bercovitch, J, *Social Conflict and Third Parties: Strategies of Conflict Resolution* (New York, Routledge, 2019).

Block, MK, Parker JS, Vyborna, O and Dusek, L, 'An Experimental Comparison of Adversarial versus Inquisitorial Procedural Regimes' (2000) 2 *American Law and Economics Review* 170.

Boghossian, P, 'What is Inference' (2014) 169 *Philosophical Studies* 1.

BonJour, L, *Epistemology: Classic Problems and Contemporary Responses*, 2nd edn (Plymouth, Rowman and Littlefield, 2010).

Boult, C and Kohler, S, 'Epistemic Judgement and Motivation' (2020) 70 *The Philosophical Quarterly* 738.

Bragger, JD et al, 'When Success Breeds Failure: History, Hysteresis, and Delayed Exit Decisions' (2003) 88 *Journal of Applied Psychology* 6.

Brandom, RB, 'Asserting' (1983) 17 *Noûs* 637.
——, *Making it Explicit* (Cambridge, MA, Harvard University Press, 1994)
——, *Perspectives on Pragmatism: Classical, Recent and Contemporary* (Cambridge, MA, Harvard University Press, 2011).
Burge, T, 'Reason and the First Person' in B Smith and C Wright (eds), *Knowing One's Own Mind* (Oxford, Oxford University Press, 1995) 243.
Burnyeat, M, 'Can the Sceptic Live His Scepticism?' in M Burnyeat (ed), *The Skeptical Tradition* (Berkeley and Los Angeles, CA, University of California Press, 1983) 117.
——, 'The Sceptic in his Place and Time' in M Burnyeat and M Frede (eds), *The Original Sceptics: A Controversy* (Indianapolis, IN, Hackett Publishing Company, 1997) 92.
Burton, JW, 'Conflict Resolution as a Political System', *Center for Conflict Analysis and Resolution, George Mason University, Working Paper* 1/1993.
Campbell, L, 'Criminal Labels, the European Convention on Human Rights and the Presumption of Innocence' (2013) 76 *MLR* 681.
Carnap, R, 'The Methodological Character of Theoretical Concepts' (1956) 1 *Foundations of Science and the Concepts of Psychology and Psychoanalysis* 38.
Carter, Jr, WM, 'A Thirteenth Amendment Framework for Combating Racial Profiling' (2004) 39 *Harvard Civil Rights-Civil Liberties Law Review* 17.
Chaitin, GJ, 'Randomness and Mathematical Proof' (1975) 232 *Scientific American* 47.
Chiao, V, 'Fairness, Accountability and Transparency: Notes on Algorithmic Decision-making in Criminal Justice' (2019) 15 *International Journal of Law in Context* 126.
Chiao, V, 'Predicting Proportionality: The Case for Algorithmic Sentencing' (2018) 37 *Criminal Justice Ethics* 238.
Choo, AL-T, *Evidence*, 4th edn (Oxford, Oxford University Press, 2015).
Clark, SJ, 'An Accuser-Obligation Approach to the Confrontation Clause' (2003) 81 *Nebraska Law Review* 1258.
Cohen, LJ, *The Probable and the Provable* (Oxford, Clarendon Press, 1977).
Cohen, S, 'How to be a Fallibilist' (1988) 2 *Philosophical Perspectives* 91.
Coicaud, JM, *Legitimacy and Politics: A Contribution to the Study of Political Right and Political Responsibility*, tr and ed DA Curtis (Cambridge, Cambridge University Press, 2002) 33.
Coleman, PT, Deutsch, M and Marcus, E, *The Handbook of Conflict Resolution: Theory and Practice*, 3rd edn (San Fancisco, CA, Jossey-Bass, 2014).
Cross, R, *Evidence*, 5th edn (London, Butterworths, 1979).
Dancy, J, *Introduction to Contemporary Epistemology* (Oxford, Blackwell Publishing, 1985).
Darwall, SL, 'Two Kinds of Respect' (1977) 88 *Ethics* 36.
Decartes, R, *Meditations of First Philosophy* (1641), ed and introduction by S Tweyman (London and New York, Routledge, 1993).
Dennis, I, 'The Right to Confront Witnesses: Meanings, Myths and Human Rights' [2010] *Crim LR* 255.
——, *The Law of Evidence*, 6th edn (London, Sweet & Maxwell, 2017).
Dreckmann, F, 'Animal Beliefs and Their Content' (1999) 51 *Erkenntnis* 93.
Dretske, F, *Knowledge and the Flow of Information* (Cambridge, MA, MIT Press, 1981).
Duff, RA, *Punishment, Communication and Community* (Oxford University Press, 2003).
——, 'Restoration and Retribution' in A von Hirsch et al (eds), *Restorative Justice and Criminal Justice: Competing or Reconcilable Paradigms* (Oxford, Hart Publishing, 2006) 43.
——, 'Presuming Innocence' in L Zedner and JV Roberts (eds), *Principles and Values in Criminal Law and Criminal Justice* (Oxford, Oxford University Press, 2012) 51.
Durlauf, SN, 'Racial Profiling as a Public Policy Question: Efficiency, Equity, and Ambiguity' (2005) 95 *American Economics Review* 132.
Easton, S, *The Case for the Right to Silence*, 2nd edn (Farnham, Ashgate Publishing Limited, 1998).
——, *Silence and Confessions: The Suspect as a Source of Evidence* (London, Palgrave Macmillan, 2014).
Edmondson, AC, 'Learning from Mistakes is Easier Said Than Done: Group and Organizational Influences on the Detection and Correction of Human Error' (1996) 32 *Journal of Applied Behavioral Science* 5.

Ehrlich, SD, *Access Points: An Institutional Theory of Policy Bias and Policy Complexity* (Oxford, Oxford University Press, 2011).

Enoch, D, 'Against Public Reason' (2015) 1 *Oxford Studies in Political Philosophy* 112.

Enoch, D and Fisher, T, 'Sense and "Sensitivity": Epistemic and Instrumental Approaches to Statistical Evidence' (2015) 67 *Stanford Law Review* 557.

Enoch, D and Spectre, L, 'Statistical Resentment, or: What's Wrong with Acting, Blaming and Believing Based on Statistics Alone' (2021) 199 *Synthese* 5687.

Enoch, D, Spectre, L and Fisher, T, 'Statistical Evidence, Sensitivity, and the Legal Value of Knowledge' (2012) 40 *Philosophy and Public Affairs* 197.

Fantl, J and McGrath, M, *Knowledge in an Uncertain World* (New York, Oxford University Press, 2009).

Findley, KA, 'Adversarial Inquisitions: Rethinking the Search for Truth' (2012) 56 *NYLS Law Review* 911.

Finnis, J, *Natural Law and Natural Rights* (Oxford, Clarendon Press, 1980).

Fisher, T, 'The Theoretical Foundations of Evidence Law' (2015/16) 39 *Tel Aviv Law Review* 107.

Frank, J, *Courts on Trial: Myth and Reality in American Justice* (Princeton, NJ, Princeton University Press, 1950).

Frede, D, 'Necessity, Chance, and "What Happens for the Most Part"' in A Rorty (ed), *Essays on Aristotle's Poetics* (Princeton, NJ, Princeton University Press, 1992) 197.

Frese, M and Keith, N, 'Action Errors, Error Management, and Learning in Organizations' (2015) 66 *Annual Review of Psychology* 661.

Friedman, RD, 'Grappling with the Meaning of "Testimonial"' (2005) 71 *Brooklyn Law Review* 241.

Galligan, DJ, *Due Process and Fair Procedures: A Study of Administrative Procedures* (Oxford, Clarendon Press, 1996).

Gerken, M, 'Discursive Justification and Skepticism' (2012) 189 *Synthese* 373.

Gerken, M and Nedenskov Petersen, E, 'Epistemic Norms of Assertion and Action' in S Goldberg (ed), *The Oxford Handbook of Assertion* (Oxford, Oxford University Press, 2020) 683.

Gettier, E, 'Is Justified True Belief Knowledge?' (1963) 23 *Analysis* 121.

Giang, PH, 'Decision Making under Uncertainty Comprising Complete Ignorance and Probability' (2015) 62 *International Journal of Approximate Reasoning* 27.

Goldberg, SC, *Assertion: On the Philosophical Significance of Assertoric Speech* (Oxford, Oxford University Press, 2015).

——, 'Should Have Known' (2017) 194 *Synthese* 2863.

——, *To the Best of Our Knowledge: Social Expectations and Epistemic Normativity* (Oxford, Oxford University Press, 2018).

Golden, L, 'Hamartia, Atë, and Oedipus' (1978) 72 *Classical World* 3.

Goldman, A, 'Discrimination and Perceptual Knowledge' (1976) 73 *The Journal of Philosophy* 771.

Goodman, PS et al, 'Organizational Errors: Directions for Future Research' (2011) 31 *Research in Organizational Behavior* 151.

Greer, S, 'The Right to Silence: A Review of the Current Debate' (1990) 53 *MLR* 709.

Gruender, D, 'Pragmatism, Science and Metaphysics' in E Freeman (ed), *The Relevance of Charles Peirce* (La Salle, IL, Monist Library of Philosophy, 1983) 271.

Guyer, P, 'Feeling and Freedom: Kant on Aesthetics and Morality' (1990) 48 *The Journal of Aesthetics and Art Criticism* 137.

——, *Kant and the Experience of Freedom* (New York, Cambridge University Press, 1996).

Haddock, A, 'Knowledge and Justification' in D Pritchard, A Millar and A Haddock, *The Nature and Value of Knowledge: Three Investigation* (Oxford, Oxford University Press, 2010) 195.

Hamer, D, 'A Dynamic Reconstruction of the Presumption of Innocence' (2011) 31 *OJLS* 417.

Harman, GH, 'The Inference to the Best Explanation' (1965) 74 *Philosophical Review* 88.

Harris, DA, *Profiles in Injustice: Why Racial Profiling Cannot Work*, rev edn (New York, New Press, 2003).

Harsanyi, J, 'Can the Maximin Principle Serve as a Basis for Morality? A Critique of John Rawls' Theory' (1975) 69 *American Political Science Review* 594.

Hart, HLA, *The Concept of Law* (Oxford, Clarendon Press, 1961).
Hawthorne, J, *Knowledge and Lotteries* (Oxford, Oxford University Press, 2004).
Hayner, PB, 'Past Truths, Present Dangers: The Role of Official Truth Seeking' in PC Stern and D Druckman (eds), *International Conflict after the Cold War* (Washington, DC, National Academy Press, 2000) 338.
Hegel, GWF, *The Phenomenology of Spirit* (1807) tr AV Miller; analysis and Foreword by JN Findlay, rev edn (Oxford, Oxford University Press, 1976).
Hermann, DHJ, 'Restorative Justice and Retributive Justice: An Opportunity for Cooperation or an Occasion for Conflict in the Search for Justice?' (2017) 16 *Seattle Journal for Social Justice* 71.
Hetherington, S, 'Epistemic Responsibility: A Dilemma' (2002) 85 *The Monist* 398.
Hieronymi, P, 'Two Kinds of Agency' in L O'Brien and M Soteriou (eds), *Mental Actions* (Oxford, Oxford University Press, 2009).
Hill, AB, 'The Environment and Disease: Association or Causation?' (1965) 58 *Proceedings of the Royal Society of Medicine* 295.
Ho, HL, *A Philosophy of Evidence Law: Justice in the Search for Truth* (Oxford, Oxford University Press, 2008).
Hyde, I, 'The Tragic Flaw: Is it a Tragic Error?' (1963) 58 *The Modern Language Review* 321.
Kant, I, *Critique of the Power of Judgment* (1790), ed P Guyer; trs P Guyer and E Matthews (Cambridge, Cambridge University Press, 2000).
Kripke, S, *Philosophical Troubles: Collected Papers*, vol 1 (Oxford, Oxford University Press, 2011).
Krygier, M, 'The Rule of Law: Pasts, Presents, and Two Possible Futures' (2016) 12 *Annual Review of Law and Social Science* 199.
Kvanvig, J, 'Assertion, Knowledge, and Lotteries' in D Pritchard and P Greenough (eds), *Williamson on Knowledge* (Oxford, Oxford University Press, 2009) 140.
Lackey, J, 'The Norms of Assertion' (2007) 41 *Noûs* 594
Landsman, S, *The Adversary System: A Description and Defence* (Washington, DC, American Enterprise Institute for Public Policy Research, 1984).
Laudan, L, *Truth, Error, and Criminal Law: An Essay in Legal Epistemology* (Cambridge University Press, 2006).
Laudan, L and RJ Allen, 'The Devastating Impact of Prior Crime Evidence and Other Myths of the Criminal Justice Process' (2013) 101 *Journal of Criminal Law and Criminology* 493.
Lesson, SB, Tinklenberg, B and Andrews, K, 'Belief and Representation in Nonhuman Animals' in S Robins, J Symons and P Calvo (eds), *The Routledge Companion to Philosophy of Psychology*, 2nd edn (London, Routledge, 2019) ch 23.
Levanon, L, 'Sexual History Evidence in Sexual Assault Cases: A Critical Reevaluation' (2012) 62 *University of Toronto Law Journal* 609.
——, 'The Law of Police Entrapment: Critical Evaluation and Policy Analysis' (2016) 27 *Criminal Law Forum* 35.
——, '"Bad Character", Tragic Errors and Deep Ignorance' (2019) 39 *Legal Studies* 676.
——, 'Statistical Evidence, Assertions and Responsibility' (2019) 82 *MLR* 269.
——, 'The Probable and the Nonarbitrary: Evidential Foundations for a Finding of Guilt' (2021) 41 *Legal Studies* 294.
Lewis, D, 'Humean Supervenience Debugged' (1994) 103 *Mind* 473.
Liao, SM (ed), *Ethics of Artificial Intelligence* (Oxford, Oxford University Press, 2020).
Lippke, RL, *Taming the Presumption of Innocence* (Oxford, Oxford University Press, 2016).
Littlejohn, C, 'A Plea for Epistemic Excuses' in J Dutant (ed), *The New Evil Demon Problem* (Oxford, Oxford University Press, forthcoming).
Lloyd-Bostock, S, 'The Effects on Juries of Hearing about the Defendant's Previous Criminal Record: A Simulation Study' [2000] *Crim LR* 734.
Massaro, TM, 'The Dignity Value of Face-to-Face Confrontations' (1988) 40 *University of Florida Law Review* 863.
Massie, P, 'Philosophy and *Ataraxia* in Sextus Empiricus' (2013) 1(4) *Peitho/Examina Antiqua* 211.

McDowell, J, *Mind and World* (Cambridge, MA, Harvard University Press, 1994).
McEwan, J, *The Verdict of the Court: Passing Judgement in Law and Psychology* (Oxford, Hart Publishing, 2003).
McKeena, M, *Conversation and Responsibility* (Oxford, Oxford University Press, 2012).
McKenna, R, 'Why Assertion and Practical Reasoning are Possibly Not Governed by the Same Epistemic Norm' (2013) 4 *Logos & Episteme* 457.
McKinnon, R, 'The Supportive Reasons Norm of Assertion' (2013) 50 *American Philosophical Quarterly* 121.
Montminy, M, 'Why Assertion and Practical Reasoning Must Be Governed by the Same Epistemic Norm' (2013) 94 *Pacific Philosophical Quarterly* 57.
Moore, MS, 'The Plain Truth about Legal Truth' (2003) 26 *Harvard Journal of Law and Public Policy* 23.
Nagel, T, 'Rawls on Justice' (1973) 2 *The Philosophical Review* 220.
Naqvi, Y, 'The Right to Truth in International Law, Fact or Fiction?' (2006) 88 *IRRC* 245.
Norris, C, 'Hilary Putnam on Realism, Truth and Reason' (2004) *Philosophy Now: A Magazine of Ideas* at https://philosophynow.org/issues/49/Hilary_Putnam_on_Realism_Truth_and_Reason.
Noyes, GR, 'Aristotle and Modern Tragedy' (1891) 13 *Modern Language Notes* 6.
Nozick, R, *Philosophical Explanations* (Cambridge, MA, Harvard University Press, 1981).
Nussbaum, M, 'Equity and Mercy' (1993) 22 *Philosophy and Public Affairs* 83.
O'Brian, WE, 'The Right of Confrontation: US and European Perspectives' (2005) 121 *LQR* 481.
Pabst Battin, M, 'Aristotle's Definition of Tragedy in the Poetics' (1975) 33 *The Journal of Aesthetics and Art Criticism* 293.
Panepinto, AM, 'The Right to the Truth in International Law: The Significance of Strasbourg's Contributions' (2017) 37 *Legal Studies* 739.
Papineau, D, 'The Disvalue of Knowledge' (2021) 198 *Synthese* 5311.
Pardo, MS and Allen, RJ, 'Juridical Proof and the Best Explanation' (2008) 27 *Law and Philosophy* 223.
Peacocke, C, *Being Known* (Oxford, Oxford University Press, 1999).
Peirce, CS and Weiss, P (eds), *Collected Papers of Charles Sanders Peirce*, vol V: *Pragmatism and Pragmaticism*, book I: *Lectures on Pragmatism* (Cambridge, MA, The Belknap Press of Harvard University Press, 1934).
Peterson, M, *An Introduction to Decision Theory* (Cambridge, Cambridge University Press, 2009).
Picinali, F, 'Generalisations, Causal Relationships and Moral Responsibility' (2016) 20 *The International Journal of Evidence & Proof* 121.
——, 'The Presumption of Innocence: A Deflationary Account' (2021) 84 *MLR* 708.
Plato, *Meno*, tr B Jowett (Champaign, IL, Infomotions Inc, 2000).
Pritchard, D, *Epistemic Luck* (Oxford, Oxford University Press, 2005).
——, 'Sensitivity, Safety, and Anti-luck Epistemology' in J Greco (ed), *The Oxford Handbook of Skepticism* (Oxford, Oxford University Press, 2008) 437.
——, 'Anti Luck Virtue Epistemology' (2012) 109 *Journal of Philosophy* 247.
Pundik, A, 'Against Racial Profiling' (2017) 67 *University of Toronto Law Journal* 175.
Putnam, H, '"Degree of Confirmation" and Inductive Logic' in PA Schilpp (ed), *The Philosophy of Rudolf Carnap* (La Salle, IL, Open Court, 1963) 761.
——, 'Realism and Reason' (1977) 50 *Proceedings and Addresses of the American Philosophical Association* 483.
——, *Reason, Truth and History* (New York, Cambridge University Press, 1981).
——, 'Pragmatism' (1995) 95 *Proceedings of the Aristotelian Society* 291.
Quirk, H, *The Rise and Fall of the Right of Silence* (London, Routledge, Taylor & Francis, 2016).
Rawls, J, *A Theory of Justice*, 2nd edn (Cambridge, MA, Belknap Press, 1999).
Rawls, J, 'The Idea of an Overlapping Consensus' (1987) 7 *OJLS* 1.
Rawls, J, *Political Liberalism*, expanded edn (New York, Columbia University Press, 2005).
Raz, J, 'Authority and Justification' (1985) 14 *Philosophy and Public Affairs* 3.
——, *Value, Respect and Attachment* (Cambridge, Cambridge University Press, 2001).
——, 'On Respect, Authority and Neutrality: A Response' (2010) 120 *Ethics* 279.

Redmayne, M, 'Confronting Confrontation' *LSE Law, Society and Economy Working Paper* 10/2010 at www.lse.ac.uk/collections/law/wps/wps.htm.

——, *Character in the Criminal Trial* (Oxford, Oxford University Press, 2015).

Rouhana, NN, 'Key Issues in Reconciliation: Challenging Traditional Assumptions on Conflict Resolution and Power Dynamics' in D Bar Tal (ed), *Intergroup Conflicts and Their Resolution: A Social Psychological Perspective* (New York and London, Psychology Press, Taylor & Francis Group, 2011) 291.

Roush, S, *Tracking Truth: Knowledge, Evidence, and Science* (Oxford, Oxford University Press, 2005).

Rybowiak, V et al, 'Error Orientation Questionnaire (EOQ): Reliability, Validity, and Different Language Equivalence' (1999) 20 *Journal of Organizational Behavior* 527.

Salow, B, 'Probabilistic Knowledge, by Sarah Moss. Oxford: Oxford University Press, 2018' (2020) 129 *Mind* 515.

Sanchirico, CW, 'Character Evidence and the Object of Trial' (2001) 101 *Columbia Law Review* 1227.

Sandel, MJ, *Liberalism and the Limits of Justice*, 2nd edn (Cambridge, Cambridge University Press, 2010).

Sangero, B, 'Safe Convictions' (2019) 30 *Criminal Law Forum* 375.

Scallen, EA, 'Constitutional Dimensions of Hearsay Reform: Toward a Three-Dimensional Confrontation Clause' (1992) 76 *Minnesota Law Review* 623.

Scanlon, TM, *What We Owe to Each Other*, rev edn (Cambridge, MA, Harvard University Press, 2000).

Schellenberg, JA, *Conflict Resolution: Theory, Research and Practice* (Albany, NY, State University of New York Press, 1982).

Schum, DA, *The Evidential Foundations of Probabilistic Reasoning* (Evanston, IL, Northwestern University Press, 1994).

Setiya, K, 'Epistemic Agency: Some Doubts' (2013) 23 *Philosophical Issues* 179.

Shoemaker, D, 'Attributability, Answerability and Accountability: Toward a Wider Theory of Moral Responsibility' (2011) 121 *Ethics* 602.

——, *Responsibility from the Margins* (Oxford and New York, Oxford University Press, 2015).

Sitkin, SB, 'Learning through Failure: The Strategy of Small Losses' in M Cohen and U Sproull (eds), *Organizational Learning* (Thousand Oaks, CA, Sage, 1996) 541.

Smith, AM, 'On Being Responsible and Holding Responsible' (2007) 11 *Journal of Ethics* 465.

——, 'Attributability, Answerability, and Accountability: In Defence of a Unified Account' (2012) 122 *Ethics* 122.

Smith, M, *Between Probability and Certainty: What Justifies Belief* (Oxford, Oxford University Press, 2016).

Smith, MR and Alpert, GP, 'Searching for Direction: Courts, Social Science, and the Adjudication of Racial Profiling Claims' (2002) 19 *Justice Quarterly* 673.

Sober, E, *Ockham's Razors: A User's Manual* (Cambridge, Cambridge University Press, 2015).

Solomonoff, R, *A Preliminary Report on a General Theory of Inductive Inference: Report V-131* (Cambridge, MA, Zator Co, 1960).

Sophocles, *The Three Theban Plays: Antigone, Oedipus the King; Oedipus at Colonus*, tr R Fagles; Introductions and Notes by B Knox (New York, Penguin Books, 1984).

Sosa, E, 'How to Defeat Opposition to Moore' (1999) 13 *Philosophical Perspectives* 141.

——, *A Virtue Epistemology: Apt Belief and Reflective Knowledge* (Oxford University Press, 2007).

Spencer, JR, *Evidence of Bad Character*, 2nd edn (Oxford, Hart Publishing, 2009).

Stanley, J, *Knowledge and Practical Interests* (New York, Oxford University Press, 2005).

Steel, S, 'Justifying Exceptions to Proof of Causation in Tort Law' (2015) 78 *MLR* 729.

——, *Proof of Causation in Tort Law* (Cambridge, Cambridge University Press, 2015).

Stein, A, *Foundations of Evidence Law* (Oxford, Oxford University Press, 2005).

Stine, GC, 'Skepticism, Relevant Alternatives, and Deductive Closure' (1976) 29(4) *Philosophical Studies* 249.

Stinton, TCW, 'Hamartia in Aristotle and Greek tragedy' (1975) 25 *The Classical Quarterly* (New Series) 221.

Strawson, PF, 'Freedom and Resentment' (1962) 48 *Proceedings of the British Academy* 1.

Summers, RS, 'Formal Legal Truth and Substantive Truth in Judicial Fact-Finding – Their Justified Divergence in Some Particular Cases' 18 (1999) *Law and Philosophy* 497.

Svavarsson, SH, 'Two Kinds of Tranquility: Sextus Empiricus on *Ataraxia*' in DE Machuca (ed), *Pyrrhonism in Ancient, Modern, and Contemporary Philosophy* (Dordrecht, Springer, 2012) 19.

Tasioulas, J, 'Where is Love? – The Topography of Mercy' in R Cruft, M Kramer and M Reiff (eds) *Crimes, Punishments and Responsibility: The Jurisprudence of Antony Duff* (Oxford, Oxford University Press, 2011) ch 3.

Taylor, RS, *Reconstructing Rawls: The Kantian Foundations of Justice as Fairness* (Pennsylvania, PA, Penn State University Press, 2015).

Thibodeau, M, *Hegel and Greek Tragedy*, tr HJ Wilhelm (Lanham, MD, Lexington Books, 2013).

Tofaris, S and Steel, S, 'Negligence Liability for Omissions and the Police' (2016) 75 *CLJ* 128.

Trotta, R, 'Bayes in the Sky: Bayesian Inference and Model Selection in Cosmology' (2008) 49 *Contemporary Physics* 71.

Unger, P, *Ignorance: A Case for Scepticism* (Oxford, Oxford University Press, 1975).

Van Den Berg, HA, 'Occam's Razor: From Ockham's via Moderna to Modern Data Science' (2018) 101 *Science Progress* 261.

Van Dyck, C et al, 'Organizational Error Management Culture and Its Impact on Performance: A Two-Study Replication' (2005) 90 *Journal of Applied Psychology* 1228.

Väyrynen, T, *Culture and International Conflict Resolution: A Critical Analysis of the Work of John Burton* (Manchester, Manchester University Press, 2018).

Vogel, J, 'Tracking, Closure, and Inductive Knowledge' in LF Steven (ed), *The Possibility of Knowledge: Nozick and His Critics* (Totowa, NJ, Rowman & Littlefield, 1987) 197.

Vogt, KM, 'Activity, Action, and Assent: On the Life of the Pyrrhonian Sceptic', draft, Princeton Colloquium in Ancient Philosophy 07 at www.katjavogt.com/pdf/katja_vogt_apraxia.pdf.

——, 'The Aims of Skeptical Investigation' in DE Machuca (ed), *Pyrrhonian Skepticism in Ancient, Modern, and Contemporary Philosophy* (Dordrecht, Springer, 2012) 33.

Walgrave, L, 'Imposing Restoration instead of Inflicting Pain: Reflections on the Judicial Reaction to Crime' in A von Hirsch et al (eds), *Restorative Justice and Criminal Justice: Competing or Reconcilable Paradigms* (Oxford, Hart Publishing, 2006) 61.

Walker, VR, 'Theories of Uncertainty: Explaining the Possible Sources of Error in Inference' (2001) 22 *Cardozo Law Review* 22.

Watson, G, *Agency and Answerability: Selected Essays* (Oxford, Oxford University Press, 2004).

Weigend, T, 'Is the Criminal Process about Truth? A German Perspective' (2003) 26 *Harvard Journal of Law and Public Policy* 157.

Weiner, M, 'Must We Know What We Say?' (2005) 114 *The Philosophical Review* 227.

Wells, GL, 'Naked Statistical Evidence of Liability: Is Subjective Probability Enough?' (1992) 62 *Journal of Personality and Social Psychology* 739.

Williams, M, 'Scepticism Without Theory' (1988) 41(3) *The Review of Metaphysics* 547.

Williamson, T, 'Knowing and Asserting' (1996) 105 *Philosophical Review* 489.

——, *Knowledge and Its Limits* (Oxford, Oxford University Press, 2000).

Woodruff, P, 'Aristotle on Character in Tragedy, or Who is Creon? What is He?' (2009) 67 *The Journal of Aesthetics and Art Criticism* 301.

Zhao, B and Olivera, F, 'Error Reporting in Organizations' (2006) 31 *Academy of Management Review* 1012.

Zuckerman, AAS, 'Trial by Unfair Means – The Report of the Working Group on the Right of Silence' [1989] *Crim LR* 855.

INDEX

www.ingramcontent.com/pod-product-compliance
Lightning Source LLC
Chambersburg PA
CBHW071257180926
51613CB00001B/55
9781509942657